Defence Diplomacy in the Long War

Defence Diplomacy in the Long War

By

Patrick Blannin

BRILL

LEIDEN | BOSTON

Originally published as Volume 2.1–2 (2017), in *Diplomacy and Foreign Policy*, DOI 10.1163/24056006-12340006.

Library of Congress Control Number: 2017949021

Typeface for the Latin, Greek, and Cyrillic scripts: "Brill". See and download: brill.com/brill-typeface.

ISBN 978-90-04-35282-7 (paperback)
ISBN 978-90-04-35406-7 (e-book)

This book is printed on acid-free paper and produced in a sustainable manner.

Contents

Defence Diplomacy in the Long War

Patrick Blannin

Abstract

One of the most dominant security issues of twenty-first century has been the U.S. led battle against transnational terrorism—the aptly named Long War. Over the past fifteen years the Long War has been examined using multiple perspectives; however, one central mechanism is missing in current analyses: defence diplomacy. Defence diplomacy enhances the diplomatic and security capacity of a state, providing the only link between executive office and the ministries of foreign affairs and defence, two vital institutions in the Long War. Using a case study of U.S. defence diplomacy in Afghanistan from 2001–2014, the paper argues simply that the practice of defence diplomacy far outweighs current theories on what it is, how it works and why it matters? The paper aims to generate a more nuanced understanding of defence diplomacy, as well as identifying it as a key component of the U.S. CT/COIN strategy to achieve its Long War policy objectives.

Keywords

defence diplomacy – relationship building – U.S. – Afghanistan – long war – coalition – COIN/CT

Any long war always entails great hazards to liberty in a democracy[1]

∵

1 Alexis de Tocqueville, *Democracy, II, 842*, cited in Alan Macfarlane, *The Riddle of the Modern World: Of Liberty, Wealth and Equality*, (London: Macmillan, 2000), p. 65.

 | DOI 10.1163/9789004354067

Introduction

Conventionally, national security is understood in terms of protecting the territory and interests of a sovereign nation through defensive actions using the various mechanisms of statecraft. However, the twenty-first century has revealed new sources of security (and insecurity) which challenge the conventional means of securing the state. While acknowledging the enduring spectre of Great Power politics, the diffusion of violent Islamist insurgencies across an arc from the west coast of Africa to South-East Asia has demonstrated the ability of non-state actors armed with rudimentary weapons to inflict serious damage to Western interests, undermining the already contested concept of 'global security.' Global terrorist networks form part of a widened security agenda which also includes large-scale intra-state ethnic/religious violence, climate change, global pandemics and extreme poverty. All of these non-traditional security issues have an associated or secondary military component which is increasingly transnational in nature. Consequently states acknowledge, sometimes begrudgingly, that their security cannot be guaranteed without enhanced sub-regional, regional and global security relationships (cooperation and coordination). To achieve the former while engaging in the latter, militaries have evolved from predominantly kinetic organisations into a key component of a 'whole-of-government' national security apparatus, forming multilateral coalitions to tackle a diverse range of traditional and non-traditional threats.[2]

Over the past fifteen years, the War on Terror (hence referred to as the Long War) has demonstrated the difficulty of securing state interests in this complex threat environment, even when equipped with the most advanced military and weapons systems. Accordingly, countering non-traditional threats has focused the attention as practitioners, policy makers and academics address these challenges to the state in the Long War. These stakeholders have generated reams of documentation since 2001; however, one central mechanism is missing in current analyses: defence diplomacy.[3] Defence diplomacy is an

2 The *Armies Coalition Operations Handbook* (4th ed.) interprets coalitions as "an ad hoc arrangement between two or more nations for common action. A coalition action is a multinational action outside the bounds of established alliances, usually for a single occasion, or for longer cooperation in a narrow sector of common interest." Coalition operations are conducted by forces of two or more nations, which may not be allies, acting together for the accomplishment of a single mission.

3 Anton Du Plessis (2008) claims "military diplomacy" refers strictly to the actions of military diplomats like military attaches while "defense diplomacy" encompasses the entirety of a country's defense establishment. This study uses the term "defense diplomacy" to reflect this comprehensive assessment of the U.S. DoD's collaboration with the State Department in theatres such as Afghanistan. Interestingly, the *2015 JCOS 1-02 Dictionary for Military &*

incredibly versatile instrument of the state but it is understudied and largely undervalued by the academic community. This paper argues that an increased focus on defence diplomacy is justified as it enhances the diplomatic and security capacity of a state, providing the only link between executive office and the ministries of foreign affairs and defence, two vital institutions in the Long War.

Defined simply as "the collective application of pacific and/or cooperative initiatives by national defense establishments and military practitioners for confidence building, trust creation, conflict prevention, and/or conflict resolution," defence diplomacy's role in the Long War is an important area of theory and practice which warrants greater study (Tan & Singh, 2012: 221). If not, the military's role as the "default responder" will continue to obscure its strategic successes whilst preserving a deficit in scholarship (U.S. DoD QDR, 2006: 86). By stressing the unparalleled versatility of defence diplomacy in the Long War, this paper addresses the scholarly deficiency and amends unwarranted negativity. Moreover, defence diplomacy is often discounted in the context of contemporary diplomacy, as well as in analyses of foreign policy or assessments of irregular combat environments.[4] Winger claims defence diplomacy "has continued to exist as an umbrella concept used to corral a loose collection of nonviolent military programs under a single title" (2014: 33). Additionally, there is also a somewhat restrictive view of diplomacy, frequently perceived as an alternative to war; yet it does not end when war begins. Former U.S. Ambassador Chas Freeman to Saudi Arabia Chas Freeman insists that "War and diplomacy are different but intimately related aspects of national policy ... diplomats and warriors who recall this will therefore act as brothers in a potentially lethal common endeavour ... they will consider together when to fight and when to talk and when to press and when to stop" (Freeman, 1994: 124).[5]

Associated Terms does not contain a definition for either defence diplomacy or military diplomacy.

4 The 2009 *U.S. Government Counterinsurgency Guide* (Preface) emphasized that irregular warfare is far more varied than conventional conflict: hence the importance of an intellectual framework that is coherent enough to provide guidance, and flexible enough to adapt to circumstances. More recently the concept of 'Hybrid' or 'Greyzone' conflicts has emerged. Although the concepts are still disputed, Dr David Killcullen described Hybrid conflicts as those involving actors "who think like a state (conventional), fight like a state but who do so using non-state (conventional) means" (*The Future of War Conference*, Ronald Reagan Building and International Trade Center, Washington D.C., 10th March, 2016).

5 Freeman's linking of the diplomat and a warrior is not unique. Ambassador Robert Murphy penned '*Diplomat Among Warriors*' documenting his decades of Foreign Service in 1964, more recently SECDEF Carter labelled the new NATO Supreme Commander U.S. Army General Curtis Scaparrotti "a proven warrior diplomat" who has a proven ability "to build bridges

Although the majority of the discourse on defence diplomacy is generated by authors guided by IR mainstays such as Strategic Studies, Security Studies or Foreign Policy Analysis, the current literature is extremely useful in providing a background to defence diplomacy, acting as a foundation for more detailed diplomacy centric assessment. This paper demonstrates that while defence diplomacy is a ubiquitous tool of statecraft during times of peace, it also fulfils a central role in the Long War providing an instrumental and complimentary relationship building role in a whole-of-government approach to foreign policy. For Willard, the "essence" of defence diplomacy is its ability to influence "future outcomes by shaping the environment to one's advantage" (2006: 11).[6] While Scharre claims that "force is a tool that can be used in many ways to achieve political aims … leverage military power to secure American interests in situations short of major combat operations" (Scharre, 2016). These are the fundamentals which "make defence diplomacy an effective geopolitical tool" (Winger, 2014: 33).

To date, no studies have directly reviewed and theorised on the role of defence diplomacy in the Long War. Clausewitz reminds us that "the primary purpose of any theory is to clarify concepts and ideas that have become … confused and entangled" (1997: 357). Therefore the paper's core proposition is simple: the *practice* of defence diplomacy far outweighs current theories on what it is, how it works and why it matters. It argues that defence diplomacy produces transformative outcomes by combining "the engine room of international relations," (Cohen, 1998) with the "bulwark guarantor of its security and independence" (Joint Publication 1, 2013: i). Three hypotheses stem from this broad argumentative position. First, that defence diplomacy was instrumental in building a fifty-one nation, ad-hoc coalition at the beginning of the Long War (hence referred to as the Coalition). Second, that defence diplomacy has sustained anti-terror coalitions over the past fifteen years, converting political objectives into direct, tactical action. Third, defence diplomacy represents one of the enduring aspects of the Long War which needs to be recognised, championed and further resourced. Testing these hypotheses generates a more

---

between allies and partners, between diverse elements within our joint force" (Remarks at EUCOM Change of Command As Delivered by Secretary of Defense Ash Carter, Stuttgart, Germany, May 3, 2016 available at http://www.defense.gov/News/Speeches/Speech-View/Article/750946/remarks-at-eucom-change-of-command).

6 Influence is the act or power of producing an effect without apparent exertion of force or direct exercise of command; For more information on how the military shapes the environment; See also: Charles F. Wald, 'The Phase Zero Campaign', *Joint Force Quarterly, Issue 43, 4th Quarter*, (2006), pp. 72–75; U.S. Advisory Commission on Public Diplomacy, 'Chapter 6. Increasing the US's Influence in the World', *Assessing U.S. Public Diplomacy: A Notional Model*, (Austin, Texas: The LBJ School of Public Affairs, 2010), pp. 41–46.

nuanced understanding of defence diplomacy, identifying it as a key element of the U.S. counter-terrorism (CT)/counterinsurgency (COIN) strategy, affording policy makers the confidence to support defence diplomacy oriented activities into their Long War strategy.[7]

Structurally, the first section of the paper provides a comprehensive literature review which elucidates the origins, definitions, objectives and myriad applications of defence diplomacy. Primary sources documents such as the UK MOD *Strategic Defence Review* (1998) and UK *Defence Doctrine* (2014), NATO's *Multiple Fronts Project* (2009), *Strategic Concept* (2010) and *JP-4.5-Host Nation Support Doctrine* (2013), U.S. *Defense Strategic Guidance* (2012), *Quadrennial Defence Review (1996, 2001, 2010), Quadrennial Diplomacy and Development Reviews* are reviewed in order to bring clarity to this papers holistic examination of defence diplomacy's role in a state's foreign/security strategy. Additionally, in relation to the U.S. centered case-study, the *National Security Strategy*, the *National Defence Strategy* and the *National Military Strategy* are prioritised as "fundamental national policy documents that chart the course of the country" (DoD, nd.: 5).[8] Examining these primary documents provide a link between a governments stated views and its actual policies, thus enabling the researcher to discern broad overarching ideas, themes or patterns. Similarly, primary sources such as U.S. DoD *Joint Publications* and NATO *Allied Joint Publications* (field manuals) detail the specific motivations and mechanisms involved in developing and implementing the foreign policy of the nations at the forefront of the struggle against transnational terrorism. The review also includes regionally oriented literature which examines the motivations, applications and outcomes of defence diplomacy. While all these resources make a contribution to improving our understanding of defence diplomacy in practice there is a distinct lack of theoretical analysis. Much of the current discourse and literature on defence diplomacy has been generated by practitioners and, as such, is descriptive and theoretically unambitious. Moreover, when diplomacy oriented scholars examine defence diplomacy it is often viewed through the Schelling's lens of coercive or preventative diplomacy.[9] Whilst this paper's

---

7 *U.S. Army FM 3-0 Operations (2001)* defines "strategy is the art and science of developing and employing armed forces and other instruments of national power in a synchronized fashion to secure national or multinational objectives" p. 2.

8 Chairman of the JCOS revealed in March 2016 that *The National Military Strategy* would no longer be a publically available document, speech available at https://www.defense.gov/Portals/1/Documents/pubs/2016%20China%20Military%20Power%20Report.pdf.

9 Schelling, T. C. *Arms and Influence*, (New Haven, CT: Yale University Press, 1966); Byman, D., Waxman, M. C. & Larson, E. V., *Air Power as a Coercive Instrument*, (Santa Monica CA: RAND Corporation, 2002), pp. 1–195; Sperandei, M. 'Bridging Deterrence and Compellence: An Alternative Approach to the Study of Coercive Diplomacy', *International Studies Review, Vol. 8,*

comprehensive review aims to establish a revised, updated theory of the military's role in diplomacy it also addresses the current academic deficiency by studying the Long War through a diplomatic lens in a focused theoretical and practical manner.

The second section of the paper examines defence diplomacy in practice. This practical validation begins with an overview of how NATO and ASEAN member states incorporate defence diplomacy into national and regional security strategies, respectively. NATO is chosen because its member states first introduced the terminology through the UK MOD's *Strategic Defence Review*, 1998. They have also vigorously engaged in the process as well as being conspicuous on most fronts in the Long War. ASEAN offers an alternative to Western-oriented examples of defence diplomacy in praxis. ASEAN nations also perceive it to be "the most useful and effective form of security multilateralism in the region" (Bisley, 2014: 12). ASEAN member states are also important regional partners in the struggle against transnational terrorism since 2001. The selection of NATO and ASEAN provides geographic breadth for the paper's overview of defence diplomacy in practice. The third section narrows the focus, presenting a case study of U.S. defence diplomacy during Operation Enduring Freedom (OEF) and as part of NATO's International Security Assistance Force (ISAF) in Afghanistan from 2001 to 2014. The U.S. is a valuable referent object for inquiry because its diplomacy is heavily militarised, it has a history of over two centuries of defence diplomacy, and it has been both a target and offensive sovereign entity in the Long War. Besides further validating theory into practice the aim of this case study is to provide an alternate lens through which to view U.S. engagement in Afghanistan post 9/11. The Afghan case study enables an examination of both external and host nation (HN) partners, providing multiple levels of analysis.

This paper has three objectives. First, to deliver an analysis of the dominant international security issue of the twenty-first century through the lens of defence diplomacy, illuminating an unexplored corner of the Long War. Second, this paper aims to complement the existing body of diplomacy focused literature, whilst answering the call for a more multi-disciplinary approach to

---

no. 2, (2006), pp. 253–280; Levy, J. S. 'Deterrence and Coercive Diplomacy: The Contributions of Alexander George', *Political Psychology, Vol. 2, no. 4*, (2008), pp. 537–552; Zyck, S. A. & R. Muggah, 'Preventive Diplomacy and Conflict Prevention: Obstacles and Opportunities. Stability', *International Journal of Security and Development, Vol., no. 1*, (2012), pp. 65–78; Cheyre, J. 'Defence Diplomacy', in F. C. Andrew, H. Jorge, T. Ramesh & C. Juan Emilio (eds), *The Oxford Handbook of Modern Diplomacy*, (Oxford: Oxford University Press: 2013), pp. 368–382.

global security issues,[10] while demonstrating its centrality in the process of "relationship building may help to consolidate the disciplinary identity of diplomacy" (Bjola, 2012: 2). Third, by examining "the apparent incongruity between the force-based orientation of defence ... and the peace-based orientation of diplomacy" (Tan & Singh, 2012: 224) the findings from this study may deflect some of the criticism directed toward the military which is negatively perceived it as the "default responder" in the Long War (DoD QDR, 2006: 86).[11] Collectively these objectives determine whether long-term institutional, operational, economic and security benefits occur when the military, the most kinetically powerful institution of the state, incorporates diplomacy to achieve a state's foreign policy objectives. The paper identifies and fills a gap in existing analyses of the Long War, revives and updates the theoretical foundations of the concept as well as demonstrating how defence diplomacy enhances the management of irregular warfare in the 21st century. This paper, it is hoped, will be of interest to both scholars across the discipline IR and to civilian and military practitioners engaged in the vitally important yet misunderstood political-military union of defence diplomacy.

---

10 Major General James P. Hunt who led Stability Operations in Iraq form 2009–2010 concluded that although military and civilian personnel all spoke English, "there is no guarantee that any of us are actually communicating," (2010: para. 8); Ryan Crocker, 'Diplomacy in a Non-Polar World', *The Yale Journal of International Affairs, Vol. 8, Iss. 2*, (Summer 2013), Ambassador Crocker addresses the gap between academia and international affairs practitioners in the U.S. p. 103; Constantinou, C. & S. O. Opondo, 'Engaging the 'ungoverned': The merging of diplomacy, defence and development', *Cooperation and Conflict*, Vol. 51, no. 3, (2015), pp. 307–324; Rovner, J. 'Warring Tribes Studying War and Peace', *War on the Rocks*, (April 12, 2016); Thornhill, P. 'A Funny Thing Happened When These Military Officers and Academics Got Together', *Defense One*, (April 3, 2016). Many stakeholders recognise the need to remove barriers between practitioners and among academics with increased inter-disciplinary outreach. Despite the increase interaction between DoD and State there are still basic problems of communication; Barno, B & Bensahel, N. 'The Military Is From Mars, Civilians Are From Venus: Avoiding Planetary Collisions In The Conference Room', *War on the Rocks*, (March 22, 2016), The authors claim they've "attended many meetings where it felt like the military personnel were from Mars and the civilians were from Venus: part of the same solar system, but from planets with vastly different landscapes and languages"; Jonathan Bate, 'Getting the Military and Social Scientists Back Together: The Need for Expeditionary Social Science', Political *Violence @ a Glance*, (September 29, 2016).

11 For more on the U.S. military's role as the default responder see Brendan Ballou, 'Why America's Nation Building Office Failed and What Congress Had to Do With It. Stability', *International Journal of Security and Development, Vol. 3, no. 1*, (2014), Art. 30, pp. 1–17.

Whilst it is important to summarise what this study will address, it is also necessary to establish clear parameters by highlighting areas not covered by the document. The paper stresses defence diplomacy as a process in conflict prevention as well as conflict management mechanism (particularly in CT/COIN), not a conflict resolution mechanism. It is generally accepted that conflict resolution and reconciliation would not be possible without diplomacy; however, as the *Report on the Legal and Policy Frameworks Guiding the United States' Use of Military Force and Related National Security Operations* released in December 2016 contends, "groups like al Qa'ida are highly unlikely to disarm and sign instruments of surrender ... are also highly unlikely ever to denounce terrorism and violence and to seek to address their perceived grievances through some form of reconciliation or participation in a political process" (U.S.G., 2016: 11). Additionally, while crisis diplomacy and/or conflict diplomacy are commonly associated with complex conflict environments, they tend to predominately focus of negotiations between adversaries. However, this paper aims to demonstrate the utility of diplomacy, more accurately defence diplomacy, in the management of conflict as a process which creates and maintains relationships by enhancing capabilities, building trust through transparency and accountability, identifying commonalities and shaping worldview's.[12] The paper analyses defence diplomacy from a strategic, operational and tactical level (the Why, What and How of warfare),[13] yet it does not focus on 'the' enemy. It argues that defence diplomacy influences the formation of national security strategy and forms part a framework to conduct CT/COIN operations, regardless of geography or adversary.[14] This framework allows stakeholders to prioritise enemy-specific tactical considerations with the help of HN and regional partners (these actors are interchangeable, with geography and/or enemy dictating their involvement).

Relatedly, causational factors are not discussed, as generally, the causes of conflict do not impact defence diplomacy at a strategic level; rendering the inclusion of causational factors unnecessary as it will not augment the paper.

12 For Bjola, the fundamental "problem of theorizing about processes of relationship-building is a question about trust: how much trust is needed to turn a relationship of enmity into one of friendship?" (2013: 13).

13 For more see: 'Levels of War' (chapter 1-Doctrine), *Basic Doctrine, Vol. 1*, Curtis E. Lemay Center for Doctrine Development and Education, (Maxwell AFB, AL: Air Force University Press, 2015), pp. 44–45.

14 Hoffman emphasises that strategists and policymakers need to recognise that every insurgency is unique and overcoming today's "irregular challenges" can't be found by laminating yesterday's framework into current doctrine and strategy," (2007: 13).

Likewise, the 'militarization' (Adams & Murray, 2014)[15] of U.S. foreign policy manifests in a reflection on the civil-military relationship in the U.S., which can include the effectiveness of the civilian control over the military (evaluating what Samuel Huntington (1957) referred to as the objective or subjective civilian control), the expansion of the military area of operations into operations other than war, or the budgetary and institutional imbalance between the DoD and State (as well as other civilian agencies). While these debates are important and ongoing, with practitioners and scholars often producing coherent arguments for and against what Adams and Murray (2014) label "mission creep" and form part of this papers comprehensive literary review, the topic is examined to answer the 'framing' question of 'how did we get here.' The paper does not make a judgement on the appropriate civil-military ratio or the decision (intentional or otherwise) to diminish the capacity of State; it simply assesses what it considers to be the situation 'on the ground.' An area which is acknowledged but not analysed in this document is the role and impact of non-state actors including NGO's and private contractors (who have contributed "fifty percent or more of the total military force"), who work with other key U.S. departments, performing political (diplomatic/military) duties in the Long War (Thannhauser & Luehrs, 2015: 427). Finally, the timeline for this paper is 2001–2014. Events before and after this period are briefly discussed to provide context and support its hypotheses.

Having established the objectives and parameters of this study and before demonstrating the role, utility and scope of defence diplomacy, an introduction to diplomacy is required to frame the argument and identify the fundamentals of the referent object. The following section briefly defines and conceptualizes traditional state-centric diplomacy to generate a general understanding of the concept which serves as the theoretical nucleus of the paper.

Diplomacy: A Timeless Existential Phenomenon

Contemporary Diplomacy

The section begins by clarifying three terms which are central to the paper: statecraft, foreign policy and finally diplomacy. Statecraft and foreign policy will be succinctly addressed whereas diplomacy requires a broader discussion. Statecraft can be simply defined as the skilful management of state affairs

15 The authors interpret this militarization as "a gradual seeping in of military perspectives and priorities into the broader foreign policy and national security strategies and policies of the United States," p. 13.

and its central role in political science has been attributed in no-small-part to Niccolo Machiavelli (Butterfield, 1955). Likewise, Harold Nicolson reflects upon Machiavellian statecraft which "ignored the practical purposes of true negotiation, and introduced an abominable filigree of artifice into what ought always to be a simple machine" (1955).[16] Contemporary scholars explore the motivation and application of the concept. Ping conceives "statecraft as the actions of a state internationally, actions that are guided by the state's desire to achieve international goals … the selection of means for the pursuit of foreign policy goals" (2003: 27). Codevilla (2008) presents statecraft as incorporating multiple levers of state power including diplomacy and military action; it's about managing reality, coupling ends and means in ways which advance the states interests. Similarly, Kerr & Wiseman define statecraft as, "the development and use of instruments … diplomacy, intelligence, force, economic leverage, and the law to secure the states interests in the international system" (2013: 358).[17] While Kilcullen views it as an amalgam "of the individual, the nation, the state and all their internal and external relationships, which unifies approaches to all areas of policy" (2007: 45).

It's also necessary in any discussion concerning diplomacy to address what Langhorne labelled "the evergreen problem about the distinction between foreign policy and diplomacy" (2009: 101). For Ernest Satow, "foreign policy is formulated by governments, not diplomats," with the diplomats role being to carry out that foreign policy through diplomacy (Roberts, 2009: 3). While Nicholson claims "Foreign policy is based upon a general conception of national requirements … diplomacy on the other hand, is not an end but a means, not a purpose but a method" (1954). Similarly, Smith, Hadfield and Dunne present foreign policy as "the sum total of decisions made on behalf of a given

16 See also: Harold Nicolson, *The Evolution of Diplomatic Method*, (London: Cassell, 1954): Greg Russell, 'Machiavelli's Science of Statecraft: The Diplomacy and Politics of Disorder', *Diplomacy & Statecraft, Vol. 16, no. 2*, (2005), Similarly, Russell contends that "Machiavelli's legacy, no less in the competitive arena of diplomacy than in the clash of political ideas, has also signified for many a preoccupation with expediency and artifice to the detriment of good faith and truthfulness in upholding interstate obligations," p. 228.

17 The seven instruments of contemporary statecraft are commonly referred to by the acronym DIMEFIL: Diplomacy, Information, Military, Economic, Financial, Intelligence and Legal. See also Cale Horne, Stephen Shellman & Brandon Stewart, Nickel and DIMEing the Adversary: Does it work or PMESII them off?, ISA's 49th Annual Convention, Bridging Multiple Divides, Hilton San Francisco, CA, (International Studies Institute, 2008), pp. 1–55; Boone Bartholomees, *Theory of War and Strategy*, (Carlisle, PA, Strategic Studies Institute, 2010); Brett Daniel Shehadey, *Putting the 'D' and 'I' Back into DIME*, Department of Homeland Security, (2013), pp. 1–10.

political unit (usually a state) entailing the implementation of goals with direct reference to its external environment" (2012: 392). Other scholars define foreign policy in relation to diplomacy. Hans Morgenthau, a foremost figure in 20th century IR theory, described diplomacy as what diplomats do whilst engaging in "one of the lesser tools of foreign policy" (Quoted in Sharp, 2009, 110). While Criekemans (2011) contends the availability of different diplomatic mechanisms influence foreign policy decisions on multiple levels,[18] Sasson Sofer explains that while the "interests, aims and concepts of foreign policy may change," changes in diplomacy occur only in the methods used in its role as a facilitator (1988: 196). For Wiseman, "foreign policy tends to be about theory (substance, strategy, ends) and diplomacy about practice (procedures, tactics, means)" (2005: 410). Finally, Constantinou and Der Derian acknowledge that although "a rigid definition between the two can be unhelpful, it would complicate the discussion if we failed to deliver an elementary "distinction between the formulation and implementation of policy" (2010: 15).

One must also recognise the distance between ideologically driven foreign policy and diplomacy. Ideology may indeed influence the foreign policy agenda of the state; however, diplomacy remains a vital mechanism for achieving a diverse spectrum of foreign policy goals.[19] For Sofer, regardless of the ideology driving its foreign policy, diplomacy remains relevant, as "the state must employ the most suitable means of achieving the national interest" (1988: 196). Kleiner describes foreign policy as the international "aspirations and aims" (2010: 1) of a state pursued through its external relations within the international system; however, other scholars identify the interconnectedness of the international and domestic constituency in the formation of foreign policy.[20] Connecting the domestic and international interests is not only a scholarly endeavour with Ambassador Ryan Crocker confirming succinctly that "foreign policies, in any democracy, are driven by domestic concerns—it's just the way it is" (2013: 103). Recognizing this relationship is important as a government seeks to placate its domestic constituency in order to prosecute its national security strategy. However, the interconnected nature of polities and politics in the 21st century may render such definitions as meaningless. Some argue, just

18 Criekemans claims diplomacy can be considered as having an 'input' and an 'output' in foreign policy formulation, p. 716.

19 Sofer explains that after de-colonisation in the mid-20th century, some newly active sovereign states initially reject diplomacy, viewing it as a symbol of Western oppression, inevitability they were compelled to engage in the diplomacy as the only legitimate means of addressing pertinent foreign policy issues (1988: 201).

20 Putnam, 1998; Huijgh, 2011; Conley Tyler, 2012; Hocking, 2013; Hammer, 2013.

as the demarcation between sovereigns becomes opaque, so too has "the once bright line between domestic and foreign policy" begun to blur (Bill Clinton quoted in Auerswald, et al., 2003: 41). Whether clear or opaque, an essential mechanism to bridge the domestic-international divide is diplomacy.

After tracing the etymology of diplomacy to ancient Greece, Satow affirms that diplomacy is "the application of intelligence or tact to the conduct of relations between the governments of independent states" (1957: 1). Diplomacy's historical legacy leads Jönsson and Hall to regard it as "a perennial international institution ... a timeless existential phenomenon."[21] diplomacy as "a relatively stable collection of social practices consisting of easily recognised roles coupled with underlying norms and a set of rules or conventions (which) proscribe behavioural roles, constrain activity, and shape expectation" (Jönsson & Hall, 2005: 3). Diplomacy exists to forge connections between estranged peoples either after systemic change or to facilitate such transformations. Der Derian claims that diplomacy acts "[L]ike the bridges of medieval cities, the diplomatic culture begins as a neutral link between alien quarters ... attempting to mediate systemic alienation" (1992: 23).[22] Diplomacy plays a central role as "an institution structuring relations among polities" (Jönsson & Hall, 2003: 196). Suri (2015) places the discipline of diplomacy within the spectrum of activities which include the practices of dialogue, reconciliation, compromise, trust-building, and persuasion, between diverse and often antagonistic groups. Tarrosy insists diplomacy "intermediates among all these various actors, it proceeds actions or decisions, or prepares the ground for further action," therefore serving as an irreplaceable lever of statecraft in relation to national security (2014: 72). Whereas Hamilton and Langhorne look beyond the sovereign state, and arrive at a working definition for 'new' diplomacy as "the peaceful conduct of relations amongst political entities, their principles, and accredited agents" (2009: 1).

---

21 Christer Jönsson & Martin Hall, *The Essence of Diplomacy*, (New York: Palgrave Macmillan, 2005), p. 3.

22 Der Derian's 'bridge' analogy was chosen as it mirrors the position of the UK MoD in the *1998 Strategic Defence Review* which indicated that defence diplomacy would be developed to build bridges between Eastern and Western Europe. "The MOD's Outreach programme (defence diplomacy) of bilateral defence assistance complements NATO's work to help promote a safer, more stable Europe, (p. 107); Daniel Baldino & Andrew Carr also deploy the 'bridge' metaphor in their analysis of whether defence diplomacy "functions as a bridge that relates military power to political purpose," (2016: 141; Sharp explores this notion by highlighting that diplomacy's role is to form a bridge between islands of the other in international society not to act as a converting force that transports them over to our side, (2013: 65).

Jönsson and Hall claim contemporary diplomacy operates as "a relatively stable collection of social practices consisting of easily recognised roles coupled with underlying norms and a set of rules or conventions (which) proscribe behavioural roles, constrain activity, and shape expectation" (2005: 25). Freeman (2015) equates the essence of diplomacy to a means seeking common ground by listening carefully and with an open mind to what others say as well as what they do, and acting accordingly. Former Spanish Minister of Defence Came Chacon Piqueras insists that although the international system is in a state of flux, diplomacy prevails as a "complex and ever-changing effort to bring allies and adversaries together for common cause, despite their differences" (In *Defence Diplomacy Plan*, 2012: 17). Similarly, Codevilla claims that "diplomacy serves to often prepare, as to avoid war" it is used to decide who wins and "usually codifies the results" (2008: 17). Diplomacy simplifies analysis of altered perspectives among states and it translates these adjustments through cooperation, reconciling the vanquished and stabilizing relationships. However, diplomacy is often used out of context, as a default all-purpose term to describe a complex process of conflict resolution. This can be evidenced by, for example, President George Bush declaring the ceasefire agreement between Hizballah and the Israeli government in August 2006 as a "victory for diplomacy" or more recently when Iran's decision to release five U.S. hostages caused President Obama to utter the same line.

Contemporary diplomacy is a product of adaptation, theorized and practiced in both its traditional and innovative forms, and carries a legacy of 'continuity and change' yet it seems to suffer from an externally imposed crisis of identity.[23] Jan Melissen recognises diplomacy's "inherently adaptive and

23 Throughout the canon of diplomacy, the phrase continuity and change is consistently conjured to describe the essence of diplomacy's durability. For some academics, continuity and change involves "a sequence of cumulative and continuous developments," James Der Derian, 'Mytho-Diplomacy', *On Diplomacy*, (1987), p. 202; Others use the phrase to frame the process of evolution, insisting, "change takes place within parameters that represent continuity," Jonsson & Hall, op. cit., p. 195–7; Hamilton and Langhorne state that despite the changes occurring in the international system "diplomacy demonstrates continuity" referring to continuity and change as 'diffusion' Keith Hamilton & Richard Langhorne, *The Practice of Diplomacy: Its Evolution, Theory and Administration*, (Hoboken: Taylor and Francis, 2010). pp. 3, 25 and 93; Berridge concludes *Diplomacy Theory and Practice* by returning to the theme of continuity and change, echoing Martin Wight who derived diplomatic theory from "the historiographical desire to establish continuity," Geoffrey Berridge, *Diplomacy theory and practice*, (Basingstoke: Palgrave Macmillan, 2010), p. 114; Sofer adopts the term, continuity, and evolution, to describe, "a continuous process of organic development and adaptation that dates back to the renaissance," Sasson Sofer,

elastic" nature but warns that a "preoccupation with the present and too great an emphasis on the notion of change may impede a deeper understanding of diplomacy" (1999: xix). Academics, practitioners and policy makers often endeavour to contain diplomacy within a neat theoretical box when the concept is so broad that it is difficult to corral. There are, however, constants, such as Hedley Bull key functions of diplomacy: representation, communication, negotiation, information management and the minimisation of friction (1977: 163–166). Definitions assist the reader in forming a basic understanding of a primary element of this paper although, as Melissen points out, while "definitions of diplomacy abound ... not all of them prove helpful in analysing today's varied manifestations of diplomacy" (1999: xvi). Der Derian agrees, dismissing the assumption "that we have reached-or even that we are approaching-after a long odyssey the best, final form of diplomacy" (1987: 3). However, this paper presents diplomacy, and those who engage in it, as a conduit by which information is conveyed to relevant parties (states). Diplomacy remains of fundamental importance to the international system; "a stable construct in an unstable world" (Soffer, 1988: 207). When adopting this realist perspective, "diplomacy fulfils an essential function as a neutral medium for the conduct of international relations" (Sharp, 2009: 54).

Two broad approaches in diplomatic studies emerged during the second half of the 20th century: positivism and post-positivism.[24] While positivists believe that the researcher and the researched subject are independent of each other, postpositivists accept that theories, background, knowledge, and values of the researcher can influence what is observed by recognizing the possible effects of biases. Positivist theorists, from Satow and Nicolson to Watson and Berridge,

---

'Old and new diplomacy: a debate revisited', op. cit., (1988), p. 205. According to Hocking, "diplomats are comforting figures in as much as they affirm continuity" Brian Hocking, 'The end(s) of diplomacy', *International Journal, Vol. 53, no. 1*, (1998), p. 169. It is evident that despite the different theoretical approaches of various academics, continuity and change reveal a universal ontology of diplomacy. Since change in diplomacy occurs slowly, with Kelley insisting the rate of change could only be characterised as "reptilian," similar to the imperceptible movements of a great ocean liner, it is possible for diplomacy to change direction whilst it remains on course to reach its destination; hence, continuity and change. John Robert Kelly, 'Three Assumptions of Continuity and Change', *Agency change Diplomatic action beyond the state*, (Lanham: Rowman & Littlefield Publishers, 2014), p. 16.

24 Smith and Owens define positivism as the creation of knowledge reliant on four assumptions; the unity of science, the neutrality of facts, the habitual nature of human society, and, regularities can be revealed through theorizing (2008: 178); Postpositivism is a metatheory which critiques and amends positivism.

have constructed a definition of diplomacy by highlighting fundamental, traditional elements and dismissing anyone or anything which does not conform to their guidelines. While postpositivist theorists would argue that a process in which people seek to reconcile and negotiate with others should be endorsed and encouraged without delegitimizing actors by applying historic labels. For postpositivist academics such as Sharp the definitions, rigid perceptions, and structures of traditional diplomacy are barriers to the creation of sustainable diplomatic theories and practices (2009: 54). Likeminded theorists such as Der Derian, Constantinou, Hocking, Langhorne and Pigman believe that the positivist approach to diplomatic studies "downplays, marginalizes, and omits key functions of the work of contemporary diplomacy" (2013: 78).[25] Pigman determines positivist diplomatic theory is useful and provides insight into modern diplomacy "but only up to a point" from where post-positivism's broader perspective allows us to comprehend the diplomacy of today and conceptualize the diplomacy of tomorrow (2010: 98). The foundations of this paper lie in traditional (state-centric) diplomacy and it concentrates on diplomacy's role in relation to a classic political-military agenda; "a 'dialogue' between sovereign states over the 'haute politique'—mainstays such as war, military alliances, territory, geopolitics, and traditional political-military concerns" (Watson, 1984: 1). However, it borrows a postpositivist perspective by accepting defence personnel as legitimate and equal participants in the diplomatic process.

A further round of conceptual housekeeping brings this section to a close with the following three paragraphs offer relevant points of clarification. The DoD's *Principles of Strategic Communication* defines dialogue as a "multi-faceted exchange of ideas to promote understanding and build relationships," (2009: 5) while Phillips stresses dialogue "involves active listening, engagement, and mutual understanding" which engenders trust and the cultivation of relationships over time (2012: 10). Cowan and Arsenault note a "distinction between a 'technical dialogue', in which ideas and information are exchanged, and a true dialogue, in which participants willingly and openly engage in true relationship-building exchanges in which feelings of control and dominance are minimized" (2008: 18).[26] Continuing the conceptual housekeeping, the paper defines and links three concepts; strategic culture, diplomatic culture and military culture. It does this because there is an assumption that while

25 Der Derian's *Antidiplomacy*, (1992) & Constantinou's *On the Way to Diplomacy* (1996) employ a postpositivist approach which seeks to reposition or erode the boundaries imposed on diplomacy by IR theory.

26 This distinction was introduced five decades earlier by Martin Buber in *The Life of Dialogue*, New York: Harper & Ron Publishers, 1958), pp. 123, 164.

there are shared civilian, political and military values, the differences are significant and widening.[27] However, this paper suggests that defence diplomacy melds diplomatic and military culture together in a unique and effective manner. Howlett defines strategic culture as "a product of a range of circumstances such as geography, history and narratives that shape collective identity, but one which also allows it a role in both enabling and constraining decisions about security" (2006: 3).[28] While Wiseman defines diplomatic culture as, "the accumulated communicative and representational norms, rules, and institutions devised to improve relations and avoid war between interacting and mutually recognizing political entities" (2005: 409–410). Finally, a CSIS report on *American Military Culture in the Twenty-First Century* expresses military culture as an amalgam of values, customs, traditions, and their philosophical underpinnings that, over time, has created a shared institutional ethos" (2000: xviii). Some question the purity of the amalgamation "On closer examination, the picture becomes more byzantine, with the presence of multiple sub-cultures (civilian and the individual cultures of the three services: navy, army, air force)" (Arklay, et al., 2011: 397).

In parallel to the traditional, state-centric theory of diplomacy at the core of this paper, several other IR oriented theories support the papers hypotheses; demonstrating the centrality of relationship building and the explaining how and why such relationships exist. Although there is a 'theory' of alliance creation, there is no unifying definition of the concept; broadly covering a spectrum from cooperation between political parties, military cooperation between states to business cooperation between private companies. From a more focused IR perspective, the situation remains opaque with literature

27 For example: Thomas Ricks, 'The Widening Gap Between Military and Society', *The Atlantic*, (July 1997), available at https://www.theatlantic.com/magazine/archive/1997/07/the-widening-gap-between-military-and-society/306158/ (Last accessed December 12, 2016).

28 See also: Angstrom, J. & Willem Honig, J. 'Regaining Strategy: Small Powers, Strategic Culture, and Escalation in Afghanistan, *Journal of Strategic Studies, Vol. 35, no. 5*, (2012). Angstrom & Honig define strategic culture "as a set of beliefs and norms which governs against whom, how, by what right and for what purposes the military force considered legitimate," p. 671. The authors demonstrate that the strategic culture of small allies of the U.S. in Afghanistan explain the variation in their strategic behaviour; David Kilcullen claims that "inherent in the notion of strategic culture is the idea that a nation's enduring circumstances give rise to a distinctive manner of perceiving, and using, national power—including military power," (2007: 47).

offering varying definitions.[29] However, there are central tenets which provide additional context to this papers discussion on defence diplomacy. At its core this paper presents alliance theory as the foundation and justification for inter-state cooperation as a form of security (national, regional, international). Classical Security Complex Theory is another useful theoretical lens to view and understand the fundamentals and functions of defence diplomacy. Buzan, Waever and de Wilde define a security complex "as a set of states whose major security perceptions and concerns are so interlinked that their national security problems cannot reasonably to analysed or resolved apart from one another" (2008: 12). The relationship building, knowledge transfer and 'shaping' mechanisms of defence diplomacy plays a role in either the creation of maintenance of such complexes. For example, defence diplomacy is best placed to navigate the internal dynamism of security complexes; across a spectrum spanning coalition building for outright conflict, though the creation of "security regimes" (CSBM's incorporating potential adversaries), through to the establishment of "a pluralistic security community" (Buzan, et al., 2008: 12).

Other IR concepts such as balancing, band wagoning or détente are also instructive.[30] Previous research has also identified the unique characteristics

---

29 Walt, Stephen M. 'Explaining Alliance Formation', in *The Origins of Alliance*, (New York: Cornell University Press, 1987), pp. 17–49; Barry Buzan, Ole Waever & Jaap de Wilde, *Security: A New Framework for Analysis*, London/Boulder: Lynne Rienner Publishers, 1998); John J. Mearsheimer, The Tragedy of Great Power Politics New York: W.W. Norton & Company, Inc, 2001); Kajsa Ji Noe Oest, 'The End of Alliance Theory?: A Literature Review of Realist Alliance Theory', *Research Paper*, (University of Copenhagen, 2007); Ali, Mehrunnisa, 'Soviet-Pakistan Ties since the Afghanistan Crisis', *Asian Survey*, vol. 23, no. 9, (1983), pp. 1025–1042.

30 For example: Stephen M. Walt, 'Alliance Formation and the Balance of World Power', *International Security, Spring, Vol. 9, no. 4,* (1985), pp. 3–43; Stephen M. Walt, 'Testing Theories of Alliance Formation: The Case of Southwest Asia', *International Organization*, Vol. 42, no. 2, (1988), pp. 275–316: Chong Ja Ian, 'Revisiting Responses To Power Preponderance: Going Beyond The Balancing-Bandwagoning Dichotomy', *Working Paper, No. 54*, (Singapore; Institute of Defence and Strategic Studies, 2003), pp. 1–34; Benjamin Pohl, 'Neither Bandwagoning nor Balancing: Explaining Europe's Security Policy', Contemporary Security Policy, No. 34, no. 2, (2013), pp. 353–373; Paula, L. Young Pectro, *Complacency: a threat to homeland security?*, (Monterey, CA: Naval Postgraduate School, 2014), p. 65 A final term which is central to: a) relations between nation states, b) the state of 21st century warfare and c) the nature of CT & COIN, is complexity. This study views a complex system as "one in which numerous independent elements continuously interact and spontaneously organize and reorganize themselves into more and more elaborate structures over time ... A complex system is one in which numerous independent elements continuously interact and spontaneously organize and reorganize themselves into

of U.S. diplomacy and this paper builds upon those studies in an attempt to contribute to the discipline of Diplomatic Studies by identifying defence diplomacy as an intrinsic and under-researched aspect of traditional diplomacy, discussing the relationship between the diplomatic sector and armed forces.[31] Additionally, terms alliance and coalitions are often conflated as both require multilateral military cooperation but there are clear differences; however, diplomacy plays a critical role in both. Conceptually, alliances are formal, treaty-based arrangements, formed for preventive/defensive purposes, while coalitions are ad hoc security agreements among states to engage an adversary.[32] Moreover, the theory and practice of war evolved during the 20th century, as former U.S. SECDEF Casper Weinberger declared in 1984 "the line between peace and war is less clearly drawn than at any time in our history." The evolution has continued in the three decades since the Secretary's statement with terms such as irregular, grey zone, unrestricted, asymmetrical, multi-dimensional permeating defence ministry and armed force publications.[33] In this era of complexity, diminished expectations of what diplomacy can achieve in irregular conflicts in general and the Long War in particular are often the product of ineffective foreign policy and/or a misunderstanding of

more and more elaborate structures over time." From this definition one can argue that defence diplomacy is a useful mechanism to offset uncertainty, increase stability and align 'likeminded' elements (states).

31 Schneider, C. 'Culture Communicates: U.S. Diplomacy that Works', in S. Mawby (ed), *Discussions Papers in Diplomacy, No. 94*, (Netherlands Institute of International Relations 'Clingendael', 2004); Wiseman, G. 'Engaging the Enemy: An Essential Norm for Sustainable US Diplomacy', C. Constantinou and J. Der Derian (eds.), *Sustainable Diplomacies*, (Basingstoke: Palgrave Macmillan, 2010), pp. 213–234; Clinton, D. 'The Distinction between Diplomacy and Foreign Policy in American International Though and Practice', In G. Wiseman (ed.), *American Diplomacy*, (Leiden: Brill, 2011); Sharp, P. 'Obama, Clinton and the Diplomacy of Change', in G. Wiseman (ed), *American Diplomacy*, (Leiden: Brill, 2011), pp. 159–177; Foley, F. 'Why inter-agency operations break down: US counterterrorism in comparative perspective', *European Journal of International Security, Vol. 1, no. 2*, (2016), pp. 150–175. These authors investigated whether U.S. exceptionalism translates into exceptional national institutions, foreign policy and diplomacy.

32 Walt defines an alliance as "a formal commitment for security cooperation between two or more states, intended to augment each member's power, security, and/or influence" (2009: 86).

33 Recently, the U.S. House Armed Service Committee conducted a hearing on *The Evolution of Hybrid Warfare and Key Challenges* on March 22, 2017 where witnesses were tasked with informing the House on the complexities of Hybrid Warfare which incorporates all these terms, available at https://armedservices.house.gov/legislation/hearings/full-committee-hearing-evolution-hybrid-warfare-and-key-challenges (Last accessed March 2017).

what diplomacy actually is; effectively blaming the messenger and the act of message giving instead of the message (Murray, 2006: 162, 234). This preliminary discussion sought to address this confusion.

The paper identifies both 'who' is involved, as well as 'how' relationships are built and maintained. The 'who' discussion helps us to look beyond the traditional ideal of the diplomatist espoused by Satow (1922), Nicolson (1955) or even Bull (1977). Whereas the 'how' prioritises the process in which this expanded network of diplomatic actors engage each other. Adopting this approach advances a conceptual framework introduced by Corneliu Bjola who sought to encourage greater scholarship in Diplomatic Studies by "demonstrating the practical value of theoretically informed accounts of the mechanisms and processes by which diplomats steer international politics along constructive versus destructive pathways of interaction" (2013: 9). Bjola offered his framework as a "more promising alternative" (Ibid.: 19) to the limitations inherent in the approaches which had hitherto "gained recognition" (Ibid.: 6). The methods which Bjola, and by extension this paper, strove to complement, were those which viewed diplomacy as either: a practical mechanism of conducting international relations, a subordinate or parallel lens to understand such relations, or the "English School' approach, which itself was a progression from rigid scholarship of the early 20th century (Ibid.: 6–7). Through adroit application of 'collective intentionality' (Mitzen, 2005)[34] Bjola envisioned "a more nuanced understanding of international relations" (Bjola, 2013: 2). This paper supports Bjola's hypothesis that "diplomacy is a way of conducting international relations, thinking about these relations and also doing enquiry" (Ibid.: 3). Additionally, while delivering a unique perspective on an issue of significant global importance in the 21st century, the paper also advances Bjola's exploratory proposal by demonstrating "what turns diplomacy into a core analytical and practical method of international engagement?" (Bjola, 2013: 1).

Throughout the Long War, the U.S. and its allies have engaged in various whole-of-government actions. These actions include building up offensive and defensive military capabilities, creating strategic alliances and coalitions whilst strengthening existing political relations. In practice, diplomacy not only contributes to these strategic activities, it is critical to them, while diplomatic theory helps us to understand the relationships we have today, and

34 Mitzen presented collective intentionality as a concept which explains why states engage in multi-actor mechanisms in pursuit of its foreign policy, how collective interest can supplement and/or supplant national interest, and how said engagement generates domestic and international legitimacy. Bjola infers "collective intentionality is a catalyst for relationships of friendship" (2013: 15).

to build the relationships we need in the short, medium and long-term. This section has discussed the fundamentals of diplomacy to support its relevance in IR more generally but also to illuminate "the power that is wielded by diplomats as relationship creators" (Bjola, 2013: 8). With this knowledge in hand, the paper transitions from a discussion of traditional diplomacy into a broad examination of defence diplomacy in theory and practice. The following section answers one question; if diplomacy is 'the profession, activity, or skill of managing international relations, typically by a country's representatives abroad,'[35] then exactly what is defence diplomacy, and is it defined by its actors, activities, outcomes or objectives? Academic definitions and practical summaries of defence diplomacy are therefore presented to answer this question. The following definitional discourse is not merely based on semantics for it has key substantive implications which lie at the core of this study.

Defining Defence Diplomacy

This section articulates the connection between diplomacy and the military. As we begin to rationalize the concept, our genesis is thus: "each state maintains a military establishment to serve national interests, counter threats, and project armed force internationally," while diplomacy is traditionally perceived as the management of relations between sovereigns to avoid war (Barkawi, 2011: 598). Centuries of international relations demonstrate that diplomacy and war have been the primary levers of statecraft (means) by which states have advanced their national interests (ends). Sun Tzu dictates "diplomacy and war are not just closely related—they comprise a continuous, seamless activity (with diplomacy) the best means of attaining his ideal of victory without bloodshed" (Handel, 2005: 24). A quote widely attributed to Frederick the Great of Prussia eloquently expresses the relationship, stating simply that "Diplomacy without arms is like music without instruments." While Clausewitz wrote that "war is nothing but a continuation of political intercourse, with a mixture of other means', he also argued that "political intercourse does not cease by war itself, it is not changed into something quite different ... it continues to exist ... through war until peace takes place" (1997: 357). Mattingly (1955) locates Clausewitz's theory in praxis, recalling how diplomats in the Middle-Ages withdrew to the rear of the battle phalanx only to re-emerge to begin negotiations when hostilities ended. In his seminal tome on COIN, *Learning to Eat Soup with a Knife*, John Nagl writes that "in conventional war, violence was a last resort, used after diplomacy had failed ... political leaders handed over to military men the problem that diplomacy had not solved" (2002: 23).

---

35 *Oxford English Dictionary* definition of diplomacy.

Conversely, the threat of military force has, implicitly and explicitly, lingered on the periphery of diplomatic negotiations. Therefore it's a complimentary rather than a binary choice by states to support their national interests by co-opting, coercing or deterring 'others' through military superiority or peacefully imparting its interests and/or will onto another. Secretary of Defence (SECDEF) Mattis observes that "if you have covenants without swords, without an effective military, then your moral voice will never be heard as loudly" (March 20, 2014),[36] By extension, an effective coalition requires more than a set of values or a common philosophy (values being irrelevant if you can't defend them); therefore it needs to act, as well as speak, in unison.

President Kennedy declared to the U.S. Congress in 1961 that 'diplomacy and defense are no longer distinct alternatives, one to be used where the other fail; both must complement each other.[37] Sofer contends that during the Cold-War era, the threat of force, rather than the subtle strategic activity of diplomacy, was seen as the essential foundation of a viable foreign policy (1998: 196). However, in contemporary 'small wars', military and political action operate simultaneously for combat and diplomacy are different aspects of the same thing. While Cottey and Forster assert that defence diplomacy is not an alternative to the more traditional roles of armed forces or to other foreign and security policy instruments, but rather as a supplement to them" (2004: 77). Raymond Aron argued that:

> the ambassador and the soldier live and symbolize international relations which, insofar as they are inter-state relations, concern diplomacy and war ... Inter-state relations are expressed in and by specific actions of individuals whom I shall call symbolic, the diplomat and the soldier. Two

---

36 See also: Wesley K. Clark, 'Aftermath: Reckoning with Iraq and Afghanistan', *American Forum*, University of Virginia's Miller Center, WPT Public Media, (Published February 12, 2015), available at https://www.youtube.com/watch?v=6ntoApe_Jwg; Retired four-star Army general and former Democratic candidate for President Wesley K. Clark argues that U.S. military 'supremacy' is vital as it demonstrates America's ability to lead, not to dominate and which facilitates the spread of a set of values to facilitate the creation "of a global civilisation which provides the opportunities for individuals to reach their potential and to live in peace and harmony...."

37 Pres. Kennedy told policymakers the "primary purpose of our arms is peace, not war-to make certain that they will never have to be used—to deter all wars, general or limited, nuclear or conventional, large or small—to convince all potential aggressors that any attack would be futile—to provide backing for diplomatic settlement of disputes—to insure the adequacy of our bargaining power for an end to the arms race. The basic problems facing the world today are not susceptible to a military solution."

> men, and only two men, no longer function as individual members but as representatives of the collectivies to which they belong …
>
> 2003: 5

Moreover, military and diplomacy are both subordinate to foreign policy according to Watson, with each being subject to criticism when they fail to reach the desired policy goals (1984: 59). Therefore to avoid adverse policy outcomes, states seek to "harmonise the instruments of national power" to achieve its policies and strategies or "to defend or extend what are assessed by a state to be in its vital national interests" (Dorman & Uttley, 2016: 197, 199). Claudia Seymour notes the importance of presenting alternatives to win/lose outcome which is likely to lead to an eruption or escalation of conflict. Seymour finds that when perceptions are "moved from zero-sum to positive sum, then options for conflict management are greatly augmented" (2003, para 8). SECDEF Mattis (2015) has said that "although you'll hear either we go to war or we negotiate, the traditional diplomatic tools do not require only two options as there's a host of ways that we carry out our or express our values."[38] In this regard, for some, the utility of defence diplomacy is clear; Peter Leahy proclaims that "in an increasingly complex global security environment defence diplomacy adds a new and very useful dimension to traditional diplomacy" (2014: 15). Theory supports Leahy's assertion.

Modern military theory (and diplomatic engagement) can be divided into strategic (grand or national strategy), operational (ways of achieving policy objectives) and tactical levels (means of achieving operational objectives).[39] *The Air and Space Power Mentoring Guide* affirms that "the three levels allow causes and effects of all forms of war and conflict to be better understood-despite their growing complexity" (1997: 1).[40] Drew and Snow express succinctly the contrast between levels as "tactics are concerned with 'doing the job right', and higher levels of strategy are concerned with 'doing the right job'" (2006: 24). Furthermore, just as various components of the defence establishment are de-

38 Comments made during discussion with Ambassador Charles Hill and General James Mattis on the Iran Deal, Democracy, and Freedom, *The Hoover Institution*, (July 16, 2015), available at https://www.youtube.com/watch?v=g5QeGKIMgUY&t=13s.

39 For detail see: David Jablonsky, 'Strategy and the Operational Level of War: Part I', *Parameters*, (Spring, 1987), pp. 65–76; David Jablonsky, 'Strategy and the Operational Level of War: Part II', *Parameters*, (Summer, 1987), pp. 52–67; J. Boone Bartholomees, JR. *Theory of War and Strategy, Vol. 1*, (4th ed.), (Carlisle, PA: Strategic Studies Institute, U.S. Army War College, 2010), pp. 1–385.

40 See also: 'Unified Action', Chapter 2, *U.S Army FM 3-0 Operations*, op. cit., pp. 2–4.

ployed in each domain in support of a common foreign policy objective, the diplomatic mechanisms and language may differ across strategic, operational and tactical realm yet they are universally supported by the fundamentals of diplomacy. Anton Du Plessis (2008: 113) echoes Martin Wight (19977: 113) stating that defence diplomacy enhances the 'master institution' (diplomacy) and 'master process (diplomatic negotiation) of international relations). Theoretically the increased level of military to military cooperation improves the "effectiveness of the armed forces of cooperating nations and the efficiency of their security and defence spending through greater mutual understanding or access to new capabilities and training possibilities" (Ministerio De Defensa Espana: 13).

However, Major General Craig Orme claims defence oriented relationships delivers benefits beyond mere tangibles, contributing "to both capability and culture … we can learn to deal with complexity, and remove prejudice and preconceptions from our policy and operational decision making" (2013: 2). In this regard defence diplomacy assists the transition from strategic objectives to tactical actions and vice-versa. Under the direction of the Ministry of Foreign Affairs (MFA), defence diplomacy is generally "the non-violent use of the state's defence apparatus to advance the strategic aims of a government "through cooperation with other countries" (2014: 8). Singh and Tan define defence diplomacy as "the cooperative activities undertaken by militaries and the related infrastructure during peacetime" (2011: 2). Similarly the Oxford Handbook of Modern Diplomacy identifies defence diplomacy as the "employment, without duress, in time of peace of the resources of defence to achieve specific national goals, primarily through relationships with others" (Cheyre, 2013: 369). Whereas Rolfe delineates military cooperation as a "sub-set of defence diplomacy" and defines the concept as "non-warlike" activities of a state's armed forces rather than the often used 'non-violent' descriptor (2015: 1).

Whether 'non-warlike' or 'non-violent,' defence diplomacy employs the predominant institutions of the state (the MFA and Department of Defence-DoD) as natural allies in the execution of diplomacy.[41] While in practice, the military appears to remain a blunt force object, routinely defence diplomacy uses the defence apparatus "to persuade rather than muscle recalcitrant foreigners into line" (Freeman, 2015). Du Plessis concludes that defence diplomacy mobilises

41 The UK MoD *Strategic Defence Review* declares "The Armed Forces and the Ministry of Defence have considerable experience and expertise in conflict prevention work but the creation of a formal Defence Diplomacy Mission will make this a core defence activity. This will give it greater priority and ensure that it is properly linked to the Government's broader policy objectives" (1998: 20).

the "trained expertise and disciple" of the military "to achieve national and foreign objectives abroad" (2008: 92). Similarly, Bisley contends that "while it may technical in its means, it is inherently political in its ends ... using defence personnel and assets to communicate, negotiate and more generally manage relations between states" (2014: 14). Willard presents defence diplomacy as "the conduct by military diplomats of negotiations and other relations between nations, nations' militaries, and nations' citizens aimed at influencing the environment in which the military operates" (2006: 9). While others scholars propose that defence diplomacy compensates for a complex global security environment, becoming an effective mechanism for achieving national interests short of military conflict.[42] In contemporary international relations, diplomacy is often referred to as 'soft power' where as military power in labelled as 'hard power' (Nye 1990: 156).[43] However, the distinction between soft and hard power has become opaque, creating "a zone of indistinction between cooperation and conflict, diplomacy and governance" (Constantinou & Opondo, 2015: 4). For Winger, Nye's terminology (Hard and Soft power) has been shackled to specific individual practices, suggesting the military has been mistakenly linked "as an institution of hard power as practice has blinded us to its capacity to be used in other ways" (2014: 8). Winger seamlessly blends the two by defining defence diplomacy as "an exercise of soft power practiced by the defence establishment of one country ... to mould the strategic thinking and institutions of another" (2014: 14).

Although active in times of peace, this paper presents defence diplomacy as compliant mechanism to integrate and manage the overall military response "in states at risk of failure, in failed states ... in states emerging from long periods of conflict such as Afghanistan, and in states in peaceful post-conflict rebuilding periods" (Reinert & Hussey, 2015: 121). The ability to manage a military response assists states in producing "a coordinated set of military actions whose direct and indirect, physical and psychological effects might achieve the ends set by the national political leadership at the national level" (Smith, 2002:

42 Edmonds M. & G. Mills, *Beyond the Horizon: Defence, Diplomacy and South Africa's Maritime Opportunities*, (Lancaster, UK: Centre for Defence and International Security Studies, 1998); Sending, O. J., Pouliot, V. & Neumann, I. B. 'The Future of Diplomacy', *International Journal, Vol. 6, no. 3*, (2011), pp. 527–542; Taylor, B., et al. 'Defence Diplomacy: Is the Game Worth the Candle?, *Centre of Gravity, Discussion papers*. (Canberra: ANU College of Asia & the Pacific, 2014).

43 Nye explains that "Soft power is something that a country has that can be generated from cultural, political and economic behaviour, but it is better thought of as a by-product rather than a raw material. Soft power is non-coercive, not simply non-military."

470). From a U.S. perspective, defence diplomacy enables it "to coordinate the military actions of the operational commanders with any allied actions and to ensure that all military actions would be perceived in the right way by other military actors, neutrals, friends, coalition partners, and allies" (Smith, 2002: 470). The *2015 National Security Strategy* outlines the importance of diplomacy in defensive military engagement, stating that only "U.S. diplomacy and leadership, backed by a strong military" can effectively deter "future acts of inter-state aggression." Similarly, Ryan Crocker, former U.S. Ambassador to Lebanon, Kuwait, Syria, Pakistan, Iraq, and Afghanistan, asserts that the U.S. is faced with a complex threat environment "in which, in some cases, military force is essential but it is being used in a political context so you've got to have the diplomacy right if your force is going to be effective" 2013: 103).

Fetic claims, "the role of defence diplomacy is to manage military forces from a diplomatic point of view" (2014: 10). K. A. Muthanna supports this statement declaring "defence diplomacy can further country specific foreign policy objectives by managing defence foreign relations and supporting the other diplomatic initiatives of government" (2011: 3). Additional academic oriented insight comes from Constantinou and Opondo who emphasize the diplomatic component of civil/military engagement, which permits states to oscillate between developmental-humanitarian plans, surveillance, policing and occasional warfare" (2015: 9). The benefits of civil/military engagement extend beyond personnel and expertise with the creation of dual-use assets proving to be an outcome of equal importance. The European Political Strategy Center highlights the European Coastguard and 'next generation' Government Satellite Communications as two recent products of Europe's "civilian/military synergies" (2015: 10). K. A. Muthanna states that the UK and other NATO nations, China, Australia and the U.S. "could be considered the world leaders" in defence diplomacy (2011: 8). With discernible commonalities, primary source documentation supports this statement as well as theory based justifications presented above.

UK *Defence Doctrine* (*JDP 0-01*) defines defence diplomacy as the application of resources from across the spectrum of defence, for the purpose of achieving positive outcomes in the development of bilateral and multilateral relationships ... (as well as) using defence assets to support diplomatic objectives and further defence interests" (2014: 12). The UK Ministry of Defence (MOD) declares defence diplomacy will reinforce the UK's long-term security by increasing international trust through relationship building. According to Matthew Ford, the MOD's 2011 Building Stability Overseas Strategy (BSOS) and the 2015 International Defence Engagement Strategy (IDES) prioritise defence diplomacy to prevent conflicts and assist post-conflict reconstruction by "working with and through overseas governments and partners" (2014: 496). The BSOS, is presented by the UK MOD's *International Defence Engagement Strategy* as a blend "of foreign policy realism and moral imperatives" (2015: 1) which prioritises security sector reform (SSR) and uses the UK's defence capabilities and assets more strategically to create an "Intervention to end all Interventions" (Bachman, 2014: 607).[44] While the IDES articulates how the defence forces network of "Defence Attachés, civilian defence advisors, Loan Service personnel, overseas exchange and liaison officers, permanently established overseas training teams allows defence (alongside other instruments of national power) … to shape the environment, promote the rules based international order and prevent instability in support of the UK's security and prosperity" (2015: 1). The IDES employs defence diplomacy to create opportunities for the UK "to achieve our ends more efficiently than through bilateral channels by combing efforts with like-minded countries" (2015: 3).

The Ministerio De Defensa Espana considers defence diplomacy is an important diplomatic instrument to foster confidence and transparency and began a program to refine its military capabilities as well as its strategic partners "through the exchange of experiences, procedures, tactics and armament" (2012: 16). This decision is guided by theory in that increased 'openness' mitigates zero-sum characteristics of the 'security dilemma' by increasing the pool of defence cooperation thus overcoming "the inherent ambiguity of some military postures and/or foreign policy intentions" (Wiseman, 2002: 17).[45] Through defence diplomacy, Spanish military personnel supplement the diplomatic process using their expertise, personal relations and networks, as well as the military intelligence apparatus, to establish and maintain existing relationships and reduce tensions and/or avoiding unintended conflicts. In recent times NATO Secretary General Stoltenberg (2015) and Chairman of the U.S. Joint Chiefs of Staff (JCOS) General Dunford (2016) have both championed the confidence building qualities of defence diplomacy "to reduce the risk of miscalculation."

Shifting regions from Europe to Asia, the Indian Ministry of Defence defines defence diplomacy as the exchange of high-level defence related visits, dialogue on security challenges and port calls; defence cooperation, i.e. those activities covered by training exchanges, combined exercises; sourcing,

---

44 *Joint Publication 1-02, DoD Dictionary of Military and Associated Terms* defines SSR as the "set of policies, plans, programs, and activities that a government undertakes to improve the way it provides safety, security, and justice," (2001: 486).

45 The concept was introduced during the late 70's & 80's, for example Jervis, Robert, 'Cooperation Under the Security Dilemma', *World Politics, Vol. 30, no. 2*, (1978), pp. 167–214.

development, production and marketing of defence equipment and other forms of cooperation" (*Annual Report*, 2004: 184). While the Peoples Republic of China (PRC) specify, in successive Defence White Papers, that the Peoples Liberation Army (PLA) actively leverages military diplomacy to build greater transparency, reduce the risk of miscalculation based on "the principles of good-neighbourliness and friendliness, mutual benefit and cooperation and long-term stability" (1998: 27). While Indonesia, an important regional actor in terms of its military, diplomatic and economic capabilities, has invested significant monetary and political capital into the process in support of its "independent and active foreign policy" (Djalal, 2012: 41).[46] As a country whose "military has traditionally been a means for achieving a government's foreign and security policy either through the threatened or actual use of coercion in diplomacy" successive recent governments posit "diplomacy [as] the [country's] first line of defense" (*Indonesian Defense White Article, 2002: 37*). The 2003 and 2008 *Defense White Article*'s present a multi-level approach consisting of its military-to-military engagement with ASEAN countries, defence cooperation with periphery nations such as Australia, China, Russia, South Korea, and the U.S as well as troop contribution to UN peacekeeping operations (*Indonesian Defense White Article*, 2008: 140, 152).

In 1989 Senator Gareth Evans, Australia's Minister for Foreign Affairs officially articulated his state's acceptance of the broadened security agenda and the role of defence diplomacy, declaring the instruments available to protect Australia's security are multi-dimensional. These include military and politico-military capability (in the border zone between defence and diplomacy); diplomacy; economic links; assistance with development and so-called 'non-military threats'; and the exchange of people and ideas—work together to help shape a security environment which is favourable to Australia's interests" (Ministerial Statement, 1989). Minister Evans dictated "diplomacy should also extend beyond the region itself to dialogue on regional security issues with those external actors capable of exercising influence within the region" (Ministerial Statement, 1989). A decade later, former Australian Chief of Defence Force Admiral Barrie declared "security can no longer be seen as a one-dimensional-threat-defence-equation. Security must be seen as a whole-of-nation concept" (1999: para 6). More recently the Australian government reaffirmed the defence force's "international engagement is both a strategic

46 See also: Lis Gindarsah, 'Strategic hedging in Indonesia's defense diplomacy', *Defense & Security Analysis, Vol. 32, no. 4*, pp. 336–353.

necessity and a strategic asset" (*Defence White Paper*, 2016: 56).[47] Although the current Australian Defence Minister Marise Paine has not spoken on the mechanism specifically, her predecessor David Johnston was a vocal supporter of defence diplomacy (National Press Club, Tokyo, June 12, 2014).

Contemporary armed forces are faced with a wide variety of opponents including violent non-state actors; local, national and trans-national (tribal, ethnic and religious). In response, military professionals have developed new practices for mediating and interacting with a broader set of actors, engaging in what Cottey and Forster refer to as "a growing range of peacetime cooperative tasks" (2004:8). However, cooperative security requires two essential factors: a certain level of trust and the ability to identify commonalities which serve as a nucleus for a diverse group of actors with competing domestic and regional agendas (King: 41). It must be recognised that states do not generically coalesce into united fronts, more so in the 21st century. Clohesy identifies "a nagging sense that the bonds of solidarity that we feel should draw us together are looser than ever. Perhaps they have finally snapped or perhaps they were never so strong in the first place" (2013: 1).

However, partners *do* receive considerable benefits when engaging in military coalitions thus U.S. "allies have an incentive to respond favourably to support the alliance while simultaneously having to make a decision that is acceptable to domestic political audiences" (von Hlatky & Darden, 2015: 31). Relationships and trust are critical elements defence diplomacy; trust between those involved in the process and trust in the process itself. As former U.S. Special Representative for Afghanistan, the late Amb Richard Holbrooke underscored, in "diplomacy, process can often be as important as substance" (1999, 178).[48] In both aspects, relationships are incrementally reinforced by an increase in the other. KA Muthanna claims that despite India's rising power status, its inability to evince trust and goodwill with its neighbours has led most of them preferring to employ defence diplomacy with China as an India-specific countervailing factor" (2011: 1). While SECDEF Mattis underscored trust as an essential element of the combined effort in the Long War declaring that "operations today move at the speed of trust" (*Conversations with History*, 2014).

Throughout the Long War the soldier and the diplomat of U.S. and Coalition states have worked in tandem to mitigate conflict and influence behaviours both within the group and towards unstable nations and adversaries. The U.S.

47 Using policy documents from the past decade, Baldino & Carr (2016: 142–143) demonstrate that successive Australian Defence Ministers from both sides of the political isle endorsed defence diplomacy.

48 See also Jonathan Powell, Talking to Terrorists: How Armed Conflict Ends, (London: The Bodley Head, 2014), pp. 203–205.

Department of State (hence referred to as State) *Strategic Plan* (2007–2012) directs this process by building "strong partnerships through robust political-military activities" (2007: 13).[49] Moreover, established diplomatic terms such as mediation, cooperation and representation are institutionalised in SSR, ceasefire enforcement as well as training and equip missions. Defence diplomacy facilitates multi-actor cooperative security arrangements, whereby the outcomes of a robust defence diplomacy mechanism are mutually beneficial whilst serving to reinforce the process itself. Tarrosy supports this statement; identifying diplomacy (the concept around which defence diplomacy revolves) as both a policy instrument and global process, referring to these two aspects as the micro-actor level perspective and the macro-system level perspective (Tarrsoy, 2012: 72). At either level; trust, capacity building, transparency, burden sharing, SSR, minimization of friction, as well as 'shaping both the strategic environment' and the worldview of others and the institutionalization of certain positive behaviours, are just some of the outcomes from establishing such structures.[50] The UK *Strategic Defence Review* labels this process as "disarmament of the mind" (1998: 106).

Defence diplomacy brings allies, former adversaries/emerging partners together through bilateral and minilateral meetings, high-level civilian or military personnel visits, Navy or Airforce stop-overs, education and training exercises (termed professional military education-PME) as well as general capacity building through industry and technological support and defence materiel (Pant, 2016).[51] Building the capacity of HN security forces (HN/HNSF) has

---

49 Bush's post-9/11 foreign policy sought to transform the international system of states by reformatting the levers of state (military and diplomacy) to best serve U.S. interests (Tan & Singh, 2012: 223). Condi Rice's 'Transformative Diplomacy' (2006) sought to essentially create and maintain like-minded democratic states which conduct themselves and respond to issues in a predictable manner. A strategy of 'partnership not paternalism' centred on working with states not for them is a more sustainable approach for international security. Tan and Singh argue "there is no denying the fact that all diplomacy is to an extent transformative in orientation, in that states seek incessantly to influence other states or regimes to modify their perspectives and policies in ways that benefit the former" (2012: 224).

50 *JP5-0 Joint Operation Planning* defines "Shaping or Phase 0 operations as "Joint and multinational operations—inclusive of normal and routine military activities—and various interagency activities are performed to dissuade or deter potential adversaries and to assure or solidify relationships with friends and allies"; however, it concludes that shaping occurs throughout 'all' the phases of operation planning, (2011: xxiii).

51 Pant claims years of progressive engagement between the U.S. and India have shifted a culture of 'presumptive no' to one of 'presumptive yes' which has led to increases in technology transfer, multi-industry commercial ventures and military training exercises.

become a key element of contemporary military operations today, exemplified in ongoing operations such as Afghanistan.[52] Increasing the capacity of others is a key relationship building component of defence diplomacy which "can help improve the quality of regional partner's militaries and consequently foster goodwill between countries and the U.S." (Suh, et al., 2016). These measures are dual purpose, delivering specific government to government outcomes, whilst indirectly shaping the strategic environment by influencing foreign publics through military led public diplomacy or more accurately 'strategic communication.'[53] A U.S. Advisory Commission on Public Diplomacy report prioritised the ability of U.S. diplomats to influence foreign audiences to offset "anti-American sentiment" generated through its foreign policy (2010. 44).

---

52 The goal of changing any HNSF is: a) an accountable, self-sustaining, capable and credible force able to meet the security challenges faced by the HN and b) being looked upon as legitimate by the domestic population. Achieving this may take years, but all activities should seek to achieve this aim from the outset. Coalition forces have recognized that conventional military action alone is not sufficient for enduring success. Success, in contemporary military operations will be determined in large part by how well and how quickly HNSF can assume the responsibility for security from Coalition. Ultimately, this legitimizes HN authority & enables the exit of Coalition.

53 Department of Defense, *Report on Strategic Communication*, (December 2009) available at http://mountainrunner.us/files/dod/1055_Dec2009.pdf. However, the DoD states openly that it "does not engage directly in public diplomacy, which is the purview of the State Department, but numerous DoD activities are designed specifically to support the State Department's public diplomacy efforts and objectives, which in turn support national objectives. DoD refers to these activities as "Defense Support to Public Diplomacy (DSPD)", p. 5; *The National Military Strategic Plan for the War on Terrorism'* JCOS, U.S. Department of State, (2006). The JCOS defines strategic communication as "the transmission of integrated and coordinated U.S. government themes and messages that advances U.S. interests and policies through a synchronised interagency effort supported by public diplomacy, public affairs, and military information operations (IO) security cooperation, in concert with other political, economic, information and military actions," p. 38; State defines public diplomacy as an action which "seeks to promote the national interest of the U.S. through understanding, informing and influencing foreign audiences" See also: Brian E. Carlson, 'Who Tells America Story Abroad? State's Public Diplomacy or DoD's Strategic Communication?, in Gordon Adams & Shoon Murray (eds.), *The Militarization of US Foreign Policy*, (Washington D.C.: Georgetown University Press, 2014), pp. 145–165; Russell Rumbaugh and Matthew Leatherman, 'The Pentagon as Pitchman: Perception and Reality of Public Diplomacy', *Stimson Center*, (September 2013), pp. 10–11 available at http://www.stimson.org/images/uploads/researchpdfs/Pentagon_as_pitchman.pdf; Phillips, C. D. *Towards a Theory of Strategic Communication: A Relationship Management Approach*, (Carlisle Barracks, PA: United States Army War College, 2012); See also authors cited in this paper: Munoz, 2012; Manor, 2016; von Hlatky, 2016.

While Wallin asserts "the military conducts operations and activities that are both directly and indirectly intended to influence the attitude and actions of foreign publics and military audiences to support foreign policy objectives" (2006: 2). Again diplomatic practice is supported by theory; for example Geoffrey Cowan and Amelia Arsenault stress "while dialogue between cultures is an admirable goal, it begins with dialogue between individuals ... These dialogic relationships provide the building blocks through which a broader "dialogue between civilizations" can evolve" (2008: 17).

Into the breach step contemporary military personnel who are professional and articulate, and exhibit a unique understanding of the "many dynamic, difficult and varied national security and foreign policy challenges" founded on shared military experiences (DoD, nd.: 1). They also perform a unique dual role as communicators in supporting U.S. military objectives whilst advancing U.S. national security interests. In this respect, the 'diplomat in uniform' is as prepared to enter the once cloistered international diplomatic realm as any graduate of any MFA training facility; both view themselves as apolitical representatives of the state (Anderson & Veillette, 2014).[54] In the Long War for example, military outreach to foreign publics through state visits, joint training operations, shore visits ect, creates a positive public image and subsequently influences political behaviour (Douglas, 2007). Members of the armed forces as well as their civilian counterparts use public diplomacy as a "tool through which political actors try to achieve their goals in the international arena" (Yarchi, 2016: 1072). Henrikson argues these "military-to-military activities foster new relationships, not just operational relations but also bonds of collaboration and genuine community with host cities" (2013: 277). Statements of support such as the one made by SECDEF Carter in February 2016 following an attack on Turkish troops by Islamic militants or his speech on the day after the BREXIT vote in Britain are examples of the public diplomacy/strategic communication practiced by the defence departments around the world.[55] Similar constructive engagement or enhanced interaction sees defence personnel entering into international political discussion to allay fears, clarify a position

54 Diplomats in uniform are also referred to the less than flattering label of 'soldiers in sandals.' p. 97.

55 Statement from Secretary of Defense Ash Carter on Bombing in Turkey. Release No: NR-057-16, 17th Feb 2016 http://www.defense.gov/News/News-Releases/News-Release-View/Article/657534/statement-from-secretary-of-defense-ash-carter-on-bombing-in-turkey?source=GovDelivery. Carter's statement read, "... We stand with our Turkish allies in the face of this horrific act, which only strengthens our resolve to deepen our ongoing cooperation in the fight against terrorism."

and/or project confidence. Although defence diplomacy is supported by sound theory, its role in foreign policy/national security is questioned which mirrors an ongoing debate on the rise, role and impact of non-state actors in the previously state-centric domain of diplomacy. The remainder of the section offers a broad critique of defence diplomacy.

A Critique of Defence Diplomacy —"Grand Expectations, Little Promise" (White, 2014)

Detractors often highlight a disparity between defence diplomacy's core assumptions and its practical outcomes. A primary assumption is that transparency, legislative oversight and an increased focus on rule of law and human rights is a positive by-product of defence diplomacy (Du Plessis, 2008; Henrikson, 2013). For example, the U.S. *Foreign Assistance Act* lists one of its primary objectives as teaching foreign military officers "basic issues involving internationally recognized human rights" (1961: 193). This issue is discussed in more detail below; however, Cooley (2008) and Bell, et.al (2016) find the assumption unsubstantiated, failing to find the 'correct' balance between ensuring personal freedoms and securing U.S. national interest. Another assumption is that defence diplomacy creates 'strategic leverage' by identifying intentions and influencing behaviours (Floyd, 2010; Knabbs-Kellar & Wirajuda, 2016). For example, Bisley states that defence diplomacy "improves information flows and enhances mutual understanding of states capabilities" reducing the risk of misinterpretation leading to poor strategic decision-making (2014, 13). However, Carr (2015) suggests that identifying and interpreting intentions is one thing, but questions the misplaced ambition of using defence diplomacy to somehow change a state's political alignment. Similarly, the multinational character of a coalition "merits particular attention because national interests and organizational influence may compete with doctrine and efficiency. Consensus is painstakingly difficult, and solutions are often national in character" ABCA *Armies Coalition Operations Handbook*, 2008). Similarly, Ford maintains the UK MOD's current defence diplomacy strategy merely "supports the U.S. exercise of global power rather than offer an alternative to it" (2014: 496).

Proponents of defence diplomacy also have to contend with the persistent uncertainty which revolves around the independent role of beliefs, interests and/or ideology; can cooperation persuade others to alter their military doctrine? For example SECDEF Mattis has previously indicated that 21st century defence personnel must be not only "willing to listen to other people's ideas but willing to be persuaded" (*Conversations with History*, 2014). Some scholars suggest that while defence diplomacy is an effective mechanism to improve partnerships at a tactical level by "enhancing operational proficiency ... they cannot be assumed to negate hard-power political considerations ... tactical interactions" which generate larger strategic behavioural shifts (Baldino & Carr, 2016: 142).[56] Similarly, the ability of the process to 'shape' the regional environment is also an area on criticism with Hugh White claiming that "military to military contacts do little if mange deeper strategic risks, and may induce a false complacency that problems are being managed" (2014: 10). While Andrew Bacevich (2016) asserts the U.S. military apparatus lacks the capacity to shape the course of events (in the Middle East), labelling it as "an absurdity, and indulging the absurdity to attend to concerns that are far more pressing."

Cottey & Forster (2004) assert that defence diplomacy can effectively mitigate conflict; however, Carr insists that only recently has defence diplomacy begun to viewed as anything other than a tool for addressing practical issues "to its new form as a solution for regional tension...," suggesting that as far as Australia is concerned, "such lofty expectations" are unhelpful" (2015: 2). In the same way, Frühling determines "the problem with the (Australian Department of Defence) White Paper's discussion of defence engagement is that it does not link activity and desired outcomes through a strategic concept" (2013: 48). Some of the criticism or underappreciation of defence diplomacy stems from the ongoing debate of the civil-military relationship. In the U.S. for example, the dispute began during the Truman administration and its power struggle with the U.S. Armed Forces, particularly General Douglas MacArthur, causing "theorists and practitioners alike struggled over the proper balance of authority," how to "formalize a successful wartime national security apparatus (and) maintain proper civil authority over a powerful military establishment" (Willard, 2006: 27).

Defence diplomacy's role in stability and reconstruction initiatives (such as in Afghanistan since 2001) as well as SSR and associated governance is also challenged (discussed further below).[57] Hills suggests it is "reliant upon an over extension of everyday military business, and is based on an assumed (rather than proven) linkage between defence, development and security" (2000: 49). Stapleton and Keating found "the widely held assumption that reconstruction and development produce a stability dividend went largely unquestioned

56 See also: Winger, op. cit.; Stephen Frühling, 'The 2013 Defence White Paper: Strategic Guidance Without Strategy', *Security Challenges, Vol. 9, no. 2*, (2013); White, op. cit.; Carr, op. cit.).

57 The *U.S. Army Field Manual 3-07 Stability Operations* defines reconstruction as "the process of rebuilding degraded, damaged, or destroyed political, socioeconomic, and physical infrastructure of a country or territory to recreate the foundation for long-term development."

(2015: 6). Criticism in this particular area has been consistent despite the Bush administration releasing *National Security Presidential Directive (NSPD) 44* which formalized and framed how State would lead a transition from initial combat operations to 'nation building' activities.[58] Stapleton and Keating claim the complexity of military/civilian assistance programs is undermined by a simplistic mantra of "If you can't solve the problem with money, spend more money," where the mere existence of the program takes priority over outcomes (2015: 5). Similarly, and investigation by Fishstein and Wilder found that "pressure to spend too much money too quickly is not only wasteful, but undermines both security and development objectives, especially in insecure environments with weak institutions" (2012: 4). While McNerney, et al. (2014) used statistical analysis to assess security cooperation data and state fragility scores for 107 countries from 1991–2008, identifying both the region and the type of assistance provided led to widely varied success rates.[59]

Another assumption is that collaboration between diplomatic and defence establishments increases the level of internal and external review and accountability which strengthen nascent institutional reforms. However, Bachman (2014) warns that British led SSR programs present opportunities for indigenous actors to exploit Western donors. In terms of international CT cooperation, states such as the U.S. rely "heavily upon the cooperation of trusted local agents—the police, military, and intelligence apparatus of the host country" (Boutton, 2016: 2).[60] Therefore, as a central state institution the military can, in theory, facilitate a fully integrated security mechanism which protects citizens and their rights, reduces violence and coordinates police, intelligence, information and judicial systems. However, Adams & Sokolsky (2015) and Watts (2016) suggest Western intervention into the reform process of partner

58 NSPD 44 states explicitly designated State as the lead agency "to prepare for, and conduct stabilization and reconstruction activities." See also the Center for Strategic and International Studies and the Association of the United States Army, *Post-conflict Reconstruction Task Framework*, (May 2002), pp. 1–22; Report of an Independent Task Force, *In the Wake of War: Improving U.S. Post-Conflict Capabilities*, (Council on Foreign Relations, 2005), pp. 1–76.

59 The report revealed Latin America, Europe, and East Asia benefited the most while partners in Africa and the Middle East experienced no gains in their stability.

60 The counterterrorism strategy of the Obama administration has heavily emphasized policies to "train, build capacity, and facilitate partner countries on the front lines," Remarks by the President at the United States Military Academy Commencement Ceremony, Office of the Press Secretary, (The White House, May 28, 2014), available from: https://www.whitehouse.gov/the-press-office/2014/05/28/remarks-president-united-states-military-academy-commencement-ceremony.

nations brings with it associated risks alongside strategic reward. Negative consequences include insulating a regime from legitimate opposition, institutionalizing intercommunal power as empowering non-state actors through the unintentional redistribution of military and non-military aid. Finney emphasises that "the military instrument of power in SSR is predominantly centered on supporting the security capabilities of vulnerable or failing states, often in peacetime and in stable post-conflict situations" (2010: 3). SSR is a complicated and protracted process (if it occurs at all) and it needs to occur in parallel with an improvement in governance. Overall improvements in governance and institutional reform require effective leadership; however, it takes more than just political nous or a strong character to produce the kind of stability necessary for an adequate return on the political and economic investment of foreign governments.[61]

Michael L'Estrange and Hugh White identify some positive aspects of the concept and both note its political appeal yet the former warns the "benefits should neither be assumed or overstated" (2013, 23) while the later contends the primary assumption is that "defence diplomacy works better than other forms of diplomacy to soothe strategic tensions, ease rivalries and facilitate cooperation on security issues" (2014: 10). Likewise Jaishankar supports an increased emphasis on defence diplomacy but cautions that "a two-way dialogue is needed to ensure that the political objectives are clearly articulated by the civilian leadership (whether political or bureaucratic) and that the military has the capability and willingness to achieve those objectives" (2016: 22). While acknowledging defence diplomacy's utility, Ford concludes that it "is and will remain an extremely imprecise lever that needs to be carefully managed if it is to be a democratically accountable tool of foreign policy" (2015: 500). In the Long War, "Western governments face difficult dilemmas in balancing military cooperation with longstanding allies and efforts at strategic engagement with potential enemies ..." (Cottey & Forster, 2004: 8). However, the paper presents defence diplomacy is the ideal mechanism to facilitate what B. H. Liddell Hart labelled the "perfection of strategy"; that is one capable of achieving strategic objectives without serious fighting (1967: 339).

While forming part of a balanced assessment, these examples also demonstrate that criticism is directed at the delivery of often unrealistic, yet expected outcomes rather than on the process or the theory which supports it. However, even among its sceptics, defence diplomacy has delivered tangible outcomes which are more readily accepted. Rolfe acknowledges a lack a clear causational

61 The 2015 Asia Foundation *Survey of the Afghan People* found that governance satisfaction levels have declined 23% since 2012 despite a change of President in 2014, p. 97.

links, but insists defence diplomacy delivers positive strategic outcomes and is "more beneficial than military force or hard power in achieving political ends, whether those ends are stability, security, influence, status or something else" (2015: 3). Dean rejects some of the assumptions yet recognises that state's focus on defence diplomacy as an important mechanism for "shaping our strategic environment" (2013: 93). While Baldino concedes that although defence diplomacy cannot directly deliver strategic outcomes, it is a vital instrument in a fully integrated multi-departmental regional outreach program which helps "to contribute to broader strategic goals" (2016: 162).[62] Additionally, some of the criticism of defence diplomacy rests on an implied binary between diplomacy and war, a topic which has been discussed above, with the paper explaining the dynamics which overcomes such either-or assumptions.

As the paper transitions into a discussion of its practical application, it's worth summarising the objectives of defence diplomacy: to build, strengthen and maintain relationships; to build interoperability and capacity among allies; to build strategic depth in a region; to gain influence in the polities where the military are prominent; to better understand 'others' strategic culture; to reinforce bilateral relations/networks of bilateral's; to facilitate capacity building in order to better contribute to shared tasks/responsibilities. Next the paper identifies "the various types of diplomacy conducted on the political-military spectrum (and the) different modes of actions at the defence-diplomacy nexus" (2008: 95). Sending et.al assert that defence diplomacy "is less about dialogue than it is about getting things done" (2011: 530). In response to this assertion the paper moves beyond a theoretical discussion to examine defence diplomacy in practice and demonstrates the primary way of 'getting things done' is through whole-of-government strategic engagement driven by the MFA and Defence Department.

Defence Diplomacy: Diplomats in Uniform

Once considered a blunt instrument, force now serves as an all-purpose chisel.

BACEVICH, 2016[63]

62 According to Baldino, this multi-departmental program would include the Ministries of Defence and Foreign Affairs and Trade, "not only diplomatic and cultural but also its trade and aid sections" as well as "other departments with relevant expertise and capacity" p. 152.

63 See also Robert Art & Kenneth Waltz, *Use of Force: Military Power and International Politics*, (Maryland: Rowman & Littlefield Publishers, 2009); John Troxell, 'Military Power and the Use of Force', in *U.S. Army War College Guide to National Security Policy and Strategy*,

Overview of Defence Diplomacy

Robert Ayson & Manjeet S. Pardesi note recently that despite an increasing focus on "maritime security competition in Asia, including in the South China and East China seas, it is easy to forget how peaceful the region has been for several decades ... an impressive record for a region that was riven by major wars in the middle of the twentieth century" (2017: 85). Research demonstrates the role of defence diplomacy maintaining peace and stability, with Asia-Pacific states committing to the process during the latter half of the twentieth century.[64] The majority of the engagement has consisted of activities commonly referred to as Military Operation Other Than War (MOOTW).[65] Defence diplomacy facilitates MOOTW which usually involve combined/joint force operations as well as the efforts of government agencies and nongovernment organizations.[66] As in traditional warfare, political objectives drive MOOTW at every level, from strategic to tactical; however, "a distinguishing characteristic of MOOTW is the degree to which political objectives influence operations and tactics" (Joint Chiefs of Staff, 1995: 4).

China, a nation with the potential to rival the U.S. militarily, has embraced the concept of defence diplomacy since the 1990's as part of its 'New Security Concept.' In 1998, The PRC *National Defence White Paper* "revised the term 'foreign military contacts' to 'military diplomacy' and put forward the policy of developing omni-directional and multilevel military diplomacy" (Zicheng &

(*2nd Ed*), (2006); Alexander L. George, 'The Role of Force in Diplomacy: Continuing Dilemma for U.S. Foreign Policy', presentation at CSIS Security Strategy Symposium, (June 25, 1998), available at http://www.pbs.org/wgbh/pages/frontline/shows/military/force/article.html; Colin Powell, 'U.S. Forces: Challenges Ahead', *Foreign Affairs*, Vol. 71, no. 5, (Winter 1992/93) for an alternative view of the military as a purely blunt force object.

64 For example: Jürgen Haacke, 'The concept of flexible engagement and the practice of enhanced interaction: intramural challenges to the 'ASEAN way', *The Pacific Review*, Vol. 12, no. 4, (1999), pp. 581–611; Michael L'Estrange, 'International Defence Engagement: Potential and Limitations', op. cit., pp. 23–34; Rhett Mitchell, 'Pacific partnership: Australia's contribution and benefits', *Headmark, No. 147*, (March 2013), pp. 9–14; Baldino & Carr, 'Defence Diplomacy and the Australian defence force: smokescreen or strategy', op. cit.

65 Although the term is commonly used by governments around the world, MOOTW is no longer in use by the DoD. It was previously codified in *Joint Publication 3-07*; however, the designator now assigned is "Stability Operations"; see footnote 127 (pp. 70–71).

66 Governments apply any combination of national power to achieve national strategic goals by integrating military efforts with diplomatic, economic, and informational agencies or organizations. For comprehensive discussions on Operations Other Than War see: Jennifer Taw & John E. Peters. *Operations Other Than War: Implications for the U.S. Army*, (Santa Monica, CA: RAND Corporation, 1995), pp. 1–70; *JP 3-07 Joint Doctrine for Military Operations Other Than War*, (June 1995), pp. 1–70.

Qingmin, 2013: 295). The White Paper proudly boasted an increase in multi-level exchange programs with partner states facilitating the movement of students, military personnel as well as senior defence officials. Since that time, China has developed exchange programs with many advanced military nations (Scobell, et al., 2014: 38–41; U.S. Office of the SECDEF, 2016: 49–50). China's MOOTW have taken its revolutionized military forces from Africa to the subcontinent, through SE Asia and even the east coast of the U.S. China's leaders recognised the country was undergoing a period of strategic opportunity supported by a relatively peaceful international order. The PRC could achieve this by concentrating on both civil and military development. Cordesman et.al claim that China's new leader, Xi Jinping, "has concentrated more on great power diplomacy (and) quickly began establishing himself as a strong military leader, going on high-profile visits to Navy, Air Force, Army, and Missile Command facilities during his first 100 days in office" (2012: 15). In January 2015, the PLA held an All-Army Foreign Affairs Work Conference to outline how China's defence diplomacy would support the vision set by the CCP's previous Central Foreign Affairs Work Conference (2014). During this event, senior officials conveyed the goals and strategic outlook for military diplomacy for the next decade, addressing themes of President Xi's speech to Party leaders, including "big power diplomacy," coordination, and policy implementation.

Analysts conclude Beijing has, and will continue, to invest heavily, in diplomatic and military terms, in the management of the order in the Indo-Pacific region. The Gwadar Port in Pakistan is a good example of steady expansion of Chinese maritime interests and influence. The Gwadar Port forms part of the China-Pakistan Economic Corridor (CPEC) and supports the security and economic prospects of China's large population which depend on external access to vital natural resources and markets (Chaturvedy, 2017). The PRC has also expanded external opportunities for PLA officers to observe and study foreign military command structures, unit formations, and operational training.[67] Moreover senior-level visits and exchanges provide China with opportunities to increase military officers' international exposure, to communicate China's positions to foreign audiences, to understand alternative world views, and to advance foreign relations through interpersonal contacts and military assistance programs. Despite increased interaction, cooperation is not expected to bridge ideological cleaves. For example the 2016 U.S. SECDEF's *Annual Report*

67 For more detail see: Office of the Secretary Of Defense, *Annual Report to Congress: Military and Security Developments Involving the People's Republic of China*, (2016), pp. 49–50. http://www.defense.gov/Portals/1/Documents/pubs/2016%20China%20Military%20Power%20Report.pdf. (Last accessed January 10, 2017).

to Congress reinforces the caveat that "although most Western militaries are considered apolitical, professional forces that first and foremost serve the state, the PLA has been a politicized "party army" since its inception and exists to guarantee the CCP regime's survival above all else" (2016: 102). Partisan motivation aside, China's MOOTW have allowed it to project its military capabilities far into the Indian and Pacific Oceans and its political/military ambition also influence the diplomacy oriented actions of nations on its immediate periphery(Storey, 2012: 287–310).

Although China does not publish a national CT strategy which outlines its objectives for international CT cooperation, it pursues a strategy which seeks to reduce instability in neighbouring states that allows terrorism to flourish as well as enhancing both domestic and regional CT capabilities. Despite its long-standing principle of non-interference in the affairs of other sovereign nations, China's CT oriented defence diplomacy takes place in both bilateral and multilateral formats. While the PRC prefers bi-lateral problem solving in search of "win-win" outcomes, it also boosts its regional standing through participation in multi-lateral fora, military exercises, and summit meetings (MFA of PRC, 2017). China's preferred multilateral forum is the Shanghai Cooperation Organisation (SCO), which comprises China, Russia, Kazakhstan, Kyrgyzstan, Tajikistan and Uzbekistan, conducting a number of bilateral and multilateral counterterrorism exercises within the SCO framework. China was instrumental in creating the Shanghai Convention on Combating Terrorism, Separatism and Extremism as well as the Regional Ant-terrorism Structure (SCO CT Factsheet, 2001, 2011). The SCO member states are important geographic stakeholders in the Long War and China also engages them through both the 'Istanbul Process' which seeks to stabilise Afghanistan and the Quadrilateral Coordination Group (QCG) for Afghan Peace and Reconciliation.[68] Some researchers suggest "Beijing prioritizes bilateral exchanges in its counterterrorism diplomacy" and the QCG enhances one of China's key bilateral CT relationships—its cooperation with the U.S (Tanner & Bellacqua, 2016: 82).[69]

China/U.S CT cooperation since September 2001 prioritises technical issues such as port and container security, information sharing about transiting extremists, terrorist financial networks, making efforts to control improvised

68 'Joint Press Release of the Quadrilateral Coordination Group on Afghan Peace and Reconciliation' Office of the Spokesperson, U.S. Department of State, Washington D.C. (January 1, 2016) available at https://www.state.gov/r/pa/prs/ps/2016/01/251105.htm.

69 See also China joins hands with three neighbours to counter terrorism, Ministry of National Defence, The People's Republic of China, (August 4 2016), available at http://eng.mod.gov.cn/DefenseNews/2016-08/04/content_4707511.htm.

explosive devices (IED) precursors, undertaking joint research initiatives, dialogues and consultations. The two major powers have also engaged in combined military exercises such as the anti-terrorist military drill "Peace Mission 2010" organised by the SCO in September 2010, in which 5000 military men took part and which was based on tactical scenarios to combat terrorism, separatism and extremismor the Quadrilateral Cooperation and Coordination Mechanism in Counter Terrorism involving Afghan, Chinese, Pakistani and Tajik armed forces (*Country Reports on Terrorism,* 2014: 57–60).[70] Tanner and Bellacqua find that "the new PRC Counterterrorism Law (December 2015) suggests that Beijing is considering a more expeditionary approach to countering terrorist threats in the future" (Tanner & Bellacqua, 2016: 100). China also uses the Conference on Interaction and Confidence-Building Measures in Asia (CICA) and the Association of South East Asian Nations (ASEAN) to develop coordinated and deeper CT cooperation throughout Asia. More broadly, the PLA has developed a robust schedule of joint exercises with approximately 30 countries since 2002. China also engages in security assistance primarily through arms sales (currently third largest export in the world-two thirds to just three counties Pakistan, Myanmar and Malaysia). Randall Shriver, a Senior Associate at the Center for Strategic and International Studies, concludes that while China's security cooperation and security assistance is increasing, the vast majority of Chinese defence engagement occurs across MOOTW, such as their involvement in the search for the downed Malaysian airliner in 2014 as well as both hosting foreign Navy's and visiting foreign ports (*Panel Discussion at The Atlantic Council,* March 7, 2017). The process aligns with China's 'win-win' approach to foreign policy allowing China to exchanges views, better disseminate the PRC's intentions, and create opportunities for future assistance and/or cooperation with SE Asian nations.

ASEAN was established in 1967 as a multilateral institution which united its member states within an economic and socio-cultural framework. "ASEAN members promoted trust and confidence and conflict prevention" in order to create regional stability away from the super-power rivalry of the Cold War (Chye, 2016: 10). Across the region, most states have actively engaged in defence diplomacy through the ASEAN to address the "mutual mistrust and tensions persisting among SE Asian states and their militaries" (Tan & Singh, 2011, 221). Singaporean Prime Minister Lee Kuan Yew initiated the formation of a SE Asian "defence spider-web" during the 1980's and bilateral and trilateral security cooperation and military exercises were taking place between

70 The Country Reports on Terrorism indicates China held dialogues with countries such as the U.S., the UK, France, South Korea, Turkey, Afghanistan, and Uzbekistan in 2014.

Singapore, Malaysia and Indonesia (Tan, 2016: 6). Since the formation of the security oriented ASEAN Regional Forum (ARF) in 1994, participating states have established regular military to military engagement although issues of sovereignty, equality and diversity of national outlooks have limited the majority of these to bilateral interactions (Chye, 2016: 10). An increasing number of defence diplomacy oriented fora have emerged in the 21st century. The ARF Defence Official Dialogue, the ARF Security Policy Conference, ASEAN Defence Ministers Meeting (ADMM & ADMM+), the Council for Security Cooperation in the Asia-Pacific (CSCAP) as well as the South Asian Association for Regional Cooperation (SAARC) are some of the more prominent multilateral civilian/military institutions/engagements.

The ADMM (est. 2006) and ADMM+ (est. 2010) were established to encourage ASEAN nations to engage on security related matters as well as enhancing regional relationships more broadly. These fora prioritise non-traditional measures including CT, improved intelligence sharing on a range of issues, regional centres for peacekeeping, discussions on a ASEAN 'Ready Group' which would enable ASEAN militaries to rapidly respond to regional disasters and a range of development areas across both military and non-military sectors. The status of these meetings has increased in the Long War as a vehicle to formulate regional CT frameworks. For example consecutive communiques from ADMM's since 2007 prioritise strengthening regional defence and cooperation "to combat terrorism in all its forms and manifestations, including through cooperation in areas such as the sharing of information and intelligence, conducting coordinated operations where feasible, and enhancing confidence and capability building mechanisms" (Joint Declaration, May 25, 2016: 6). Although member-states have established various avenues for military cooperation which have improved transparency and interoperability, U.S. DNI James Clapper maintains ASEAN engagements are hindered by differing analyses of the regional threat environment (2016: 16–17). Similarly, Lindsey Ford notes, although discussions in relation to enhanced cooperation are robust and the "trend-line is positive," the internal dynamics of the grouping slow the transition from concept to reality (March 7, 2017). Ford identifies the debate over ASEAN's raison d'etre as one of the inhibiting factors. Ironically, the strengthened relationships achieved through defence oriented engagement would provide both a forum to engage in this debate as well as working towards the generation of a united or at least aligned world view. This is crucial for ASEAN's longevity and continuing regional relevance, as generating consensus "is the whole point of the organisation" (Ford, March 7, 2017).

Another important regional player is Australia, a country which has fought in every Western conflict since the Boer War and also champions defence diplomacy globally. John Watts claims one cannot "overstate just how important security cooperation is to Australia's perspective and Australia's approach to pursuing its national interests" (March 7, 2017). Dedicating an entire chapter of the 2016 Australian Defence White Paper, *Positioning for Tomorrows Challenges* to defence engagement supports this claim. Watts insists, from both an academic and practitioner perspective, that the concept of PME "is ingrained and at the heart of Australia's strategic perspective" (March 7, 2017). For Watts, Australia engages globally in defence diplomacy to counter the fact "it does not possess, nor does it seek to possess the military capability to ensure its security and prosperity" (March 7, 2017).[71] Therefore the Australian government views defence engagement as an investment in the future, "a force multiplier, a way to use the capabilities we have to achieve our ends in the most effective and efficient way possible" (Watts, March 7, 2017). Watts identifies the trust and respect that Australia gains by engaging in a full spectrum of defence oriented diplomacy as the most important, if under-recognised outcome of Australia's "effective, robust, risk mitigation strategy" (March 7, 2017).[72] Australia is heavily invested in multi-domain training exercises such as RIMPAC, Talisman Sabre, Pacific Partnership and Pitch Black. RIMPAC, which commenced in 1971, is a prominent biennial combined exercise led by the U.S. Pacific Fleet involving Australian forces and 24 other countries including Canada, Denmark, France, India, Indonesia, Japan, Malaysia, New Zealand, People's Republic of China, Republic of Singapore, the Philippines, Thailand, Tonga, UK. The theme for RIMPAC 2016 was 'Capable, Adaptive Partners' while the Australian Department of Defence affirms the exercise "reflects the closeness of our alliance with the U.S. and the strength of our military relationships with other regional defence partners (and) is a unique opportunity to build interoperability and cultivate ties with the armed forces of Pacific Rim countries" (Aus Def RIMPAC, 2016).

All of the exercises mentioned above along with many more bilateral, trilateral, and multilateral military to military engagements between the armed forces of Australia and their partners aim to strengthen regional ties, enhance interoperability and develop a common interest in regional/global security and stability. Bisley claims that many states within the region perceive defence diplomacy to be "the most useful and effective form of the recent wave

71 Australia ranks 13th in annual investment in its defence apparatus and physical armed forces which are dwarfed by the size of the territory it's required to protect.

72 The 'full spectrum' refers to training, exercising, basing, information sharing, strategic dialogue, security forums, joint operations and defence materiel.

of multilateralism in the region" (2014: 12). For example, "India has leveraged military diplomacy in its external relations almost since Independence, by virtue of its inheriting a large, professional military force from the British Raj" according to Dhruva Jaishankar (2016: 18). While K. A. Muthanna (2011) and Shashank Joshi (2015) confirm India has increased its defence diplomacy in parallel with its rising political and economic profile. This is, according to Jaishankar, "a clear by-product of better diplomatic relations, wider international interests, greater budgetary resources, and the acquisition of key pieces of equipment" (2016: 21). Evidence suggests China, Australia, ASEAN nations and India engage in defence diplomacy to increase regional integration and/or maintain a peaceful status quo.

One of the most prominent examples of regional defence diplomacy is the Five Powers Defence Arrangement (FPDA) involving Singapore, Malaysia, the United Kingdom, Australia and New Zealand which has been in place since 1971. The FPDA and its Consultative Council allows the actors involved to react to threats or to develop combined military exercises as well as humanitarian assistance and disaster relief (HADR) deployment through a familiar permanent body. Formerly classified communications, between the Australian Prime Minister and Minister of Defence, reveal that relationship building, cooperation and unity of effort were fundamental objectives of the nascent cooperative defence treaty (NAA: M4251-44, 1971). This objective directly parallels military doctrine which dictates unity of effort is achieved through "consensus building, rather than direct command authority, and is the key element of successful multinational operations" (*U.S. Army FM-0*, 2001: 2–49). The FPDA is an example of how defence diplomacy can be used to identify 'collective interests' under the guise of the CT in general and the Long War in particular. Following on from the 9/11 attacks and the especially since the Bali bombings in October 2002, the FPDA consolidated their efforts against the scourge of international terrorism redirecting their focus onto non-traditional security from "other sources of regional instability" (Singh & Tan, 2011: 246). Long War oriented operations overshadowed efforts to combat the potential threat posed by Indonesia, which was a primary reason for the FPDA's formation in 1971.

The combined exercises undertaken by FPDA states facilitate capacity building by strengthening personal relationships and enhancing professionalism across government departments tasked with state security. For example, Singaporean Armed Forces and the Australian Defence Force, which have cooperated in conflict situations from East Timor to Afghanistan, engage in regular personnel exchanges and training exercises such as Exercise Wallaby and the tri-force exercise Trident which have contributed to the signing in 2015, of the bi-lateral Comprehensive Strategic Partnership. FPDA also facilitates annual and biennial exercises such as Bersama Shield and Suman Warrior.[73] Another regional stability mechanism in SE Asia is the U.S. Pacific Fleet's Cooperation Afloat Readiness and Training (CARAT) program which is closely coordinated between congress, State and DoD. CARAT is a series of bilateral naval exercises designed; to increase U.S. Sailors' understanding of SE Asian cultures; to enhance regional cooperation and interoperability; and strengthen professional skills at every level; to promote cooperation and interoperability between participants prioritising operational planning, command and control as well as tactics. Military officials declare CARAT demonstrates U.S. commitment in SE Asia while increasing operational readiness and the capabilities of U.S. forces as well as building lasting, working relationships, which will add to security and stability in the region.[74]

Regional defence spending continues to trend upwards (27.5% rise between 2010–2014) and increased intra-Asian defence cooperation set against the backdrop of China's regional objectives, the U.S.'s 'pivot' to Asia as well as a host of dynamic situations such as the infiltration of ISIL in SE Asian and North Korean belligerence (North Korea is China's only treaty ally in the region) (IISS, 2015: 209).[75] Asian countries now spend $100 billion a year more on defence than all of the European members of NATO combined. Bilateral security cooperation has increased over the past year including recent agreements between Singapore and Vietnam, Australian and Japan and India and South Korea which all aim the enhance capabilities through training, officer exchanges, knowledge and equipment transfer, joint R&D, servicing as well as engaging in public diplomacy through ship visits, air displays, ect. Although analysts highlight the level of training across the region is not advanced, with some describing it as "low hanging fruit," this paper would note that the region will benefit from state's involvement in the process of defence diplomacy

73 For more detail see: McMahon, A. 'Regional co-operation at the forefront of military exercise', Key Enablers, Defence Connect, (April 28, 2017), available at https://www.defenceconnect.com.au/key-enablers/616-regional-cooperation-at-the-forefront-of-military-exercise (Last accessed April 28, 2017).

74 For more information on CARAT see: http://www.globalsecurity.org/military/ops/carat.htm; http://navaltoday.com/2016/08/02/carat-2016-moves-over-to-indonesia/; http://www.embassyofindonesia.org/wordpress/?p=4874.

75 The IHS *Global Defence Trade Report 2016* and SIPRI's *Trends in World Military Expenditure* indicate ASEAN defence imports increased by 71% between 2009 and 2016, for more information see: http://books.sipri.org/files/FS/SIPRIFS1604.pdf; http://trade.gov/topmarkets/pdf/Defense_Asia_Pacific.pdf; https://www.cogitasia.com/analyzing-southeast-asias-military-expenditures/

regardless of the type of training exercises undertaken (Ford, March 7, 2017).[76] The examples presented are some of an "almost limitless range of defence diplomacy in the region" (Bisley, 2014 12). ASEAN is an example of an institution established to offset the effects of Cold War rivalries while the following example was an alliance forged to tackle the threat head-on.

Shortly after the official end of WWII, George Keenan declared the success of the Soviets "will really depend on degree of cohesion, firmness and vigour which Western World can muster" (February 22, 1946).[77] After several years of trial and error, NATO was formalised in April 1949 as a collective defence mechanism "to keep the Russians out, the Americans in, and the Germans down" (Nye, 2002: 39).[78] NATO was the first peacetime military alliance the U.S. entered into outside of the Western Hemisphere and the twenty-eight member trans-Atlantic group is arguably the most successful military-political alliance in history. In 1956 the foreign Ministers from Canada, Italy and Norway released a report into the nascent alliance which found that in order to survive and thrive, NATO needed to expand beyond a simple U.S. military guarantee by "developing political institutions and a habit of political consultation, which would underline the permanent common values and common interests of the members," creating a complex framework which emphasised cooperation across a diverse range of areas and issues both military and non-military (Shea, November 6, 2003).[79] During the Cold War, the U.S. and the USSR actively engaged in multilateral and bilateral defence cooperation with their respective allies around the world, primarily through NATO and the Warsaw Pact.[80]

Both superpowers were adept at engaging within their own spheres of influence; however, the U.S. began to develop relations with the Soviets and China during the 1970's and 80's, and these relationships "intensified

76 During the panel discussion both Lindsey Ford and Randall Shriver spoke of the relatively low level of training exercises undertaken.

77 In *The Long Telegram*, Keenan emphasised "if the adversary has sufficient force and makes clear his readiness to use it, he rarely has to do so."

78 Nye writes that NATO's first Secretary General Lord Ismay declared the purpose of NATO was "To keep the Americans in, the Russians out, and the Germans down."

79 See also Isabel Zucchero, '(The Other) Three Wise Men', *The NATO Association of Canada*, (December 13 2016), available at http://natoassociation.ca/the-other-three-wise-men/.

80 For more detail see: John K. Skogan (ed.), Civil-military relations in the post-communist states in Eastern and Central Europe: a conference report, (1993), http://hdl.handle.net/11250/284340; Mendelson, 'U.S.-Russian Military Relations: Between Friend and Foe', *The Washington Quarterly*, Vol. 25, no. 1, (2001), pp. 161–172, http://dx.doi.org/10.1162/016366002753358393; Sidorov, et al. Russian-American security. (Hauppauge, N.Y.: 2010), pp. 41–42.

significantly after the collapse of the Soviet Union" through NATO multilateralism or bilateral relations with states within the U.S./NATO security orbit (Cottey & Forster, 2004: 20). For example, Russia became a NATO Partnership for Peace (PfP) member in 1994.[81] Adams and Murray locate the PfP at the core of defence diplomacy, defining it as a "military socialization and training" initiative" (2014: 10). The PfP program encouraged practical bilateral cooperation between individual Euro-Atlantic partner countries and NATO establishing individual relationship with their own priorities for cooperation with NATO members spending substantial sums to support defence diplomacy activities, both within the PfP and other bilateral programmes (IISS, 1999: 1). Averaging approximately 25 per year between 1994 and 2000, PfP engagements during the early post-Cold War period were an effective legitimacy reinforcing/creating mechanism.[82]

Aside from its core relationship building characteristics, a key element of defence diplomacy is its ability to signal and clarify intentions. Scholars examining 'declaratory diplomacy' identify the potential of strategic public declarations to generate confidence and security building measures (CSBM's), with public statements by senior military personnel effectively "re-enforce private commitments by national leaders, defining and publicising their commitment to lessening tension and improving bilateral relations" (Krepon & Drezin, 1999: 156). They also have the ability to overcome social, political and military cultural differences. These measures are important as war in isolation is difficult to plan and even more difficult to predict and map, in part because of the complexity and dynamism of human interactions. Clausewitz states that "no other human activity is so continuously or universally bound up with chance" than war, with chance being a significant factor in points of friction transitioning from war on paper and war in reality (1997: 85). To counter this reality, NATO (especially the U.S.) sought to assure Russia that NATO expansion would not

81 The U.S. instituted a parallel program called the Warsaw Initiative Fund (WIF) which the DoD could draw funding for military training programs with former Soviet satellites.

82 The IISS '*The Strategic Survey*' (1999) describes how defence diplomacy seeks to extend understanding and trust towards countries in transition to democratic government. By ensuring that the CEE (Central & Eastern European) states develop effective and democratically accountable armed forces in cooperation with their neighbours and even old adversaries, it is intended to prepare them for integration into European and transatlantic institutions, pp. 40–41, 47; 'Founding Act on Mutual Relations, Cooperation and Security between NATO and the Russian Federation signed in Paris, France', *NATO*, (May 27, 1997). An important milestone in the fledgling Russian/NATO relationship was the signing of Founding Act on Mutual Relations, Cooperation and Security (NATO–Russia Founding Act) in 1997.

impact Russia's strategic situation.[83] For example, "Western troops did not permanently deploy in substantial numbers beyond the Cold War NATO-Warsaw Pact boundary line," military hardware toured but was not stationed in Eastern Europe and NATO went to great lengths to re-assure Russia that NATO's missile defense systems "were intended to defend against Iran, not Russia" (Frum, January 10, 2017). Weber, Hallams and Smith emphasise that, despite the dynamic nature of the contemporary security environment, during "the more than two decades since the end of the Cold War, the alliance has maintained its standing through operations, enlargement, partnerships and a reaffirmation of the transatlantic relationship" (2014: 773). Moreover, NATO is unique because it makes collective decisions and deploys its forces collectively which would be difficult, if not impossible, without a high degree of interoperability in the Long War.

Within hours of the 9/11 attacks NATO invoked Article 5 of its charter (mutual defence clause), committed to a conflict outside of its traditional European borders.[84] This commitment should not be underestimated as the alliance had "rejected out-of-area ops during the Cold War and debated vigorously the concept of Global NATO" (Mattox, 2015: 290).[85] The first operations undertaken by NATO was to mobilise a fleet of Airborne Warning And Control System (AWACS) to traverse the east and west coasts of the U.S.[86] More importantly, its defence diplomacy shifted from addressing post-Cold War destabilisation to the Global War on Terror and its primary mission as part of the International

83 The IISS *Strategic Survey* (1999) identified an "enlarged role for European armed forces and military establishments in supporting the foreign and security policy strategies of their governments," p. 38.

84 Article 5 of the North Atlantic treaty (1949) obligates members to "assist the party or parties so attacked by taking forthwith, individually, and in concert with the other parties, such action as it deems necessary, including the use of armed force, to restore and maintain the security of the North Atlantic area," http://www.nato.int/cps/en/natohq/official_texts_17120.htm See also: Theo Farrell & Sten Rynning, 'NATO's Transformation Gaps: Transatlantic Differences and the War in Afghanistan', *Journal of Strategic Studies, Vol. 33, no. 5*, (2010), p. 695. The authors identify that the NATO's military commitment in Afghanistan reveals divergence between collective defence operations and open-ended collective security campaigns.

85 See also: Michael Clarke, 'The Global NATO Debate', Politique étrangère, (May 2009), pp. 57–67 available at https://www.cairn.info/revue-politique-etrangere-2009-5-page-57.htm#re8no8.

86 AWACS are essentially a modified Boeing 707 which create mobile, long-range radar surveillance and control centre for air defense. The operation lasted for 8 months; See AWACS: NATO's 'Eye In The Sky', (NATO, October 27, 2016), available at http://www.nato.int/cps/en/natolive/topics_48904.htm.

Security Assistance Force (ISAF) in Afghanistan which was forged during the Bonn Conference in December 2001 (NATO took over command from the U.S. in August 2003).[87] However, this transition revealed weaknesses in the alliance. At the time European members had 1.4 million soldiers on paper, but could only deploy 55 000 on a permanent basis. Schmidt recalls that the U.S. was underwhelmed with the capabilities of its European allies, quickly forging a "multinational, European-centred NATO Response Force, trained and equipped to U.S. standards, able to deploy quickly and fight effectively alongside U.S. forces" (Schmidt, 2007: 98, 104).[88] Although united in objective, most European contributions to OEF were incorporated on a bilateral basis. Bensahel notes "the UK and France contributed a wide variety of types of forces to the operations, while most other countries provided smaller contingents, often with specialized capabilities and skills" (2003: 10).

Some view the initial U.S. rejection of the alliance ultimately as a positive experience. For example Williams claims "that the decision to bypass NATO after 9/11 galvanised the alliance" and led to "an accelerated process of transformation" (2008: 75). NATO produced a draft *Military Concept for Combating Terrorism*, in November 2002 which supported four pillars—antiterrorism, consequence management, CT, and military cooperation with civil authorities. In support of this mission, at its height, Coalition forces numbered more than 130,000 troops drawn from 51 NATO and partner nations. In accordance with its initial UN mandate, the *Military Concept for Combating Terrorism* and subsequent *Strategic Vision (2008)*, ISAF provided support to the Government of the Islamic Republic of Afghanistan (GoIRA) and international community in SSR. This support included mentoring, training and operational support to the Afghan National Army (ANA) and the Afghan National Police (ANP) in order to build a professional, independent and sustainable force that could provide security throughout the country through NATO's Training Mission Afghanistan (NTM-A) and ISAF's Joint Command (IJC).[89]

---

87 The Bonn Agreement, formalised in UNSC Res.1386, recognised the need to support the fragile political situation in Afghanistan by establishing "an International Security Assistance Force to assist the Afghan Interim Authority in the maintenance of security in Kabul and its surrounding areas, so that the Afghan Interim Authority as well as the personnel of the United Nations can operate in a secure environment."

88 Schmidt argued that even though NATO accepted command of ISAF peacekeeping mission in Afghanistan, its European members have been reluctant to enmesh with the US. led OEF counter terrorism campaign, not that the U.S. ever intended to pursue OEF through NATO.

89 For more detail see: *ISAF's Strategic Vision*, (Bucharest Summit, (April 3, 2008), available at http://www.nato.int/cps/en/natolive/official_texts_8444.htm.

The paper claims NATO's Afghan mission has raised the profile and capability of the alliance; forging strong relationships with non-European, non-NATO allies such as Japan, South Korea, New Zealand and Australia as well as becoming a forum for discussing topics across the broader political/foreign policy sphere. In 2016 NATO approved about US$ 390 million to support Afghan forces, fund more than 37 projects for the Afghan army, including salaries and incentive pay, infrastructure sustainability and logistic sustainability enforcing its commitment to the Long War. The funding also covers medical supplies and training continuing the commitment of NATO allies and partners to support the financial sustainability of the Afghan national defense and security forces. At its Warsaw summit in July, NATO allies decided to continue the Resolute Support mission in Afghanistan beyond 2016 and confirmed funding for Afghan forces until 2020 (Torbati & Emmott, July 9 2016). The NATO/Afghan joint Enduring Partnership parallels ORS and provides a framework for long term political consultations and practical cooperation between NATO and Afghanistan.[90] NATO has also initiated, and continues its external outreach initiatives based on the twin pillars of political dialogue and practical cooperation. NATO's Mediterranean Dialogue, Training Cooperation Initiatives, Individual and Partnership Cooperation Programmes, Individual and Partnership Action Plan on Defence Institution Building and the Istanbul Cooperation Initiative are example of the alliance's ongoing civil/military engagement with Middle East and North African states which prioritise cooperation in HADR, counter terrorism, disarmament, cyber defence as well as broad spectrum capacity building and doctrine dissemination.[91] The relationships formed and the interoperability generated through these programs has a direct impact on NATO operations in Afghanistan.

90 For more detail see: A new chapter in NATO-Afghanistan relations from 2015, *NATO Media Backgrounder*, (June 2015), available at http://www.nato.int/nato_static_fl2014/assets/pdf/pdf_2015_06/20150622_1506-media-bckgr-afghanistan.pdf.

91 For more detail see: Rhett Mitchell, 'Pacific partnership: Australia's contribution and benefits', *Headmark, No. 147*, (March 2013), pp. 9–14; *Individual Partnership and Cooperation Programme Between Japan and NATO*, (May 6 2014). available at http://www.nato.int/nato_static/assets/pdf/pdf_2014_05/20140507_140507-IPCP_Japan.pdf; The Istanbul Cooperation Initiative Fact Sheet, *North Atlantic Treaty Organization*, (April 2014) available at http://www.nato.int/nato_static/assets/pdf/pdf_2014_04/20140331_140401-factsheet-ICI_en.pdf; Partnership Action Plan on Defence Institution Building, NATO & the Canadian Defence Academy, (October 2008) available at http://www.nato.int/nato_static_fl2014/assets/pdf/pdf_2015_10/20151013_151013-pap-dib-eng.pdf (Last accessed December 12, 2016).

Identifying and disseminating the positive outcomes associated with defence diplomacy may encourage member states to meet their funding commitments from the 2014 Wales Summit. Current and former SECDEF's (Mattis & Carter) and the current Secretary of State (Tillerson) have been openly critical of alliance members for 'not paying their share.'[92] Such 'subtle' external interventions may help reverse what some have termed "a growing 'transformation gap' between the U.S. and the European allies" (Farrell & Rynning, 2010: 674).[93] Meeting these funding commitments will guarantee NATO remains "the strongest alliance the world has ever known and is the hub of an expanding global security network" U.S. NSS: 9). Bridging the 'transformation gap' is critical for NATO to ensure the "historical legacy of the alliance continues to exercise a hold over its members … sustaining a reservoir of goodwill and sense of shared destiny" (Schmidt, 2007: 106). Over the last 6 decades, through economic crises, regional conflicts and systemic political upheaval, NATO has established its role as the primary institution where Western states and their partners can cooperate, educate, communicate and build relationships. For Lindley-French, NATO's engagement in Afghanistan post-9/11 emphasised the core advantages of the alliance being "a body of standards, structures, knowledge and protocols for multinational military coalitions that is unrivalled in history" (2006: para 9). NATO's Supreme Allied Commander of Europe, Commander Breedlove recently reaffirmed the multidimensional effects of regional security alliances, stating "it is no mere coincidence that Europe's stability and prosperity have developed alongside the worlds most capable and effective political-military alliance" (May 2, 2016).

NATO's European members recognise the importance of multi-departmental cross-regional diplomacy; a mechanism which may enhance the EU's

92 For example: Readout of Secretary Carter's meeting with German Minister of Defence Ursula von der Leyen, Press release No: NR-079016, (8th March, 2016), available at https://www.defense.gov/News/News-Releases/News-Release-View/Article/688855/readout-of-secretary-of-defense-ash-carters-meeting-with-german-minister-of-def (Last accessed December 18, 2016). SECDEF Carter applied direct pressure to the German domestic policy by encouraging them to lead by example to maintain upward trajectory in defence spending throughout 2016–2018; Press Conference by Secretary Mattis at NATO Headquarters, Brussels, Belgium, Department of Defence, Press Operations, (February 16, 2017), available at https://www.defense.gov/News/Transcripts/Transcript-View/Article/1085679/press-conference-by-secretary-mattis-at-nato-headquarters-brussels-belgium (Last accessed March 12, 2017).

93 See also David Gompert, Richard Kugler & Michael Libicki, *Mind the Gap: Promoting a Transatlantic Revolution in Military Affairs*, (Washington D.C.: National Defence University Press, 1999), pp. 1–99.

aspiration of collective self-defence. The UK and Spain provide examples of the scope of defence diplomacy in post-Cold War Europe. During the late 1990's the UK Ministry of Defence (MOD) *Strategic Defence Review* (SDR) defined and developed its vision for defence diplomacy, deploying its armed forces in strategic support of diplomacy "in efforts to deter or manage crises, from humanitarian missions to UN embargoes and peacekeeping" (1998: 23). A follow-up policy paper identified conflict prevention and peacetime diplomacy as core defence activities and created a defence diplomacy mission "to give greater priority, impetus and coherence to these types of activities, and to ensure alignment with the Government's foreign and security policy objectives" (UKMOD, 2000: 2). The SDR prioritised "education and training initiatives, to help develop the skills and structures needed by modern democratically accountable forces ... (including the) establishment of a defence diplomacy scholarship scheme at the Joint Services Command and Staff College and providing extra manpower for short term in-country tasks" (1998: 20). In line with the SDR recommendations, the UK expanded the scope and coverage of its defence diplomacy and began to cooperate with many non-traditional military partners such as Bahrain, Oman, Sierra Leone Nigeria and South Africa as well as creating opportunities for cooperation with Russia and China.

For the MOD, defence diplomacy offers "a cost effective means of exerting influence," through the development of "a cadre of civilian and military personnel with appropriate ability and experience to meet the likely increase in demand for in-country advisers" (SDR, 1998: 16–17). For example, in 2000, the MOD formulated a comprehensive ship visit program (Naval Task Force 2000) "visiting over 30 countries including Egypt, Israel, Oman, Australia, China, Malaysia, New Zealand, the Philippines, the Republic of Korea, India, Japan, USA, Vietnam, Russia, Singapore, Thailand, Panama and Venezuela" (UKMOD, 2000: 13). Twelve years later, the MOD evaluated their defence diplomacy program, determining that "our defence diplomacy efforts have contributed to important long-standing relationships and enabled international partners to make a more effective contribution to international stability" (2012: 19). Recently, Stephen Lovegrove, the Permanent Secretary of the UK MOD articulated the depth of UK's defence engagement and interoperability, declaring "Our people work together, train together, study together, deploy together, fight together and die together" (March, 6, 2017). The MOD prioritises and values engagement with multilateral organisations outside NATO as well such as through the Commonwealth, ASEAN, the FPDA, and increasingly the African Union.

The first written reference to defence diplomacy in Spain appeared in the *2003 Strategic Defence Review*. Initially underdeveloped, its strategic debut occurred in the *National Defence Directive 1/2008* and was subsequently ratified in a section of *Defence Policy Directive 1/2009*. The Ministerio De Defensa Espana prioritized traditional bilateral activities with allies and partners "based mainly on dialogue and cooperation … to accomplish Spain's defence policy objectives in support of its foreign policy" (2012: 18). The *Defence Diplomacy Plan* outlines the objectives of Spanish defence diplomacy as preventing conflicts, encouraging reforms and capacity building of strategic partners and identifies joint military exercises as an important diplomatic instrument to foster confidence and transparency.[94] The Spanish government supports the call for some sort of 'European Defence Union' which pursues a common security and defence policy. Proponents highlight the defence union would produce positive outcomes through improved communication and training, increased interoperability, and enhanced technological R&D as well as a mutually beneficial 'buy local' defence acquisition program (European Defence Agency, January 2017). With some calling for the demise of NATO "there is a growing demand for the European Union to become more capable, more coherent and more strategic as a global actor" (EU External Action, August 2016). Policymakers progressed towards this reality when the European Commission tabled the Defence Action Plan (EDAP) in November 2016. The EDAP aims to boost collaboration on defence capability and support the European defence industry. The EU has been an active participant in the Long War with its mentoring and training program, the European Union Police Mission in Afghanistan (EUPOL Afghanistan) since 2007 playing a central role in Afghan SSR (EU External Action, December 2016). This section has discussed how states from around the world have engaged in the process but the story of the Coalition efforts in the Long War cannot be told without the U.S. What follows is a brief examination of the history, structure

94 The *2012 Defence Diplomacy Plan* presents the aims of Spain's defence diplomacy as:
(1) Maintain an ongoing dialogue with countries that are significant to Spain's foreign actions on bilateral & multilateral issues of mutual interest in the sphere of defence; promoting reciprocal understanding, knowledge & confidence.
(2) Help institute and consolidate a stable world order through cooperation in defence issues with countries in the sphere of Spanish actions abroad.
(3) Support the efforts of other countries in the area of defence; to consolidate their democratic structures & the rule of law as a means of contributing to the control and prevention of conflicts.
(4) Facilitate an appropriate legal framework to support & regulate development in the areas of defence, bilateral relations, political dialogue & cooperation with nations sharing historical and cultural links with Spain.
(5) Support Spanish industry in its relationship with countries. (p. 70).

and doctrine of the U.S military establishment, its relationship with State and how these elements affect U.S. defence diplomacy.

U.S. Defence Diplomacy: Containment to Engagement

> *You have no idea how much it contributes to the politeness and pleasantries of diplomacy when you have a little quiet armed forces in the background.*
>
> HARLOW & MAERZ, 1991

Shoon Murray writes that "since the end of the Cold War, accelerating after 9/11, the Pentagon's geographic combatant commands have become increasingly involved in regional engagement strategies, efforts to build capacity in other countries, strategic information, and the disbursement of humanitarian, development, and security assistance" (2014: 1). The Pentagon labels these non-combat roles as 'Military Diplomacy.' For Murray, this expansion raises one question; whether they cause friction with the "traditional" diplomatic role of State. Moreover, scholars have lamented the 'militarization' of U.S. diplomacy during the latter half of the twentieth century; a trend which has continued into the new millennium.[95]

Civil-military historian Richard Kohn has stressed that "regional commanders have come to assume such importance in their areas—particularly in the Pacific, the Middle East, and Central Asia—that they have effectively displaced American ambassadors and the State Department as the primary instruments of American foreign policy" (2002: 17). A U.S. Senate report found the "bleeding of civilian responsibilities overseas from civilian to military agencies risks weakening" both the Secretary of State and the SECDEF (U.S. Senate Report, 2006: 2). Pulitzer-prize winning journalist Dana Priest warned that "[O]n Clinton's watch the military slowly, without public scrutiny or debate, came to surpass its civilian leaders in resources and influence around the world" (2003: 42). While Melvin Goodman highlights that under Clinton's predecessor

95 Andrew Bacevich, The New American Militarism: How Americans Are Seduced by War, op. cit.; George Withers, Adam Isacson, Lisa Haugaard, Joy Olson, & Joel Fyke, Ready, Aim, Foreign Policy', A joint Publication from the Center for International Policy, the Latin America Working Group Education Fund and the Washington Office on Latin America, (March 2008), pp. 1–16; Nicholas Cull, Public Diplomacy-Lessons from the Past. *CDP Perspectives on Public Diplomacy*, (Los Angeles, USC Center on Public Diplomacy, 2009), pp. 1–62; Paul Sharp & Geoff Wiseman, *American diplomacy,* (Leiden: Brill, 2012), pp. 1–322; Chas Freeman, 'Too Quick to Draw: Militarism and the Malpractice of Diplomacy in America', op.cit; Rosa Brooks, *How Everything Became War and the Military Became Everything: Tales from the Pentagon*, New York: Simon & Schuste, 2016), pp. 1–438.

George W. Bush, the DoD "moved aggressively to eclipse the State Department as the major locus of U.S. foreign policy" (2004: 1).[96] This action, according to its detractors, weakened the role of State and other foreign policy oriented agencies, creating a situation in which the "long-term security interests of the U.S. have been imperilled, weakening the international coalition against terrorism" (Goodman, 2004: 2). Former Ambassador Chas Freeman claims that "changes in the U.S. political system that reinforce the militarised approach to foreign policy make it difficult, if not impossible for the U.S. to formulate strategic initiatives or to implement them through diplomacy and other measures short of war" (2012: 413). However, not all agree it's been a disruptive exercise. Constantinou and Opondo view this is a complimentary process, with "the militarization of diplomacy and development and diplomatization of the military" (2015: 2). The authors claim "this military-diplomatic apparatus presents something more than a state's or empire's attempt to 'enhance its value' at the periphery of the international system ... creating new sites of diplomatic engagement that exceed the governmental domain" (2015: 2).

The paper emphasises that U.S. foreign policy has 'always' been pursued through a closely aligned 'military/diplomatic apparatus,' from the Munroe doctrine, the Marshall Plan and the U.S.' global campaign to counter Communism during the Cold War and finally into the Long War, buttressed by a doctrine echoing Theodore Roosevelt's mantra of "speak softly but carry a big stick" (Roosevelt, January 26, 1900). One prominent example is Roosevelt's 'Great White Fleet' which saw 16 U.S. battleships complete a 14 month global voyage in 1908 which clearly signalled U.S. capabilities and intentions to an international and domestic audience (Holmes, 2008: 54).[97] The U.S. Combat Services Institute provides more evidence, producing a comprehensive, mutli-author case study analysis of the diplomatic role of the U.S. military in *Armed Diplomacy: Two Centuries of American Campaigning* (2003). Miller (2013) details the success of U.S. armed state-building from Cuba in 1898 through to its departure from Iraq in 2011, examining what strategies have been employed and which arm of government led these actions, while Grimmett (2007) lists hundreds of instances where U.S. military has been deployed to protect U.S.

96 Goodman claims "a militarized foreign policy offers Americans a country on a perpetual war footing, but not one that is more secure," p. 3.

97 See also: Mark B. Sherkey, *Strong Horses, Systems Thinking, Strategic Communication'*, School of Advanced Military Studies, (Fort Leavenworth, Kansas: United States Army Command and General Staff College, 2009), pp. 1–100.

citizens or promote U.S. interests.[98] Documents such as these are important as the current generation of armed forces personnel learn the lessons of past U.S. civil/military engagement in Latin America, Africa and Asia. For example, Colonel Lawyn C. Edwards from the U.S. Combat Studies Institute emphasises contemporary military issues and operations are "illuminated" by examining the (U.S.) Army's 'national building' activities during the Reconstruction of the post-Civil War South and the trans-Pacific West; through U.S. counter-guerrilla warfare in the American Civil War; the Philippines, Korea, and Latin America; to the U.S. occupation of Germany after WWII and American interventions in Mexico, China, Russia, Panama and Afghanistan" (2003: v).

History has a significant role to play in this paper's discussion on defence diplomacy. Former U.S. SECDEF William J. Perry asserted that preventative military to military outreach (defence diplomacy) "is nothing new—it has been a central idea of military strategists for over two thousand years" (March, 1996: viii). One relevant example is the role of military/defence attaché which was established as part of nineteenth century European diplomacy. The U.S. "began assigning military attachés to posts in the 1880s" and contemporary military attaché's and associated staff support the national diplomatic mission by understanding the social, military and political-military realities and intentions of HN states (Bureau of Diplomatic Security, 2011: xxiv). In practice, the military attaché serves as the ambassadors' advisor on military issues and his/her primary contact with the HN military. The job profile of a military attaché mirrors that of a 'traditional diplomat,' highlighting the complimentary relationship between the Foreign and Defence ministries. This example is one of many which should be remembered, and therefore learned; the military works in parallel with other instruments of state power and it's this relationship, rather than overt displays of its force, which has imbued the U.S. military with increased influence and credibility. William Inboden declares the "diplomatic successes" of the U.S., "building and maintaining a stable and peaceful international order over the past century, have been enabled by America's military

98 Grimmett's assessment excludes the eleven occasions where it has formally declared war against a foreign nation; see also Mark Edmonds, 'The Army's Role in Nation Building', USAWC Strategy Research Project, (Carlisle Barracks, PA: The U.S. Army War College, 2009), pp. 1–35; Other comprehensive lists include Senator Barry Goldwater, 'War Without Declaration. A Chronological List of 199 U.S. Military Hostilities Abroad Without a Declaration of War. 1798–197', *Congressional Record, Vol. 119*, (July 20, 1973); U.S. Department of State, *Armed Actions Taken by the United States Without a Declaration of War, 1789–1967*, Research Project 806A, Historical Studies Division, Bureau of Public Affairs, (1968).

dominance" (2016: 15). Inboden's assertion was echoed by SECDEF Mattis in testimony before the Senate Appropriations Committee, stating "Our military must ensure that the president and our diplomats always negotiate from a position of strength" (March 22, 2017). Defence diplomacy creates the junction between State and the Pentagon. The individual components of U.S. Armed Forces engage in defence diplomacy through a mix of traditional and new mechanisms (digital diplomacy, ect.) of diplomacy to establish a physical and/or online presence globally.

Despite this nexus, Willard acknowledges the process is not seamless and identifies "potential points of friction related to the integration of such efforts into the broader diplomatic framework" (2006:3). Part of the problem stems from a perception that "The ultimate purpose of the U.S. Armed Forces is to fight and win the Nations wars" (JCOS, 2013: 1–13).[99] Yet defence diplomacy uses these forces to enhance global security, stability and prosperity by building and maintaining relationships, creating trust between friendly armed forces and stressing the value of partner countries. Current Chairman of the JCOS, Gen. Dunford stated "at the very minimum, I want to enhance our collaboration and cooperation from a common understanding and then move towards a better integration of our efforts, because I believe, given the breadth and scope of the challenge, integrating our capabilities is the best way to succeed" (DoD, April 26, 2016). The path to success is outlined in the President's *National Security Strategy of the United States* (NSS), a capstone document which articulates U.S. foreign policy. The NSS guides the policy and strategic activities required to deliver the desired foreign policy goals of the U.S. The NSS prioritizes "promoting freedom, justice and human dignity" and these central pillars are replicated in the DoD's bi-annual *National Defence Strategy* (NDS) and State's quadrennial *Strategic Plan* which are used to coordinate and operationalise efforts of the various departments. These are key documents in the development of U.S. CT and COIN the Long War.

A successful CT strategy relies on strong relationships with foreign governments and the people they represent. Consequently, U.S. embassies have become the frontline in the Long War CT campaign tasked with building and maintaining relationships and as such, demands on foreign service staff, from the ambassador down, have increased, as has the influx of inter-agency

99 *Joint Publication 1* also dictates that U.S. Armed Forces can be involved in combat which includes the combination of offensive and defensive operations and missions to achieve objectives. Combat missions can vary in scale from individual strikes to extensive campaigns and can employ the full range of capabilities available to the military instrument of national power.

personnel (with uniformed personnel at times outnumbering their civilian colleagues), since 2001 (U.S. Senate Repot, 2006: 10). Consequently, the Senate recommended the president only nominate ambassadorial candidates "who are qualified for the sensitive and important post-9/11 role of the ambassador" (U.S. Senate Repot, 2006: 2).[100] Additionally, State has a global network of diplomatic missions and posts staffed with representatives of numerous national agencies which are invaluable sources of both issue specific and general information. The central point of contact within State for intelligence, analysis, and research is the Bureau of Intelligence and Research (INR). INR produces intelligence studies and analyses, which provide valuable information in support of strategic and operational objectives.[101] This brief example highlights the desired outcome of the integration, overlap or fusion of the armed and diplomatic services. However, the Senate report prepared for the Foreign Relations Committee cautioned that "blurred lines of authority between State and Defence could lead to inter-agency turf wars that undermine the effectiveness of the overall U.S. effort against terrorism" (2006: 1). Mitigating these detrimental outcomes requires a thorough understanding of roles and responsibilities of the actors involved.

This paper locates contemporary U.S. defence diplomacy and interagency cooperation on the National Security Act of 1947 (NSA '47') as well as the 1986 Defense Reorganization Act (*Goldwater-Nichols Act*). In addition to creating the National Security Council, NSA '47' also directed a major reorganization and streamlining of the existing military structure. The restructure would create a "unified direction under civilian control ... provide more effective, efficient, and economical administration ... and provide for the unified strategic direction of the combatant forces" (National Defense University, 2000: I-25). The objective was pursued, in large part, by merging the War and Navy Departments to create a single chain of command under a National Military Establishment; later renamed the Department of Defense. This action effectively removed uniformed military representation from cabinet level positions within the government, replacing it with a single civilian Secretary of Defense

100 Although the report seemed to diminish in situ ambassadors by insisting that new appointees demonstrate "the qualities of experienced judgment, knowledge of interagency missions and activities, and a solid grounding in the culture and politics of the region to which the candidate is expected to be assigned," p. 3.

101 Additionally, all-source reporting via Foreign Service channels at U.S. embassies or consular posts is useful, particularly during the formulation of end state and commander's objectives, target development, and assessment phases of the joint targeting cycle in COIN and CT operations.

(SECDEF).[102] The enhanced powers of the SECDEF legislated in 1958 (Public Law 85-599) increased the power and influence of the civilian leaders in the Pentagon.[103] This period of transformation also produced the U.S. strategy of 'containment,' which was introduced in *The Report to the National Security Council* (NSC *68*), a Top-Secret report completed by State's Policy Planning Staff in April 1950 and recognised as one of the most influential documents composed by the U.S. Government (USG) during the Cold War (*Truman Papers,* April 12, 1950: 21).[104]

Containment was designed to undermine what George Keenan described as the Soviets "elaborate and far flung apparatus for exertion of its influence in other countries, an apparatus of amazing flexibility and versatility, managed by people whose experience and skill in underground methods are presumably without parallel in history" (February 22, 1946).[105] Keenan heavily influenced U.S. foreign policy yet his notion of diplomatic centric containment, operationalised and implemented by Truman, morphed into President Eisenhower's 'domino theory' which further prioritised superior military capabilities deployed throughout the world. *National Security Council Report 68* (NSC 68) recognised the limitations of U.S. statecraft; bluntly stating that the U.S. found itself "at a diplomatic impasse" therefore a coalition would be sought with "rest of the free world (to) increment our own capabilities (April 12, 1950: 22, 24). Although NSC 68 recommended to President Truman that the U.S. containment strategy should prioritise "all means short of war" it remained "cardinal in this policy that we possess superior overall power in ourselves or in combination with other like-minded nations. One of the most important ingredients of power is military strength" (April 12, 1950: 21).[106] Successive administrations remained committed to the military dominated containment, supported by increased funding of the DoD so that it could address the disparity between

102 Amendment of the term National Military Establishment to Department of Defense occurred in 1949.

103 *Public Law 85-599*, (Government Publishing Office, August 6, 1958), available at https://www.gpo.gov/fdsys/pkg/STATUTE-72/pdf/STATUTE-72-Pg514.pdf (Last accessed December 1, 2016).

104 See also: John Lewis Gaddis, *Strategies of Containment: A Critical Appraisal of American National Security Policy during the Cold War*, (New York: Oxford University Press, 1982).

105 In *The Long Telegram*, Keenan asserts that containing Soviet expansion would, be "undoubtedly the greatest task our diplomacy has ever faced and probably greatest it will ever have to face."

106 This mind-set would ultimately manifest in the Gulf of Tonkin Resolution (the 20th century equivalent of the 2001 AUMF), which allowed President Johnson 'all steps necessary' to roll back Communism and force the West's enemies to yield to their goals and interests.

its actual offensive/defensive military strength and a growing list of international commitments. The goal of the U.S. outlined in NSC 68 was (and remains) achieving a tolerable state of order among nations without war and of preparing to defend ourselves in the event of an attack" (April 12, 1950: 44). Inboden declares the Truman Doctrine's enduring legacy is his "adept employment of military power as a diplomatic instrument of statecraft" (Inboden, 2016: 19), while others refer to the concept as "armed diplomacy" (Nau, 2013).

The durability of the Truman Doctrine is open for debate. For example Rahbek-Clemmensen argues that conventional military forces played only a marginal role in the peaceful dissolution of the USSR, reflecting that "conventional force is but one of many tools available for the state. Diplomacy, economic strength, and technological innovation also play a significant role" (2013: 49). While Rojansky suggests the Cold War ended to a great degree because Russians came to view the U.S as "a successful and prosperous society, whose model they hoped to emulate and whose partnership they desired to manage global challenges" (2016: para. 11). As previously mentioned, the U.S. began to develop relations (including military) with the Soviets during the 70's and 80's and a bilateral military to military relationship was formalized in a 1988 meeting between U.S. SECDEF Carlucci and his Soviet counterpart Marshall Yazov (UKMOD, 1998: 39). However, John Mearsheimer suggests Soviet willingness to engage diplomatically with the U.S. had more to do with maintaining the status quo and reducing the potential of U.S. aggression against a weakening nemesis. (2001: 50). As the relationship between the two Cold-War foes deepened, the political and security panorama changed again with the dissolution of the Warsaw Pact and the breakup of the Soviet Union yet the engagement continued. During the early 90's relations between the U.S. and former Warsaw Pact nations intensified significantly through NATO multilateralism or bilateral relations with states within the U.S./NATO security orbit.

Former U.S. Under-Secretary for Defence Policy, Douglas Feith, explained the outreach to Russia during the end of the 20th century as "the U.S. aiming to develop a more cooperative relationship, where we on a regular basis are exchanging information on these things in the way that we exchange information with other friends and allies" (DoD News, January 16, 2002).[107] Scholars maintain that U.S. "alliances have proven to be astoundingly durable, in spite of major changes in the international security environment following the end of the Cold War" (von Hlatky & Darden, 2015: 31). The reason for this period of enhanced cooperation and dialogue is a subject for debate with Russia and

107 See also: Barry R. Posen & Stephen W. Van Evera, 'Reagan Administration Defense Policy: Departure from Containment', *International Security, Vol. 8, no. 1* (Summer 1983), pp. 3–45.

the U.S./NATO producing claims and counter-claims regarding NATO expansion, reunification and basic status of forces issues.[108] Differences in narrative not-withstanding, the role of defence personnel in a diplomatic process during "a geopolitical event of the first magnitude" demonstrates their utility in mitigating negative/unintended outcomes in times of strategic ambiguity (Moens, 1991: 531). Reveron claims there are several Cold War era legacy programs, such as U.S. security assistance missions conducted by its armed forces, which indicate that effective cooperative programs can and do endure regional/global instability by helping partner nations to do the oft cited but seldom explained 'heavy lifting.' In the 21st century many states rely on the U.S. for "either the actual provision of security or the training and equipment necessary to guarantee their national security" (Reveron, 2016: 43).

U.S. post-Cold War foreign policy comprised more than Russian engagement, with Operations Desert Shield and Desert Storm delivering success in the Gulf. 'Victory' was obtained by establishing the largest and most successful war coalition since the Second World War.[109] Although foreign policy progress was being made in the immediate post-Cold War period, thanks in large part to renewed multi-level diplomatic outreach, some were uncomfortable with

108 During a series of formal and informal discussions in 1990, the U.S. allegedly sought to reassure the Soviets by pledging that NATO would not inch eastward which ran counter to U.S. strategic intentions in a unified Europe; essentially rolling back post-Soviet influence. Itzkowitz Shifrinson suggests that Russia's actions in the 21st century "may stem from feelings of insecurity and real worries that the West is an unreliable partner" (2016: 9). For more detail see: Joshua R. Itzkowitz Shifrinson, '*Deal or No Deal? The End of the Cold War and the U.S. Offer to Limit NATO Expansion*', *Quarterly Journal: International Security, Vol. 40. no. 4*, (Spring 2016), pp. 7–44; Michael MccGwire, 'NATO Expansion: 'A Policy Error of Historic Importance', *Review of International Studies, Vol. 24, No. 1*, (January 1998; Michael Cox & Steven Hurst, 'His Finest Hour?' George Bush and the Diplomacy of German Unification', *Diplomacy & Statecraft, Vol. 13, no. 4*, (2002), pp. 123–150; Mark Kramer, "The Myth of a No-NATO-Enlargement Pledge to Russia', *Washington Quarterly, Vol. 32, no. 2*, (April 2009), p. 41; Mary Elise Sarotte, 'Not One Inch Eastward? Bush, Baker, Kohl, Genscher, Gorbachev, and the Origin of Russian Resentment toward NATO Enlargement in February 1990', *Diplomatic History, Vol. 34, no. 1*, (January 2010), pp. 119–140; Mary Elise Sarotte, 'A Broken Promise? What the West Really Told Moscow about NATO Expansion', *Foreign Affairs, Vol. 93, no. 5*, (September/October 2014); Kristina Spohr, 'Germany, America and the shaping of post-Cold War Europe: a story of German international emancipation through political unification, 1989–90', *Cold War History, Vol. 15, no. 2*, (2015), pp. 221–243.

109 U.S. Army *FM 3-0 Operations*, details how these two Op's brought "more than 800,000 military personnel form 36 nations to combine their will, forces, and resources to oppose Iraqi armed forces." pp. 2–42.

a foreign policy which sought to promote democracy globally (Staten, 2005).[110] Many denounced this strategy as an invitation for a never-ending crusade or as "international social work worthy of Mother Theresa but not of the world's sole superpower" (Mandelbaum, 1996: 18). The debate over the U.S.'s post-Cold War role continued in parallel with two important changes in the U.S. First, the de-funding of the DoD and State stemming from the idea that there would be less need for aggressive global defence policy, the so called 'peace dividend', second, the election of Bill Clinton in 1992 (Wallin, 2015).

The Clinton administration initially struggled to define a strategic vision for the U.S. in the post-Cold War era and it came under increasing pressure from neoconservatives. The 'neocon's' planned to "exercise a more assertive, pre-emptive, and unilateral foreign policy that drew upon the hegemonic power and military capabilities of the United States to reshape the global political system" (Staten, 2005). For example the draft *Defense Planning Guidance* prepared in 1992 under the aegis of Paul Wolfowitz, then U.S. Undersecretary of Defense Policy, detailed how international order, and therefore the future security environment, could be shaped "in ways favourable to [the United States]" (Bacevich (b), 2016). In addition, the *Defence Strategic Guidance,* drafted the same year by then Deputy Under Secretary of Defense, I. Lewis 'Scooter' Libby, detailed how the U.S. would "preserve its freedom" by "helping other countries preserve or obtain freedom and peace" as both a means and an end in itself (February 29, 1992: 1). Finally, SECDEF Dick Cheney's *Defence Strategy for the 1990's* (1993) presented a doctrine to secure the 'New American Century.'[111] The New American Century sought to "apply the military instrument of power to an increasing range of non-warfighting missions," diverting from the conservative approach of the Weinberger Doctrine which supported the "use of military power based upon a careful calculation of national interests" (U.S.G., 2011: 43).

Despite the 'guidance' offered by the neocon's, the Clinton administration developed an alternate 'grand strategy.'[112] Firstly SECDEF Aspin implemented

---

110 Staten claims that U.S. foreign policy ebbs and flows from missionary mindset inspired by idealism through to a more limited policy which reduces, redefines and reprioritizes U.S. goals.

111 See also: Donnelly, T. 'Rebuilding America's Defences: Strategy, Forces and Resources for a New Century', *A Report of The Project for the New American Century*, (Washington D.C.: PNAC, 2000); Cohen, E. *Choosing to Lead: American Foreign Policy for a Disordered World*, (Washington D.C., The John Hay Initiative, 2015).

112 The debate over the existence of a 'grand strategy' let alone what it is ongoing and beyond the scope of this discussion. In its simplest form, grand strategy can be conceived as a set of guiding principles and priorities which provide structure to a state's decisions and responses to global events. For example, since WWII U.S. grand strategy has revolved

his *Bottom up Review* (1993) of the U.S. 'defense strategy, force structure, modernization, infrastructure, and foundations' and secondly it released *the National Security Strategy of Engagement and Enlargement* (1995) which provided a framework for the U.S. to advance its global and domestic interests into the new millennium.[113] The current defence diplomacy structure of the U.S. evolved from the Clinton administration's 'Prevent, Deter, and Defeat' (1996) policy which outlined a profound change to U.S. defense. SECDEF Perry's 'preventative defence' was the first component of a three pronged strategy to ensure the security of the U.S. and its allies, deterrence being second and military conflict as a distant third and last resort (Carter & Perry, 1999: 39).[114] Predictably, Clinton's defence policy prioritised the military element of national power; however, it also emphasised its role in fostering international relationships in non-combat situations. For example, the *National Military Strategy of the United States of America: Shape, Respond, Prepare Now: A Military Strategy for a New Era* introduced the term 'peacetime military engagement,' defined as "encompassing all military activities in peacetime that involve other militaries that have the purpose of shaping the international environment" (1997: 7). 'Shaping' missions and activities would enhance "the ability of the U.S. armed forces (and others) to 'prepare for' deliberate operations, or 'respond to,' international crises" (Szayna, et al., 2004: 9). Supporters of preventive defence, including Perry's successor William Cohen, argued the strategy was capable of preventing expensive conflicts in the future by promoting peace and stability through friendly interaction, influencing the future actions of states through military oriented relationship building. These new channels of communication would reduce misunderstandings and misperceptions. Kattelman

around maintaining its overwhelming military, economic, and political advantage. For Liddell Hart (1967), the objective of grand strategy is to "coordinate and direct the resources of a nation, or band of nations, towards the attainment ... goals defined by fundamental policy," p. 322.

113 *The National Security Strategy for Engagement and Enlargement* declared; "Never has American leadership been more essential—to navigate the shoals of the world's new dangers and to capitalize on its opportunities. American assets are unique: our military strength, our dynamic economy, our powerful ideals and, above all, our people. We can and must make the difference through our engagement; but our involvement must be carefully tailored to serve our interests and priorities," p. i.

114 Preventative defence is similar in concept and function to preventive diplomacy which is a diplomatic activity intended to minimize conflict or prevent escalation of disagreements into violence (CSBM's & CBM's); See also: Geoff Wiseman, 'What is Non-Provocative Defence?', *Concepts of Non-Provocative Defence*, (London: Palgrave Macmillan, 2002).

suggests that intra-alliance dialogue is just as important as dialogue between the alliance and external actors for confirming intentions (2016: 805).

Following two terms of Clinton's 'peaceful engagement' which included humanitarian military interventions in Somalia, Yugoslavia, Haiti and Bosnia as well as military operations in Afghanistan, Iraq and Sudan, the foreign policy strategy of George W. Bush was in its infancy when al Qa'ida conducted its attacks on September 11.[115] In response, military pre-emption/deterrence, economic sanctions, and a whole-of-government approach to national security emerged and Secretary of State Colin Powell was a prominent campaigner for swift, decisive military action. The Bush administration's approach to national security also required yet another transformation of the DoD less than a decade after the previous 'comprehensive' re-alignment.[116] SECDEF Rumsfeld articulated DoD's 'transformation' as:

> a process that shapes the changing nature of military competition and cooperation through new combinations of concepts, capabilities, people and organizations that exploit our nation's advantages and protect against our asymmetric vulnerabilities to sustain our strategic position which helps underpin peace and stability in the world.
>
> U.S. DOD, APRIL 2003: 3

However, some questioned whether this latest transformation would leave the U.S. "prepared to fight the most dangerous but least likely threats and unprepared to fight the least dangerous but most likely threats" (Reynolds, 2006: x). A key component of the 'transformation' was strategic communication which the *Report of the Defense Science Board Task Force on Strategic Communication* defined as:

> vital to America's national security and foreign policy ... it describes a variety of instruments used by governments for generations to understand global attitudes and cultures, engage in a dialogue of ideas between

115 The concept of humanitarian military intervention is articulated in: Adam Roberts, 'Humanitarian War: Military Intervention and Human Rights', *International Affairs, Vol. 69, no. 3,* (1993), pp. 429–449.

116 For more detail see: Jervis, R. 'U.S. grand strategy: Mission impossible', *Naval War College Review, Vol. 51, no. 3,* (1998); Handel, M, *Masters Of War: Classical Strategic* Thought, (London Frank Cass Publishers, 2005); Franke, V. C. & Dorff, R. H. *Conflict Management and "Whole of Government": Useful Tools for U.S. National Security Strategy?* (Carlisle PA: U.S. Army War College, 2012).

> people and institutions, advise policy makers, diplomats, and military leaders on the public opinion implications of policy choices, and influence attitudes and behaviour through communication strategies.
>
> U.S. DEFENSE SCIENCE BOARD, 2004, 11

Although Rumsfeld's 'transformation' and the use of strategic communication left the DoD well positioned to engage and comprehend key audiences, re-energize established relations and forge new ones, and influence the direction of a stalling Long War, some still believed the U.S. was "being out-communicated by a guy in cave" (Brooks, 2016: 90). This changed with the arrival of SECDEF Robert Gates late in the Bush administration and increased with the transition of power in 2009. It was therefore the newly elected Barak Obama who pursued a policy of 'engagement' through an adaptive blend of diplomacy and defense (U.S.G. 2011, 1). The dynamic security environment inhibits experimentation, and in reality, "because security is the essential precondition for stability and development, the military literally became the tip of the spear on U.S. efforts to reduce the global consequences of security deficits" (Reveron, 2016: 34). The priority placed on defence oriented diplomacy is understandable given that the vast majority of the US$ 1.6 trillion approved by congress in the first fourteen years of the war were allocated to the DoD (Belasco, 2014). Moreover, capacity building, a central component of defence diplomacy, emerged as a major strategic concept in the DoD *Quadrennial Defense Review's* (QDR) of 2006 and 2010, the biannual *National Security Strategy* and the *National Defence Strategy* and the *2012 Defense Strategic Guidance.* As a result, U.S. "uniformed personnel and military establishments are on the ground throughout the world, requiring a complex network of formal and informal bilateral and multilateral arrangements" (Marks, 2014: 66).

Since 2009 the Obama administration pursued an alternate path to somehow end up in the same position as President's Clinton and Bush, by recognising:

> The ongoing shifts in relative power and increasing interconnectedness in the international order indicate a strategic inflection point. This requires America's foreign policy to employ an adaptive blend of diplomacy, development, and defense. While the strength of our military will continue to underpin national security, we must continuously adapt our approaches … the full spectrum of power to defend our national interests …
>
> U.S.G., 2011: 3

The administration adapted to shifting global conditions by initiating the "transition from containment to engagement" (Henrikson, 2013: 266). The use of engagement as a policy 'headline' in the *National Security Strategy 2010* was not new and the Obama administration merely picked through the discarded remnants of Clinton 'Engagement and Enlargement' strategy of the mid-90's.[117] The 2010 *U.S. National Security Strategy* broadly defines engagement "as the active participation of the U.S. in relationships beyond our borders" (U.S.G., 2013: 11). As it ended the first decade of the twenty-first century, the Obama administration embraced 'engagement' as it pursued "a strategy of national renewal and global leadership ... that rebuilt the foundation of America's strength and influence" whilst maintaining its military superiority which has underpinned global security for over half a century. Henrikson claims the Obama administration gave "new status and formal recognition" to engagement, with this form of diplomacy becoming "a virtual policy itself, as distinct from being a policy precursor or the instrument of policy" (Henrikson, 2013: 266).

In the 2011 U.S. National Military Strategy titled *Redefining America's Military Leadership*, Chairman of the JCOS, Admiral Mike Mullen, asserted that U.S. forces must "deepen security relationships with our allies and create opportunities for partnerships with new and diverse groups of actors" (U.S.G., 2011: i). The *Strategy* emphasised the ability of the U.S. to use its unique "convenor" role to use its "relationships, values and military capabilities ... to bring others together to help deepen security ties between them and cooperatively address common security challenges" (U.S.G., 2011: 1). Admiral Mullen's reasoning is echoed by Paterson who asserts that the "U.S. has a moral obligation to ensure the training it provides to foreign forces is in keeping with U.S. values on democracy, human rights, and civil-military relations" (2016: 3). Hallams & Schreer concur, claiming this form of strategic engagement affords the U.S. the potential to leverage its global leadership, intra-allied cohesion and trust, burden-sharing and credibility to form ad-hoc, threat specific groupings (2012: 327).

This overview demonstrates there has been an incremental shift in U.S. foreign policy post-Cold War, whereby coercive diplomacy morphed into cooperative military engagement. Jentleson defines coercive diplomacy as the use of military power short of war to effect a change in a target country's policies or political makeup through the use of carrots and sticks (usually more stick) (2006: 2).[118] McCready asserts that failed coercive diplomacy leaves a state with

117 For more detail see: U.S. Government, *The National Security Strategy for Engagement and Enlargement*, (Washington D.C.: U.S. Government Printing Office, 1995), available at http://www.dtic.mil/doctrine/doctrine/research/nss.pdf.

118 See recent commentary, Eliot Cohen, 'Should the U.S. still carry a 'big stick'?, *Los Angeles Times*, (January 18, 2017), available at http://www.latimes.com/opinion/op-ed/la-oe-cohen-trump-big-stick-20170118-story.html.

only two options: back down or go to war" (2005: 84). In comprehensive case study analysis, Art and Cronin (2003) and Cragin & Gerwehr (2005) detail why this strategic shift may have occurred, offering the Balkans, Somalia, Haiti, North Korea, China-Taiwan, Iraq and Afghanistan as evidence that coercive diplomacy fails to prevent conflict. Moreover, Martha Crenshaw identified the limitations of coercive diplomacy on groups such as the Taliban as the motivations and values of a "loose alliance of non-states and autonomous individuals with ambiguous and complex interrelationships" (2003: 310). Another impediment to coercive diplomacy is a lack of credibility, which is exacerbated by intra-Coalition disunity. For example, Chaudhuri and Farrell note the limitations of ISAF prior to the establishment of its Joint Command was that it was "divided into five regional commands ... with little coordination between them ... a number of military task forces from different troop-contributing countries" which led to weak" unity of effort and command (2013: 275). While *FM 3-0 Operations* emphasises that "unity of command is unlikely in multinational operations ... The president of the U.S. retains command authority over U.S. forces. Most nations have similar restrictions ... To compensate for limited unity of command, commanders concentrate on achieving unity of effort" (ABCA, 2008).[119]

The paper determines that U.S. 'defence engagement', offers an alternative to unilateral diplomatic or military intervention, giving partners "an awareness of the other side's capabilities and intentions" (Henrikson, 2013: 266). The concept manifests into doctrine with The *2011 Military Strategy* identified a "multinodal world (where) the military's contribution to American leadership must be about more than power ..." (U.S.G., 2011: 5). While the *2015 U.S. National Security Strategy* dictates "[T]he use of force is not the principal means of U.S. engagement abroad, nor always the most effective for the challenges we face ... our first line of action is principled and clear-eyed diplomacy ..." (U.S.G., 2015: 4). Consequently the National Command Authority (The President and SECDEF) has additional options across a "spectrum between large-scale conflict and diplomacy" (Michel, March 17, 2016). Thus we return to the concept of 'shaping,' which *JP5-0 Joint Operation Planning*, defines as various activities "performed to dissuade or deter potential adversaries and to assure or solidify relationships with friends and allies" (2011: xxii). Quite simply, the relationships

119 The ABCA Handbook emphasises that "in coalition operations, consensus building to ensure compatibility at the political, military, and cultural levels between partners is key. A successful coalition must establish at least unity of effort, if not unity of command ... with the optimum level of input and upfront accountability from all likely participants will provide a firm base for a successful operation."

built within the Coalition establish a unified and credible, front that can simultaneously deter, compel and assail.

Throughout the second period of the Obama administration military officials have reiterated their support for Coalition train and equip initiatives with commanders on the Iraqi frontlines in 2017 insisting "their strategy of training and fighting "by, with, and through" local forces is working ..." (Baron, July 23, 2013).[120] Some analysts determine "the legacy of Obama's presidency in Afghanistan is a strong Afghan Army and weak Afghan state" (Miller 2016: para. 5). However, Schadlow asserts that political order is the essential condition for military victory. Central to strategic victory in all wars fought by the U.S. has been the creation of a favourable political order which requires a strategy for the use of non-military tools of statecraft whereby "combat operations and governance operations are both integral to war and occur in tandem" (Schadlow, 2003: 86). This paper presents defence diplomacy as a mechanism to achieve Schadlow's objective. What is clear at the end of President Obama's time as Commander in Chief is that his 'Disrupt, Dismantle & Defeat' strategy (the so-called Obama doctrine which prioritised SOF, and 'leading from behind' (Goldberg, April, 2016)) of pursuing U.S. security interests "by with and through local forces" has relied heavily on effective defence diplomacy.[121]

Although the Obama White House insisted "NATO is the strongest alliance the world has ever known and is the hub of an expanding global security network," President Trump has been vocal in his criticism of trans-Atlantic alliance and his administration will assess whether to commit to multidimensional security and stabilization operations and what form that commitment will take (U.S.G., 2015: 25). Trump vigorously campaigned on a platform of rebuilding the capability of U.S. forces, which he claims have been decimated by the Obama administration in parallel with U.S. economic downturn and

120 For more detail see: Kevin Baron, 'Want Syria? Convince General Dempsey', *Defence One*, (July 23, 2013), available at http://www.defenseone.com/politics/2013/07/want-syria-convince-dempsey/67298/; Marcus Weisberger, 'Dempsey's Final Instruction to the Pentagon: Prepare for a Long War', *Defence One*, (July, 1, 2015), available at http://www.defenseone.com/business/2015/07/dempseys-final-instruction-pentagon-prepare-long-war/116761/; Marcus Weisberger, 'Odierno Wades Into GOP Battle Over Iraq War', *Defence One*, (August 12, 2015) available at http://www.defenseone.com/threats/2015/08/odierno-wades-gop-war-over-iraq-war/119083/.

121 Department of the Army, Army Special Operations Forces Unconventional Warfare, FM 3-05.130, (Washington D.C., September 2008) pp. 1–2; Gen. In his *Commanders Initial Assessment* to President Obama, Stanley McChrystal claimed that the only way to achieve sustainable stability and development for the Afghan population was 'by with and through' a legitimate Afghan government.

subsequent sequestration (O'Toole, May 30, 2016). Budget constraints since 2008 have amplified previous warnings that a U.S. "military force that lacks the ability to employ ground forces that can survive and manoeuvre rapidly on future battlefields will deprive U.S. political leaders of a decisive tool of diplomacy" (Kagan, et al., 2000: 30). Inboden (2016) for example, claims a diminished and weakened defence capability has undermined American diplomatic and economic power and influence. While SECDEF Mattis testified, that "Sequestration has done more damage to our readiness, than the enemies in the field" (March 2017). President Trump's commitment to rebuilding the armed forces at a considerable ongoing cost to DoD's bottom line which will be recouped through spending cuts in other departments.[122] However, the President may heed the comments of his own SECDEF who reminded policymakers "if you are going to under-fund the state department then please by more ammunition because we are going to get into more fights" (March 20, 2014).

Some seek to moderate the conjecture, believing that "despite the Trump administration's emphasis on strengthening the U.S. military, defense policy cannot exist by itself-it should be nestled within an overall U.S. strategic policy" (Suh, et al., March 16, 2017). Further speculation on the future direction of U.S. policy in South Asia is not within the remit of this paper, moreover, as Senator John McCain recently commented, he "had long ago given up trying to interpret the remarks of the President of the United States, I only pay attention to what he does" (March 23, 2017). In reality, the U.S. Army is adding 28,000 soldiers in 2017, including 16,000 active duty troops who will complement the U.S. global military presence where at least "100 U.S. troops are stationed in more than 20 countries across the world and there's at least one American soldier in

122 For more detail see: Anthony Capaccio, 'Trump's Bigger Army Could Cost $12 Billion by Fanning's Math', *Bloomberg Politics*, (January 19, 2017), available at https://www.bloomberg.com/politics/articles/2017-01-19/trump-s-bigger-army-could-cost-12-billion-by-fanning-s-math; Joe Gould, 'McCain Hits Trump Budget Office Pick Mulvaney on Defense', *DefenceNews*, (January 24, 2017) available at http://www.defensenews.com/articles/indonesian-defense-chief-plays-down-a400m-acquisition-reports; Rebecca Kheel, Retired Generals Urge Congress Not to Cut Funds for Diplomacy', *The Hill*, (February 27, 2017) available at http://thehill.com/policy/defense/321395-retired-generals-urge-congress-to-fully-fund-diplomacy; Sean O'Keefe, 'Trump's Defense Budget Plan in Perspective, *Bipartisan Policy Center*, (February 28, 2017), available at https://bipartisanpolicy.org/blog/trumps-defense-budget-plan-in-perspective/#.WLYZXrv54jQ.twitter; (Last accessed February 30, 2017); Pat Towell & Lynn M. Williams, 'The Trump Administration's March 2017 Defense Budget Proposals: Frequently Asked Questions', *CRS Report R44806*, (Washington D.C.: Congressional Research Service, April 3, 2017), pp. 1–10.

nearly 175 countries" (Watson, January 2017). For example, 2017 sees "the biggest U.S. and NATO arms build-up on the European continent since the 1980s ... a reversal of the long build down that reduced the U.S. force in Europe from more than 300,000 in the late 1980s to barely 100,000 in the aftermath of 9/11" (Frum, January 10, 2017). Likewise, the U.S. Army Corp of Engineers is "building more infrastructure than it has built in the past four decades ... building 145 infrastructure projects ranging from training range renovation to housing for NATO troops in Poland, the Baltic States, and the Balkans worth $276.4 million" (Braw, 2016: 3).[123] SECDEF Mattis made clear his support for the trans-Atlantic alliance declaring "If we did not have NATO today we would need to create it" (Wright & Herb, January 12, 2017).

The Trump administration is committed to make the U.S. 'great again,' achieving 'peace through strength' which ensures U.S. foreign policy produces positive domestic outcomes.[124] It also remains to be seen whether President Trumps stated policy direction and his 'transactional' approach to diplomacy will impact current engagement initiatives as well as future State and DoD military oriented outreach.[125] The President needs to be reminded that even though the U.S. has "the most modern and professional military in the world, battlefield success has rarely translated into strategic victory over the last three decades" (Hooker & Collins, 2015: 6). The two objectives of the new administration are not mutually exclusive, with previous foreign policy officials, Secretaries of State and Defence enforcing this reality.[126] For example former

123 Braw writes that the "U.S. has quadrupled its funding for the European Reassurance Initiative to $3.4 billion, which includes military pre-positioning to Europe," p. 5.

124 'Peace through strength' is an ancient phrase and concept implying that strength of arms is a necessary component of peace. The phrase is quite old; it has famously been used by many leaders from Roman Emperor Hadrian in the first century AD, to Ronald Reagan in the 1980s, and has been resurrected by the Trump administration and conservative think-tanks such as The Heritage Foundation, see: https://www.whitehouse.gov/1600/presidents/ronaldreagan; https://reaganlibrary.archives.gov/archives/speeches/1983/32383d.htm; http://www.stateoftheunionhistory.com/2015/11/1983-ronald-reagan-peace-through.html; William Inboden, 'The Role of a Strong National Defence', *2016 Index of U.S. Military Strength*, (The Heritage Foundation, 2016), pp. 15–22.

125 Transactional diplomacy prioritises short term benefits over shared values and history, is more aligned with a Realist, isolationist rather than Liberal, globalist world view and may diminish the role of State whilst solidifying the military as the predominant foreign policy tool.

126 For more detail see: Robert Gates, Secretary of Defense, Landon Lecture at the Kansas State University, (November 26, 200, available at http://www.defenselink.mil/speeches/speech.aspx?speechid=1199; Shared Responsibility, Pooled Resources (SRPR) Memorandum

Secretary of State John Kerry insists that "global leadership is a strategic imperative for America, not a favour we do for other countries. It amplifies our voice and extends our reach ... and it really matters to the daily lives of Americans" (January 24, 2013). Senator Kerry's sentiments echoed previous comments by Tom Kelly, Principal Deputy Assistant Secretary, Bureau of Political-Military Affairs who stated quite simply that "at the forefront of the United States' foreign policy is the notion that America helps itself by helping others" (April 17 2014). Finally, the *2015 US National Security Strategy* reinforced both statements by State officials, emphasising:

> We will lead with capable partners. In an interconnected world, there are no global problems that can be solved without the United States, and few that can be solved by the United States alone' ...'we and our partners must make the reforms and investments needed to make sure we can work more effectively with each other while growing the ranks of responsible, capable states
>
> U.S.G., 2015: 3

In a complex threat environment where the projection of decisive military power encompasses many variants, U.S. forces disseminate its core values through the persuasive power of example, with military power complimenting the other instruments of statecraft "when applied in concert" (U.S.G., 2015: 5). For example, the Long War has led to "massive investments in CT and COIN by the U.S.-led international coalition, in cooperation with regional partners, have included the entire spectrum of instruments available in the state toolbox (Brynjar, 2016: 74). A 2016 RAND report examines the multi-nodal risk, determining the U.S. is potentially confronted by several traditional and non-traditional actors in a multi-front assault and defence diplomacy may be the only mechanism to pacify these threats (Binnendijk, 2016). The capacity building and universal doctrine delivered through defence diplomacy provides the U.S. with the global posture, forward presence, and strategic depth required without having to rapidly aggregate, (already constrained) capabilities. With foresight, the U.S. has reinforced defence diplomacy as a tool of conflict prevention as well as forming the core of its stability operations.[127]

---

for the Secretary of State from the Secretary of Defense, titled "Options for Remodelling Security Sector Assistance Authorities', (December 15, 2009).

127 *U.S. Army Field Manual 3-07* defines stability operations as one "that integrates the cooperative efforts of the departments and agencies of the USG, intergovernmental and nongovernmental organizations, multinational partners, and private sector entities to

Emphasising defence diplomacy's theoretical foundations and demonstrating the practical benefits is important beyond the scope and particular case study of this paper. As the global threat dynamic transitions again, with the 5th domain (Land, Air, Sea, Space & Cyber) becoming increasingly relevant, stakeholders need to determine what's the military's role in this realm; will defence diplomacy remain relevant? This paper projects two areas in particular where defence diplomacy will be prominent. Firstly, Information Operations are an integral aspect of irregular warfare and oft cited linkages between diplomacy and propaganda will come to the fore (Berridge, 2010: 182; Carlson, 2014:149–150). Moreover, Nichiporuk labels public diplomacy (strategic communication) as a multi-strike weapon in Information Warfare operations (2002: 202). Secondly, at a time when international cyber norms remain inchoate, U.S. defence diplomacy has a critical role to play in shaping offensive and defensive behaviour as well as maintaining the gap between advanced and emerging cyber actors. The U.S. formally established its independent Cyber Command in 2016, creating another entity for traditional defence cooperation mechanisms such as dialogues, exchanges and working groups to generate norms of behaviour and deterrence capabilities. However, greater transparency and cooperation in this nascent sphere requires a high degree of trust among partners as information sharing and the transfer of technology can identify vulnerabilities which can be exploited by both nation states and nefarious non-state actors. Attribution of cyber-related aggression is difficult therefore establishing CBM's, "fostering transparency, trust and predictability among militaries" should be prioritised (Heinl, 2016: 22–23). Identifying and championing the positive outcomes of defence diplomacy, with its inbuilt trust and cooperation generators, will ensure it remains a central tool for states to pursue its security in a multidomain threat environment.[128]

Whether looking at conventional or unconventional warfare today or into the future, U.S. initiated security cooperation ensures partners are interoperable with U.S. forces when the U.S. leads international military coalitions

achieve unity of effort toward a shared goal." Stability Operations replaced the previous designator; Military Operations Other Than War (MOOTW) which was codified in Joint Publication 3–07, other nations continue to use MOOTW.

128 For more detail see: U.S. Army, 'Multi-Domain Battle Combined Arms for the 21st Century', *MDB White Paper*, (February 24, 2017) available at http://www.tradoc.army.mil/MultiDomainBattle/docs/MDB_WhitePaper.pdf (Last accessed March 20, 2017); Chris Telly & Samuel Mebrere, Training "No Hurdle" Joint Offense', *War on the Rocks*, (January 31, 2017), available at https://warontherocks.com/2017/01/training-no-huddle-joint-offense/ (Last accessed February 3, 2017). The author's discussion on improving 'joint' operational integration in multi-domain warfare is also applicable to 'combined' operations.

such as the Long War Coalition in Afghanistan.[129] This section has discussed the spectrum of defence diplomacy throughout NATO and ASEAN as well as highlighting the potential of defence diplomacy to reinforce U.S. national security by improving the capabilities and influencing the mind-set of strategic partners in the Long War. The following section combines the theoretical element of section one with section two's discussion of the general practical elements to present an overview of defence diplomacy in Afghanistan since 2001 with the aim of validating the concept. The following case study employs the core principles of defence diplomacy to demonstrate U.S. engagement with its Coalition partners as well as with Afghanistan's nascent civil/military institutions. It also establishes the central role of defence diplomacy in U.S. foreign policy; building sustainable relationships, maintaining global stability and economic growth, exporting democracy and ensuring U.S. homeland security. The case study examines how the U.S. military, the most kinetically powerful institution of the state, used its 'diplomats in uniform' to pursue parallel military and political lines of effort in pursuit of its foreign policy objectives.

Defence Diplomacy in the Long War

The Afghan Coalition

> *There is only one thing worse than fighting with allies and that is fighting without them*[130]

Defence diplomacy provides a unique lens to view how the U.S. has pursued its national security strategy in Afghanistan since 2001 and can be a useful metric to gauge 'successes' in the Long War. Mahapatra concluded that U.S. defence diplomacy in Afghanistan was "designed towards ending the U.S. military

---

129 *DoD Directive 5132.03* defines security cooperation as "The full continuum of activities undertaken by the Department of Defense to encourage and enable international partners to work with the United States to achieve strategic objectives. It encompasses all DoD interactions with foreign defense and security establishments, including all DoD-administered security assistance programs, that build defense and security relationships promoting specific U.S. security interests, including all international armaments cooperation activities and security assistance activities; that develop allied and friendly military capabilities for self-defence and multinational operations; and that provide U.S. forces with peacetime and contingency access to host nations," (Defence Security Cooperation Agency, 2014:1).

130 Sir Winston Churchill, (April 1945).

operations without ceding total authority to the Taliban ... feeling assured that no second 9/11 takes place" (2011: 39). How have U.S. military engagements supported this objective? Moreover, despite President Obama labelling the war in Afghanistan as "the good war," seldom are U.S. and Coalition successes recognised or even identified.[131] As the previous section revealed, defence diplomacy involves a number of aspects and tasks not specifically related to 'traditional' military domain, dealing with strategic and political issues including those related to humanitarian aid and development. Long War oriented defence diplomacy revolves around the construction and reproduction of defence relations between Coalition states. U.S. *Joint Publication 3-16 Multinational Operations* notes that building a multinational force "starts with the political decisions and diplomatic efforts to create a coalition or spur an alliance into action. Discussion and coordination between potential participants will initially seek to address basic questions at the national strategic level" (2007: 50). Essentially, nations weigh their national interests and then determine if, when, and where they will expend their nation's resources for reasons both known and unknown to other nations. Defence diplomacy helps states commit by reducing ambiguity, creating and maintaining defence relations and practices, while widening and deepening the interdependence necessary to sustain relationships.

After fifteen years the Coalition has been reduced in number yet the cooperation between new and existing security partners continues in large part due to the process to unite Coalition partners behind a common mission long after the anger in the immediate aftermath of the 9/11 attacks has faded. The U.S. has adopted a multidimensional, multi-organizational, and multilateral/multinational whole-of-government and whole-of-alliance/coalition approach in the Long War in general and the Afghan theatre in particular. Kattelman notes the theory of 'alliance building' explains the alignment of collective interests in the Long War. Collective interests continue to influence the stability and duration of coalitions beyond initial participation by emphasizing a sense of "tactical and strategic purpose" (2016: 805). Similarly, former SecDef Gates declared "the effectiveness and credibility of the United States will only be as good as the effectiveness, credibility, and sustainability of its local partners" (June 2010: 2).The following section tests Gates' theory by briefly discussing

131 Obama labelled Afghanistan as "the good war," with a direct link to the Sept. 11 attacks. In contrast, the Iraq war was "a war that has not made us more safe, but has distracted us from the task at hand in Afghanistan"—as Obama told a rally in Pennsylvania in April 2008.

the 'effectiveness, credibility, and sustainability' of Australia, the UK, Canada, and India.

The U.S. serves as a focal point for Australian international defence engagement and Australia has been, and remains, a senior military partner of the U.S. in Afghanistan. Kelton and Jackson claim Australia's decision to join the Coalition was "strategically and politically motivated to counter the rise of terrorism, enhance regional security, support the U.S., and, by doing so, augment its alliance relationship" (2015: 225). Bisley contends that the current "never-better strategic relationship" between the U.S. and Australia is in large part due to the "links forged" during OEF (2014: 13). Former Australian Chief of Army Peter Leahy cites his personal experience of being "able to expedite the acquisition of military capabilities and ammunition" during his deployment in Afghanistan because of the relationships formed through ongoing dialogue with foreign counterparts (2014: 16). Even though Australian soldiers have been deploying offshore on combat operations for well over a century, Ash Collingburn argues "some of the Army's most valuable and enduring contributions in conflict have been building local capacity through training" (September 12, 2016). A major part of Operation Slipper, Australia's campaign in Afghanistan during the Long War, was advising and assisting Afghan National Security Forces in COIN operations against the Taliban, primarily through its mentoring of the Afghan National Army's 4th Brigade in Uruzgan Province until the closure Multi-National Base—Tarin Kot in 2013. It has also developed its unilateral Mentoring & Reconstruction Taskforce as well as participating in combined reconstruction and stability efforts.[132] Captain Lachlan Joseph, an ANA Officer Academy Mentor articulated the long-term benefits of the Australian Train and Advice mission in Afghanistan, emphasising that "these officer cadets are not only going to be young military leaders but they'll also most likely move into politics and other realms that will continue to reinforce the development of the country" (Dept. Def, March 28, 2017). The worldview and professionalism of these future leaders has been shaped by the relationships forged with Coalition personnel.

132 From 2014, Australia has continued to contribute to the NATO-led Train, Advise and Assist mission directed by the Department of Foreign Affairs and Trade and AUSAID. Australia signed the Long-term Comprehensive Partnership with Afghanistan in May 2012. As part of this responsibility, Australia has committed US$100 million annually for three years from 2015 to support the continued development and sustainment of the Afghan National Security Forces, Commonwealth of Australia, *Defence White Paper*, 2016: 17); See also Commonwealth of Australia, *Australia in the Asian Century*, (Canberra: Department of Prime Minister & Cabinet, 2012).

Reflecting upon Australia's military engagement in Afghanistan, Collingburn claims that although "most Australian soldiers wouldn't willingly choose a training role over combat ... training is important and our soldiers have learned a lot about the art of war from training others" (September 12, 2016). Australia's improved 'interoperability' resulting from their engagement with the U.S. produces benefits beyond Afghanistan as it and the U.S. pivot to the Asia-Pacific. This paper proposes Australia's involvement over the past fifteen years has complimented its broader defence diplomacy objectives of building trust across governments and societies in the region and beyond, increasing transparency, establishing reliable and practical defence habits (such as establishing a Joint Operations Command and Special Operations Command as well as developing and disseminating innovative operating doctrine such as *Complex Warfighting* and *Adaptive Campaigning*) and finally, enhancing cooperation based on common values (IISS, 2005: 419).[133] The Australia U.S. military relationship is dynamic and enduring and this bond will be elevated in the years to come if the Obama's administrations comprehensive 'pivot' (a multidimensional reallocation of resources) transforms into a strategy whereby the military 'trumps' diplomacy and trade. Statements from senior DoD and State officials support this preliminary projection.[134] Frances Adamson, Secretary of Australia's Department of Foreign Affairs and Trade, observed during recent international visits, "I have found again and again that other countries want to do more with us. In part, this is because of who we are and how we work: we're capable, effective, reliable, we have little baggage; we are nowhere maligned and generally liked" (March 15, 2017). Nowhere is this more evident than in its military relationships with partner nations around the globe.

Just as Australia increased its bilateral defence relations globally prior to September 11, so too had the UK. However, the involvement of British Forces in ISAF and OEF, and their defence engagement with the U.S. (and its Coalition partners) in Afghanistan, has generated mixed assessments. The Brits have stood shoulder to shoulder with the U.S. in both OEF and ISAF and the British

133 The *IISS Military Balance* highlights that "large portions of the new U.S. future land warfighting concept appear to have been drawn directly form the Australian *Complex Warfighting* doctrine"; See also Albert Palazzo, 'The future of war debate in Australia: Why has there not been one? Has the need for one now arrived?, *Australian Defence Force Journal, No. 189*, (2012), pp. 5–20.

134 For example Acting Assistant Secretary of State for Asia Susan Thorton (March 17, 2017) stated the Trump administration had not determined how to frame its approach to Asia or whether the Trump administration will seek to develop its own whole-of-government strategy for Asia.

military campaign in Helmand Province from mid-2006 to mid-2009 is often the basis of assessments (Farrell & Gordon, 2009).[135] The British deployment in Helmand, which supplanted a U.S. contingent, consisted of 3,150 troops (building to a maximum of 8,300 by October 2008) and its primary job was protecting the Provincial Reconstruction Team (PRT) in the provincial capital of Lashkar Gah, securing the economic and political centre of Helmand (an Afghan Development Zone-ADZ), as well as maintaining/creating security throughout the vast reaches of the province.[136] As a lead actor in ISAF and OEF, the UK was in a position to disseminate a combined COIN/CT doctrine which is a key outcome of defence diplomacy. The principles of COIN are clearly delineated in the 2009 *ISAF Commander's COIN Guidance* which states "Protecting the people is the mission. The conflict will be won by persuading the population, not by destroying the enemy" (2009: 1). However, Catignani found that UK forces "had been unable or unwilling to execute non-kinetic population-centric operations due to their lack of understanding" of these principles" (2011: 513).[137]

Similarly, a British former Commander of ISAF, General David Richards recognised "there has been a radical change in the way wars are fought ... The lexicon of today is non-kinetic effects teams, precision attack teams, Counter-IED, combat logistic patrols, information dominance, counter-piracy, and cyber-attack and defence, yet these changes had not translated into cultural internalisation" (August 26, 2009).[138] Contrarily, Catignani highlights the "potential strategic effect of tactical operations within asymmetric conflicts" which

135 The authors assert that any "comparisons between the British performance in Helmand and that of the U.S. in the east have tended to ignore the different scale of challenges in each region, making meaningful comparisons difficult," p. 18.

136 The British PRT was staffed primarily by military personnel with only a handful of civilians from the UK's Afghan Stabilisation Unit, the Foreign Office, and the Department for International Trade.

137 The author defined military innovation as "how they adopt new doctrine, routines, programmes and organisational structures in order to improve military performance in the face of operational challenges," p. 515.

138 These types of assessments suggest that traditional military hierarchy was responsible for a lack of adaptation, an assumption which is supported by a general perception that 'policy guide's execution.' Yet Farrell writes that the Defence White Paper provides the authoritative policy direction for British military change along the lines of U.S. military transformation which would mitigate structural impediments to adaptation (2008: 778); In the previously mentioned *2003 Transformation Planning Guidance*, SECDEF Rumsfeld wrote: "We must think differently and develop the kinds of forces and capabilities that can adapt quickly to new challenges and to unexpected circumstances," (2003: 1).

transfers culpability from policy makers to lower-level practitioners (2011: 519).[139] Obviously this brief discussion does not capture the complexity of a situation in which Britain is undergoing a process of military transformation involving a "major investment in networking of the armed forces, a fundamental shift in military mind-set from doing things (often violently) to achieving effects (ideally non-violently)" (Farrell, 2008: 777). While there has been considerable research devoted to identifying the enablers of military innovation, with scholars prioritising top-down or bottom-up approaches, this paper suggests 'horizontal' nature of defence diplomacy would facilitate innovation on either level, often simultaneously. Furthermore, while Dorman (2015: 12) concludes the British involvement in Afghanistan has undermined the credibility of its armed forces domestically as well as abroad "in the eyes of potential opponents and allies," the MOD declares its involvement in Afghanistan has facilitated greater efforts in "upstream prevention activity" in countries where a traditional British military presence would not be warranted or justified; such as global CT operations (2015: 4).

Another key ally in the Long War is Canada, whose relationship with the U.S. is unique and multifaceted (geographic, economic, political and security oriented) and serves as a litmus test for Long War defence diplomacy. Manwaring notes the Canadian whole-of-government approach and the NATO whole-of alliance model to homeland defense and global security are primary organizational principles used to establish a comprehensive North American process for active intergovernmental and multilateral policy cooperation (2006: 3). Invoking Article 5 of the NATO charter brought Canada into the Long War, but it remained to achieve political and status gains with a strategic objective; "to raise its profile in the international community and among its NATO partners (especially the U.S.)" (Bercuson, et al., 2011: 1). Analysts determine that Canada rebuilt its military prowess and reputation during the Long War, with Canadian Armed Forces (CAF) undergoing a radical transformation as a result of the Afghan campaign (Fleming, 2011: 4). However, Qurban-Ali questions whether Canada "is better respected; whether they have increased its international political clout; or more secure domestically as a result its thirteen year military commitment in Afghanistan" 2015: 23). Other research found that Canada's military presence in Afghanistan revealed a gap between rhetoric and reality. After 7 years in-country engagement the *Independent Panel on Canada's Future in Afghanistan* concluded that "Canada and its key allies should assert a

139 The author identified the "transient and informal" nature of this adaptation "made it very difficult" for these lessons to translate into military innovation, p. 536.

stronger and more disciplined diplomatic position … ensure greater coherence in the civilian and military effort" and that the "importance of Canada's engagement in Afghanistan has earned Canadians considerable influence among the countries cooperating in Afghanistan's progress" (2008: 37–39).

Although Canada's defence ties with the U.S. are lengthy and deeply integrated, Alexander Moens asserts their bilateral defence relationship continues to be essentially ad hoc, concluding that:

> the Canadian Armed Forces can bring little added value to the supersized American armed forces, even as American soldiers and officers realize the high quality of Canadian personnel and the tasks they perform. U.S. military preparedness remains essentially American, period.
>
> 2016: 3

While it's true the "CAF suffered from a lack of combat ready personnel and a lack of specialized equipment and personnel, the need for which put pressure on allies, most notably the Americans," Lindley-French claims "unless Canada wishes to become an isolationist power, the utility of allies and partners to the fulfilment of Canadian security and defence objectives is vital" (2016: 3). Finally, while noting that the missions "objective was to promote good governance and achieve stability in Afghanistan," Qurban-Ali found that "the Canadian military's international visibility, profile and credibility" increased as a result of its engagement in ISAF and OEF (2015: 23).

India was an important regional member of OEF, yet India's offer of "unsolicited, unlimited military cooperation" following the 9/11 attacks, was neutralised by the complexity of the India/Pakistan relationship, which led the U.S. to prioritise its established military relationship with Pakistan (Koshy, 2006: 90). Consequently, India's contribution to the Long War has largely occurred through traditional diplomatic channels, with India being a vocal supporter of Coalition objectives as well as encouraging states to support UN CT instruments. Their support has borne fruit as the dynamics Long War returned India to the U.S. strategic orbit. Subsequently, the Obama administration initiated its first political-military dialogue with India in six years, enabling their Indian counterparts work through the challenges of interagency processes on national security issues. Indian officials indicate that these exchanges are especially helpful in helping them to coordinate the same issues within their own government, as well as giving them a better idea of how the U.S. deals with its own large and complicated bureaucracy. The Indian military is also increasingly interested in buying equipment from the U.S. and its Coalition partners with foreign military sales to India growing from only US$363 million in military sales from 2002–2006 to more than US$9 billion by 2014 (Kelly, April 17 2014).[140]

Most recently, the U.S. and India actioned the first two projects under their Defence Technology and Trade Initiative (DTTI) with the U.S. "officially designating India as a major defence partner" (Carter, December 8, 2016). The two countries will work together to create "unique and transformative military technologies" such as the future infantry combat vehicle and the future vertical lift aircraft (Pandit, December 31, 2016). The future cooperation between India and the U.S. appears to sound. For example, Christine Fair finds that on a broad, conceptual level "the two states have similar worldviews ... Both states are non-revolutionary, status quo states. Both states, to a different extent, work through multilateral institutions to effect gradual change. Both states have foreign policies with a 'moral streak'" (2004: 81). The U.S. Joint Strategic Vision for the Asia-Pacific and Indian Ocean Regions reflects the growing strategic convergence of U.S. and India's interests.[141] Former SECDEF Carter declared that "India, like the United States, seeks to be a net exporter of security, and the two countries will continue to work with other partners to shape a regional security architecture that will allow all to rise and prosper" (January 25, 2015). Most importantly, both countries have been impacted by transnational terrorism and share similar perceptions of the threat.

The ongoing lessons learned by Australia, Canada, the UK, India and the rest of the Long War Coalition resulting from their defence cooperation in Afghanistan improves their ability "to navigate the scope and limitations of their roles within a rapidly changing global theatre" (Qurban-Ali, 2015: 24). Elsewhere in Asia the U.S. has applied these lessons and committed to building healthy, stable, reliable, and continuous military-to-military relations. The U.S. and China maintain a robust schedule of military-to-military exchanges and dialogues "to encourage China to exhibit greater transparency with respect to its military capabilities and intentions" (Kelly, April 17 2014). Tom Kelly, U.S. Deputy Assistant Secretary of the Bureau of Political-Military Affairs, states that U.S. military, diplomatic, and defense officials "participate in a range of

140 For example India has purchased 22 Apache attack helicopters and 15 Chinook heavy-lift helicopters at a cost of US$ 3.1 billion; India signed a contract to buy 36 Rafale twin-engine fighter jets from France for US$ 8.8 billion in 2016 and a US$ 2 billion deal for an air defence system was penned with Israel Aerospace Industries in early 2017.

141 'U.S.-India Joint Strategic Vision for the Asia-Pacific and Indian Ocean Region', Statement by President Obama, (Office of the Press Secretary, The White House, January 25, 2015), available at https://obamawhitehouse.archives.gov/the-press-office/2015/01/25/us-india-joint-strategic-vision-asia-pacific-and-indian-ocean-region (Last accessed February 11, 2017).

combined civilian-military dialogues with the Chinese in which we work to build mutual trust and understanding" (April 17 2014). The U.S. also engages in regular exercises with the Republic of Korea and Japan, countries in which the U.S continues to station several thousand defence personnel. Additionally, annual and/or ad-hoc meetings between military representatives such as the Pacific Armies Management Seminar (PAMS) provide a forum for exchanging the views of regional officials. Willard claims that the PAMS presents an opportunity "to establish and enhance a set of strong interpersonal relationships among the future leaders ... a solid contributor to the shared goals of regional stability [and] is just one example of the diplomacy conducted around the world every day by the U.S. military" (2014: 2).

U.S./Afghanistan Defence Diplomacy

> Security cooperation remains a critical foreign policy tool that allows the United States to advance its national security interests worldwide ... Building partner nation security capacity is one of the most important strategic requirements for the United States to promote international security, advance U.S. interests and prevail in the war against terrorism.[142]

The U.S. does not have the historical legacy of the British or Russia in South Asia in general and Afghanistan in particular. Galster claims U.S. policy maker's post-WWII (until the Iranian revolution in 1979) did not regard Afghanistan security as strategically important, given the friendly relations the U.S. had with Afghanistan's neighbours. In the depths of the Cold War, the U.S. sought "to bolster its image and influence ... it got an opportunity to reduce the Soviet power and influence in the event of the Soviet intervention in Afghanistan" in 1979 (Mahapatra, 2011: 41). The U.S. was extensively involved in arming and training the Afghan mujahedeen (resistance fighters) against the Soviet occupation throughout the 1980s, a program strictly framed in terms of the U.S.-Soviet strategic rivalry.[143] The Reagan administrations covert aid program

142 U.S. Department of State, 'Introduction', *2007 Report to Congress: Section 1206(f) of the 2006 National Defense Authorization Act*, (Washington D.C.: Bureau of Political-Military Affairs, July 3, 2007).

143 The CIA lead the program as the Department of State had no official presence on the ground in Kabul after the kidnapping and murder of Ambassador Adolf 'Spike' Dubbs in 1979. See Declassified CIA and DIA assessments: http://nsarchive.gwu.edu/NSAEBB/NSAEBB57/us1.pdf (Last accessed December 2, 2016). http://nsarchive.gwu.edu/NSAEBB/NSAEBB57/us2.pdf http://nsarchive.gwu.edu/NSAEBB/NSAEBB57/us3.pdf http://

grew from about US$20 million per year in FY1980 to about US$300 million per year between FY1986–FY1990 (Kratzman, 2016: 3). Given its anti-Soviet stimulus, it's not surprising that U.S. interest in Afghanistan was severely reduced with the demise its foe (two years after the Soviet's withdrew its troops from Afghanistan) (Galster, 2001).[144]

The U.S. restricted its 'official' presence in January 1989 citing security concerns yet the perception was the U.S. had no remaining interests once Soviet forces had withdrawn. However, Katzman reveals that U.S. was the largest single provider of assistance to the Afghan people during the 1990's, though no U.S. aid went directly to the Taliban government when it was in power during 1996–2001, monies were provided through relief organizations (2016: 52). While civil war racked Afghanistan between 1989 and 2001 the U.S. followed a limited political strategy for managing the long-term consequences of the country. Although the U.S. intelligence community and elements of both the Bush 41 and Clinton administrations had followed events in Afghanistan closely, the events of September 11 "triggered the most rapid and dramatic change in the history of U.S. foreign policy" forcing the Bush 43 administration to divert its full attention and significant resources to South Asia (Walt, 2001: 56). Moreover, the broad international anti-terrorist front that formed after the attacks enabled Western forces to be deployed close to certain parts of Asia that had been considered Russia's traditional sphere of influence (Lachowski, 2007; Pettyjohn, 2012).

Although Bush's Global War on Terror was multifaceted, OEF in Afghanistan was prioritised. Despite the fact that NATO had conducted protracted but ultimately successful operations in the Balkans during 1990's culminating with the air campaign in Kosovo in 1999, U.S. SECDEF Rumsfeld declared "this war (Afghanistan) will not be waged by a grand alliance united for the single purpose of defeating an axis of hostile powers. Instead, it will involve floating

---

nsarchive.gwu.edu/NSAEBB/NSAEBB57/us7.pdf http://nsarchive.gwu.edu/NSAEBB/NSAEBB57/us11.pdf. http://nsarchive.gwu.edu/NSAEBB/NSAEBB57/us12.pdf (The final CIA brief summarizes lessons learned from the U.S. involvement in the Afghan rebel train and equip mission).

144 Galster claims that policy makers post WWII (until the Iranian revolution in 1979) did not regard Afghanistan security as strategically important given the friendly U.S. relations with Afghanistan's neighbours. Galster writes that "a top official in the U.S. Embassy in Kabul claimed that the Soviet leadership might cancel their pull-out to prevent their client government (Najibullah) from unravelling … the diplomat's suspicion illustrates a point: U.S. policy toward Afghanistan right up to the end of the Soviet occupation was based on a deep mistrust of Moscow's goals, a mistrust which continued well after the withdrawal."

coalitions of countries" (September 27 2001). Hallams explains U.S. led action with selected coalition partners was designed to avoid the "war by committee" disputes that plagued the Balkan campaign (2009: 40). While Williams writes that the U.S. emerged from the Balkans "with a belief that its operational freedom and flexibility had been hampered operating within alliance constraints" (2008: 65). SECDEF Rumsfeld was vocal in his disdain for a "grand alliance" (September 27, 2001) and "there was simply no desire to see U.S. aims and objectives undermined by working through" NATO (Williams, 2009: 69). General Wesley Clark, NATO's former Supreme Allied Commander of Europe recalls how a senior Pentagon official declared that "no one is going to tell us where we can or can't bomb" in the days after 9/11 (2002: 19). While Saideman and Auerswald claim that there are "few things over which Rumsfeld and Canadians concur, but the problem of caveats in Afghanistan is one of them" (Saideman & Auerswald, 2012: 67). Despite bold statements from the upper echelons of the Pentagon,[145] Mahapatra claims that overwhelming military force paralleled nuanced diplomatic outreach as "the Bush administration's military offensive was accompanied by sophisticated defence diplomacy" (2011: 42).

As well as assisting in the formation of the Coalition, this paper proposes that defence diplomacy has enhanced the U.S. Long War strategy of 'winning hearts and minds' through three lines of effort: Security, Governance and Development.[146] Since October 2001 the different elements of U.S./Afghan engagement have been legislated in support of their strategy, legislation which impacts directly on the process of defence diplomacy. Some are benign such as the Status of Forces Agreement (SOFA), which authorized a semi-permanent U.S. presence in Afghan territory in September 2002 (NATO's ISAF established to conditions for foreign military presences on Afghan soil with the Bonn

145 Pentagon's Director of NATO Policy, Colonel Mark Sullivan stated "when a nation acts in an autonomous way outside of the alliance it can act much more swiftly, it's not just the decision making, it's the ability to bring resources to bear … we were able to act much more quickly by not going through NATO" (Interview cited in Williams, 2009: 69).

146 JCOS FM 3-24 *Counterinsurgency*, (2014). Although 'winning hearts and minds' is the common term used, "legitimacy not hearts and minds along with political power are the central issues in insurgencies and counterinsurgencies," p. 2. Legitimacy can be measured by six indicators: the security of the population; just and fair selection of leaders; popular participation in the political process; a culturally acceptable level of corruption; a culturally acceptable level of political, economic and social development; a high level of regime acceptance by major social institutions, p. 37; The three lines of effort are detailed in *The Strategic Framework for U.S. Efforts in Afghanistan*, U.S. Government Accountability Office, (Washington D.C., June 15, 2010), available at http://www.gao.gov/assets/100/96809.pdf.

Agreement signed in December 2001),[147] the U.S. Strategy for Afghanistan and Pakistan (March 2009), the Integrated Civilian-Military Campaign Plan for Support to Afghanistan (August 2009) and the formal agreement for Operation Freedom Sentinel (September 2014).[148] While others are contentious such as the Authorisation for the Use of Military Force (AUMF), Section 1206 of the *2006 National Defence Authorisation Act* and the Commanders Emergency Response Program (CERP) which granted the DoD authority to train equip and disburse federal funds in Iraq and later Afghanistan without the knowledge or endorsement of State.[149]

In 2012, the U.S. and Afghanistan signed a legally binding executive agreement called the Enduring Strategic Partnership Agreement (SPA) which provided a framework for the future relationship between both countries.[150] The document reaffirms their commitment to cooperate to defeat al Qa'ida, confirms the U.S's commitment to support Afghanistan's social and economic development and designates Afghanistan as a "Major Non-NATO Ally" a formal

147 For more detail see: Erik Rosenfeld, 'Applications of U.S. Status of Force Agreement to Article 98 of the Rome Statute', *Washington University Global Studies Law Review*, Vol. 2, no. 1, (January 2003), pp. 273–293 available at http://openscholarship.wustl.edu/cgi/viewcontent.cgi?article=1276&context=law_globalstudies, "SOFAs are international agreements between states that create obligations concerning the jurisdiction over foreign state's military or civilian citizen" p. 280; Chuck Manson, *Status of Force Agreement (SOFA): What is it and how has it been utilized?*, (Washington D.C.: Congressional Research Service, 2012).

148 For a comprehensive list of U.S./NATO legislation up to and including 2010 see *The Strategic Framework for U.S. Efforts in Afghanistan*, op. cit., available at http://www.gao.gov/assets/100/96809.pdf.

149 Public Law 107-40, 107th Congress, Congressional Record, Vol. 147, (September 18, 2001), available at https://www.gpo.gov/fdsys/pkg/PLAW-107publ40/pdf/PLAW-107publ40.pdf; National Defense Authorization Act for Fiscal Year 2006, Public Law 109–163, 109th Congress, (January 6, 2006), p, 325, available at https://www.gpo.gov/fdsys/pkg/PLAW-109publ163/pdf/PLAW-109publ163.pdf; *The Commanders' Emergency Response Program, ATP 1-06.2*, Department of the Army, (Washington D.C., (2005), pp. 1–93; Nina M. Serafino, *Security Assistance Reform: "Section 1206" Background and Issues for Congress*, (Washington, DC: U.S. Library of Congress, Congressional Research Service, February 11, 2011), pp. 1–30, available at http://www.fas.org/sgp/crs/natsec/RS22855.pdf; The CERP returned authority to DoD which was removed in 1984 by the Comptroller General who ruled the Army had violated fiscal law and the Foreign Assistance Act when it used its Operation and Maintenance Funding to do humanitarian assistance. The Foreign Assistance Act, and its Humanitarian and Civic Assistance funding were coordinated and distributed by State.

150 The White House, '*Fact Sheet: The US-Afghanistan Strategic Partnership Agreement*', available at https://www.whitehouse.gov/the-press-office/2012/05/01/fact-sheet-us-afghanistan-strategic-partnership-agreement.

commitment to continue to foster U.S.-Afghan "close cooperation."[151] The SPA is an important diplomatic measure to reinforce the obligations and assurances made by the two nations since 2001. U.S. forces remain in Afghanistan at the invitation of the GoIRA, and their presence is governed by both the U.S.-Afghanistan Bilateral Security Agreement (BSA) and the NATO-Afghanistan Status of Forces Agreement (SOFA), which were both signed on September 30, 2014, and ratified by the Afghan Parliament on November 27, 2014.[152] After fifteen years of war, overall policy objectives remain relatively static; however, strategies have evolved and OEF transitioned into OFS, additionally the corresponding NATO mission ISAF transitioned into Operation Resolute Support (ORS) in December 2014.

Today, Army General John Nicholson commands U.S. & Allied Forces in Afghanistan, the latest in a long line of commanders which began with General Tommy Franks in 2001 (followed by Generals Mikolashek, Barno, Eikenberry, McNeill, McKiernan, McChrystal, Petraeus, Allen, Dunford, and Campbell).[153] These Commander's, two presidents, five SECDEF's and four Secretaries of State, the U.S. has carefully cultivated its political/military relationships regarding Afghanistan since 9/11, navigating a complex South Asian theatre involving inter-connected regional and global issues. The U.S. (with and through NATO) achieves this through intra-group engagement, burden-sharing, trust and capacity building initiatives within the region, serving as an essential combat multiplier that instils confidence whilst enhancing capabilities. The continuing objective of U.S. Forces Afghanistan (USFOR-A) in Afghanistan under Operation Freedom Sentinel (OFS) (as it was under OEF) is to work with the international community to provide financial and advisory support to the GoIRA to generate a well-trained, equipped, and sustainable Afghan National

151 *Enduring Strategic Partnership Agreement Between The United States of America and The Islamic Republic of Afghanistan*, available at https://www.whitehouse.gov/sites/default/files/2012.06.01u.s.-afghanistanspasignedtext.pdf (Last accessed December 8, 2016).

152 U.S. Department of Defence, Report on Enhancing Security and Stability in Afghanistan. DoD Report to Congress, (June 2015), p. 1.

153 A similar situation has occurred in Iraq and Army Lieutenant General Stephen Townsend is the current, and ninth, U.S. Commander of coalition forces since overthrew the Saddam Hussein regime in March/April 2003. One again General Tommy Franks stepped up to the plate, and like Afghanistan, he moved aside for Generals Sanchez, Casey, Petraeus, Odierno (Operation Iraqi Freedom-March 2003–August 2010), and finally General Austin (Operation New Dawn September-2010-December 2011) who led coalition forces until the end of 2011 when President Obama terminated the U.S. military occupation. In 2014, Generals James Terry, Sean MacFarland and currently General Townsend direct Operation Inherent Resolve's counter-ISIL mission.

Defence and Security Force (ANDSF).[154] Achieving this goal will enable the ANDSF to independently secure Afghanistan, engage in counterterrorism operations against al Qa'ida and to enhance regional stability, and to ensure that "Afghanistan does not again become a safe haven for terrorist attacks on the homeland, U.S. persons overseas, its allies and partners."[155] However, the GoIRA needs to be able to provide security, maintain the state's monopoly of legitimate force, and operate in accordance with democratic principles and rule of law Hanlon & Shultz Jr, 2016). This paper asserts that defence diplomacy is central to achieving the strategic objectives of the ad-hoc Long War Coalition by ensuring combined capabilities match combined commitment. One vital mechanism which supports both the Coalition and its objectives has been military exchange programs.

Foreign military personnel across the ranking spectrum attend U.S. military academies to update skills and establish networks which bolster future relations. As a result of this familiarity, "military leaders have common experience and common frames of reference that facilitate dialogue and relationships less hindered by political realities" (Reveron, 2014: 68).[156] From a DoD perspective, the U.S. Army emphasises that "military-to-military exchanges build trust, improve understanding and communication, and pave the way toward greater cooperation" (May 16, 2011). While State justifies these exchanges

154 The Afghan National Defense and Security Forces is the official designation for the Afghan security forces used in the BSA and is the GoIRA preferred designation for the overall force. The U.S. Government now uses this term instead of the previously used Afghan National Security Forces (ANSF).

155 Department of Army, *ADR 3-05*, op. cit., pp. 3–7. To implement SSR programs in Afghanistan, the U.S. country team designs SSR strategies, plans, programs, and activities. They coordinate with appropriate USG departments and agencies as well as the chief of mission's authority in the host nation. The Department of State (DOS) leads and provides oversight for these efforts though its bureaus, offices, and overseas missions. The DoD provides coercive and constructive capability to support the establishment, to restructure or reform the armed forces and defense sector, and to assist and support activities of other USG agencies involved in SSR; Department of Defence, *Report on Enhancing Security and Stability in Afghanistan*, Report for Congress, (June 2015), p. 10. One notable element of OFS is U.S. forces no longer target individuals solely on the basis of their membership in the Taliban which is an indication that a negotiated political process inclusive of the Taliban is well underway. The *2015 Report on Enhancing Security and Stability in Afghanistan* does stipulate "if a member of the Taliban threatens U.S. or coalition forces, or provides direct support to al Qaeda, U.S. forces may take appropriate action." p. 4.

156 Reveron outlines how foreign military personnel "rely on a unique blend of charitable American political culture, latent civil-military capacity and ambitious military officers," p. 66.

as a key component of SSR, finding that "more professional militaries are less likely to block necessary political reform efforts" (2013: 245). In summary, key exchange programs such as the U.S. Military Personnel Exchange Program seek to: Strengthen alliances and coalition partners by building partner capacity and maintaining or enhancing relationships, increases defense cooperation by integrating U.S. and partner nation military personnel, provides a framework through bilateral exchanges of military personnel in support of multinational operations.[157] Another formal exchange mechanism is the International Military Education and Training program (IMET). Funding for the IMET is derived from the civilian foreign affairs budget, directed by the Secretary of State and operationalised by the DoD (U.S. Senate Report, 2006: 7). The IMET program was introduced in 1976 in an attempt to foster closer relations with foreign militaries. The program exposes "students to the U.S. professional military establishment and the American way of life, including amongst other things, U.S. regard for democratic values, respect for individual and human rights and belief in the rule of law, exposure to U.S. military procedures and the manner in which our military functions under civilian control" (DSCA, 2013). In 2014 the IMET taught roughly 4,000 foreign military officers, or 7% of the more than 56,000 foreign officers trained by the DoD annually at a cost at more than US$100 million per annum. (Chadwick, January 17, 2017). Exchanges generate transparency and openness, with participants (approx. 60, 000 per year) essentially integrating themselves into the partner nation's military over a period of 1 to 3 years, although Wallin notes that foreign military personnel do not participate in combat unless "expressly authorized" by the USG" (2014: 19).

The Regional Defense Combating Terrorism Fellowship Program (CTFP) and the Ministry of Defence Authority (MODA) are two 'joint' education initiatives. The CTFP is designed to assist partner nations in their "struggle against violent extremism through targeted, non-lethal, combating terrorism (CbT) education and training" (DoD (c), 2015: 1). The MODA was designed around a program introduced specifically for Afghanistan and legislates the movement of senior DoD officials abroad to assist foreign counterparts to create and

---

157 For more detail see: Department of the Army, Army Military Personnel Exchange Program with Military Services of Other Nations, (July 14, 2011), available at http://armypubs.army.mil/epubs/pdf/r614_10.pdf; U.S. Government Accountability Office, 'Building Partner Capacity: Key Practices to Effectively Manage Department of Defense Efforts to Promote Security Cooperation', *GAO-13-335T*, (February 14, 2013), pp. 1–24 available at http://www.gao.gov/products/GAO-13-335T; Paul, Christopher, Colin P. Clarke, Beth Grill, Stephanie Young, Jennifer D. P. Moroney, Joe Hogler & Christine Leah, *What Works Best When Building Partner Capacity and Under What Circumstances?*, (Santa Monica, CA: RAND Corporation, 2013), available at http://www.rand.org/pubs/monographs/MG1253z1.html.

strengthen their defence institutions.[158] Finally, the Joint Combined Exchange Training (JCET) is a parallel Special Operations Forces (SOF) run program which has traditionally been the DoD point of contact for CT (Story, 1999). The JCET was the first U.S. training program to "require background screening of all foreign participants' (Amnesty International, 2002: iv). While the theory behind military exchanges is sound, the assumed 'two-way' concept can be more one-sided which limits U.S. personnel exposure to foreign doctrine. For example, few American officers participate in personnel exchanges with Pakistan, for a variety of reasons, including security concerns. Although U.S. military exchange programs present opportunities for gathering intelligence as participants disseminate a wealth of experience and personal knowledge about foreign operations, "a key question is whether or not it influences the thought process or actions of foreign militaries in a way that helps secure U.S. strategic interests" (Wallin, 2014: 20). The U.S. Army addresses this concern, declaring exchanges encourage greater participation in the decision making process, but more importantly, "collaborative tools give subordinate commanders and staff the capacity to gain a greater understanding of the thinking behind U.S. directives'" (U.S. Joint Warfighting Center, 2006: V-3).

Despite the prominence of various programs between Coalition partners and the HN (Afghanistan), Wallin notes that the effects of these exchanges may only become apparent over a long term period (2014: 21). Additionally, exchange programs cannot deliver guarantees of influence on participants' actions. For example, in a small number of cases, individual's trained under IMET programs have been accused of human rights abuses (Chadwick, 2017). Paterson determined that "training and equipping foreign forces without providing accompanying education on human rights standards and IHL invites the improper use of force" (2016: 2). The DoD's Assessment, Monitoring, and Evaluation (AM&E) process improves identification and reporting of abuses, such as the *Human Rights Report for International Military Education and Training Recipients for CY 2015*, which have led to course modifications which prioritise respect for human rights.[159] In addition, State's Office of Democracy, Human Rights and Labour, the Bureau of Political-Military Affairs and the

---

158 *National Defences Authorisation Act for FY 2012*, PL 112–81, Section 1081, (December 31, 2011), Section 1081 (a) authorizes "the Secretary of Defense may, with the concurrence of the Secretary of State, carry out a program to assign civilian employees of the Department of Defense as advisors to the ministries of defense (or security agencies serving a similar defense function) of foreign countries," pp. 303–304.

159 For more detail see: Federation of American Scientists, International Military Education and Training (IMET), available at http://www.fas.org/asmp/campaigns/training/IMET2.html.

DoD triangulate data to improve oversight and transparency in order to "apply lessons learned and best practices to inform security cooperation resources and policy decisions" (Ross Jr, January 17, 2017).[160] Carol Atkinson conducted comprehensive research on the matter; identifying a trend in which states that send military officers to study at military institutes in the U.S. are more likely to see improvements in human rights than those states which do not (2010: 16). Paterson concludes that soldiers without the proper training or education jeopardize their legitimacy among the civilian population. Maintaining/establishing domestic legitimacy and the illusion of sovereignty is essential for the GoIRA to maintain support from its external benefactors.

USG oversight mechanisms regulate, to a certain degree, who/how the U.S partners in the Long War. For example, Willard identifies "the executive branch of government desire to engage Indonesia as a potential partner in the war on terror, as well as assisting the country's fledging institutions of democracy ... (yet) the legislative branch restricts funds, training, and engagement activities targeted for Indonesia due to the poor human rights record of the Indonesian security forces" (2014: 36). As of FY2014, all U.S. funding for the ANDSF (including training, equipment and other forms of assistance) is subject to the 'Leahy Law,' an amalgamation of amendments to the *Foreign Assistance Act of 1961* and the *1997 Foreign Operations Appropriations Act* and prohibits U.S. forces from training suspect foreign personnel as well as withholding U.S. funding for any unit of a foreign force that, according to credible information, has committed a gross violation of human rights.[161] Violations are identified through a vetting process (the International Vetting and Security Tracking (INVEST) database) managed by State's Bureau of Democracy, Human Rights, and Labour in collaboration with the HN embassy.

Erica Gaston concludes that "the Leahy law has accomplished far less than its champions hoped for, but far more than its critics presume" (March 5,

160 Paterson (2016: 32) highlights that U.S. law requires the Secretary of Defense to submit an annual summary of JCETs to Congress each year. The Assistant Secretary of Defense for Special Operations and Low Intensity Conflict collects the JCET info from the regional commands and submits it to Congress on behalf of the Secretary of Defense. The report is submitted to the Armed Services and Foreign Relations Committees of the Senate and the Armed Services (National Security) and Foreign Affairs Committees of the House of Representatives.

161 For more detail see: Paterson, (2016: 33–38); *An Overview of the Leahy Vetting Process*, U.S. Department of State, (Humanrights.gov, September9, 2013), available at https://www.humanrights.gov/dyn/an-overview-of-the-leahy-vetting-process.html (Last accessed February 10, 2017).

2017). While the head of U.S. Special Operations Command, Admiral William McRaven, argued that Leahy exclusions limit support to important partners for U.S. forces in many countries, and can be counter-productive by preventing the type of human rights training that might prevent abuses (Stewart, March 6, 2013). Despite the complex delivery mechanism, the primary motivation and strategic goals of military exchanges in the Long War remain national/regional stability, interoperability and relationship building within an alliance. Ash Collingburn concludes that "developing local capacity and confidence to fight their own battles, protect their population, and secure their own borders and territory is critical to long-term success" (September 12, 2016). Defence personnel exchange programs, often dismissed as '"military tourism," support interoperability with the forces of both the HN and external partners (IISS, 1999: 43). Interoperability is also enhanced by training, equipping and advising Afghan security personnel.

The U.S. in-country train and equip mission commenced in early 2002, shortly after U.S. and Coalition special forces 'defeated' the Taliban, with the makeup of the nascent Afghan National Army (ANA) being articulated at the Bonn II Conference on rebuilding Afghanistan in December 2002. Participants authorized a 70,000 strong force which would be expanded to 195,000 by the end of 2012 (Kucera, 2004: 6). The primary source of the training was initially provided by CIA operatives and U.S. Army Special Operation troops. In July 2003 the responsibility to train the ANA transferred to Combined Joint Task Force Phoenix whose mandate consisted of training, coaching, mentoring and logistics (U.S. DoD, September 30, 2009). After three years of training, a 2005 CRS Report for Congress concluded, "most analysts agree that the ANA had developed into a credible fighting force"; however, the presence of a significant foreign troop contingent (majority U.S.) masked their vulnerabilities (Feickert, 2005: 9). As the security situation declined in 2006 the DoD revised its plans and increased its train and equip allocations to over "US$7.6 billion in 2007, over a threefold increase compared with fiscal year 2006," which in turn was greater than the combined assistance package from 2002–2006 (Cordesman, 2007: 6).

During this period the U.S. updated its strategy and disarmed and demobilised over 14,000 Afghan Militia Forces (AMF) which had provided special operation support for the U.S. since the early days of OEF (Grenier, 2015: 54). This initiative was implemented to increase recruitment rates for the ANA; however, the demobilisation of the AMF created security vacuums which the ANA, and the Coalition struggled to fill. With the security situation deteriorating President Obama announced a "comprehensive" strategy in March 2009, which centered on deploying an additional 21,000 U.S. forces.[162] That number would be increased to 30,000 by December 2009 following advice from U.S. and NATO commander General Stanley McChrystal in his *Commanders Initial Assessment*, (August 30, 2009).[163] The 'surge' of troops paralleled a shift in military strategy with a concerted population-centric COIN approach replacing the enemy-centric approach of CT (although SOF would maintain CT operations under OEF and later OFS).[164] The shift in strategy also required those tasked with training the ANA (the U.S. and their Coalition partners) to also transition from CT to COIN training. This difficult task was made more so when the USG announced "a gradual transition to Afghan security leadership and a corresponding drawdown of U.S. forces (which) … would focus the Afghan government on training its own forces."[165]

The U.S contributed US$4.1 billion for the ANDSF for FY2015 and US$3.65 billion for FY2016 and has pledged about US$3.45 billion for FY2017. Additionally, U.S. partners pledged US$1 billion annually for the ANDSF during 2017–2020 at the NATO summit in Warsaw in July 2016 (U.S. Senate Report, September 15, 2016). Despite the financial support, the multi-ethnic ANA (made up of Pashtuns, Tajiks, Hazaras, Uzbeks and smaller ethnic groups) has struggled to develop into a credible fighting force, suffering persistent complications such as low morale and fluctuating desertion rates (Chaudhuri & Farrell, 2011).[166] The ANA has managed to build and maintain a certain level of autonomy; however, most battalions routinely receive assistance from U.S. and NATO military

162 For more detail see: White Paper of the Interagency Policy Group's Report on U.S. Policy toward Afghanistan and Pakistan', (Washington D.C.: The White House, February 2009), available at http://www.whitehouse.gov/assets/documents/Afghanistan-Pakistan_White_Paper.pdf (Last accessed December 12, 2016).

163 General McChrystal's assessment stated that about 44,000 additional U.S. combat troops would be needed to provide the greatest chance for success.; See also Remarks by the President in Address to the Nation on the Way Forward in Afghanistan and Pakistan, (December, 1, 2009) available at. https://www.whitehouse.gov/the-press-office/remarks-president-address-nation-way-forward-afghanistan-and-pakistan (Last accessed December 12, 2016).

164 The '*Commander's Initial Assessment*' defined the nature of the fight as "not a cyclical, kinetic campaign based on a set 'fighting season.' Rather it is continuous, year-long effort to help GoIRA win the support of the people and counter insurgent coercion and intimidation," p. 11.

165 During the November 2010 NATO summit in Lisbon, policy-makers decided on a gradual transition to Afghan leadership that would be completed by the end of 2014.

166 The authors claim ANA desertion levels were exacerbated by "corruption, drug abuse, ethnic rivalry and poor leadership at all levels," p. 274; The Pajhwok News Service announced on March 6, 2017 that the first Afghan Sikh had formally joined the ANA.

personnel. This had led to situation where, perhaps incorrectly, U.S. and NATO forces began to "mirror image Afghan security forces into a Western-style defence enterprise" (Grenier, 2015: 55).[167] The number of ANSDF personnel is often used to demonstrate progress (or lack-there-of) of U.S. efforts in the Long War yet the numbers need to be viewed in context. Some analyst's stress that the comprehensive train and equip mission had produced nothing more than an "auxiliary force" (Giustozzi, 2007) plagued by "dangerously low morale, inadequate weapons, poor trading and ineffective leadership" (Grenier, 2015: 55). While others claim that as "the tactical proficiency of the soldiers have improved, the army is among the more stable institutions in the country" (Zimmerman, 2015: 21).

However, the ANDSF have taken heavy casualties: between January 1 and November 12, 2016, they lost 6,785 service members and an additional 11,777 were wounded (SIGAR, 2017: 98).[168] General John W. Nicholson, the current U.S. commander of U.S. forces and ORS, testified that ANDSF recruitment has generally kept pace with losses and attrition (February 9, 2017). One reason, according to Dr M. Homayun Qayoumi, Chief Advisor to Afghan President Mohammad Ashraf Ghani, is that "the Afghan people know and believe that this is their fight and they should make that sacrifice" (March 3, 2017). Although Max Boot finds "there is no doubt that the losses severely strain Afghan forces and raise doubts about whether they can maintain the current tempo of operations" (February 23, 2017). Moreover, Nicholson acknowledges 70 percent of all offensive operations are carried out by Afghan National Army Special Operations Command, which numbers only 17,000 men out of a total force of between 175,000 and 195,000. The current size of the ANDSF (ANA & ANP combined) is about 320,000, roughly 10% below target levels. The ANA (all components) has about 175,000 personnel as of June 2016, including its

167 Kratzman (2016: 30) notes other major concerns raised in DoD and other reports are:
(1) That about 35% of the force does not re-enlist each year, and the rapid recruitment might dilute the force's quality;
(2) Widespread illiteracy within it, which prompted an increasing focus on providing literacy training (as of 2010);
(3) Casualty rates that U.S. commanders call "unsustainable," including 5,500 combat deaths in 2015;
(4) Inconsistent leadership that sometimes causes Afghan commanders to overestimate insurgent strength or to panic at the first sign of insurgent assault; and
(5) A deficit of logistical capabilities, such as airlift, medical evacuation, resupply, and other associated functions.

168 The Afghan casualty number is nearly three times as many fatalities in less than year as U.S. forces have suffered in Afghanistan in the last fifteen-and-a-half years.

special operations component which was trained by U.S. Special Forces. The Afghan Air Force (AAF) numbers about 7,000 personnel and approximately 124 aircraft.[169] Nearly 20 air crews were added to the force this year and their training and education in U.S. schools helped further professionalize their force allowing the AAF to increase its organic strike missions by 268 percent, dropping 430 bombs (SIGAR, 2017: 14). Similarly, the numbers don't tell the full story with General Nicholson declaring that the force is still "some years away" from being fully functional which limits the capacity of the AAF to provide crucial air support for the ANA engaged in combat.[170]

The current U.S. military presence in Afghanistan adds an additional layer of context to the discussion of U.S. military 'in-country' engagement in the Long War. With the end of the U.S. and NATO combat mission in 2014 the majority of U.S. military personnel currently in Afghanistan operate under U.S. Embassy Kabul authority tasked to: protect U.S. installations, process Foreign Military Sales (FMS) of weaponry to Afghanistan, and to train Afghans on the use of that weaponry.[171] President Obama amended prior troop reduction plans on several occasions; from about 1,000 troops in 2011 to 5,500 by the end of 2016. Finally, in June 2016, President Obama committed 9,800 personnel would remain through 2016, then decreasing to 8,400 thereafter. In January 2017 most military personnel on the ground in Afghanistan are assigned to the 13,000-person NATO-led training and support mission Resolute Support; however, approximately 15% of the U.S. contingent operates within OFS (although the actual figure is classified) (SIGAR, 2017: 91). While train and support remains the mission banner, President Obama introduced an important caveat into his withdrawal framework which authorized all U.S. forces in Afghanistan to carry out combat missions if and when they, or the GoIRA, are presented

169 Including eight A-29 Super Tucano light attack aircraft, four C-130 transport planes and 47 Mi-17 (Russian-made) helicopters as well as 3 Mi-35 Cheetah helicopters donated by India. The figures are approximate as result of the dynamic security situation in Afghanistan. According to the SIGAR (Jan 2017), USFOR-A reported that two Mi-17 helicopters had been lost in combat in late 2016, ten Mi-17s are currently in for overhaul or heavy repair and one C-130 is in the depot for major repairs.

170 While the DoD acknowledged that AAF close air attack and armed overwatch capabilities are still developing; however, an increase in its close-air attack capability has bolstered ANDSF ground forces' motivation and enhanced their will to fight, (Nicholson, February 9, 2017).

171 'Statement by the President on Afghanistan', The White House Office of the Press Secretary, (May 27, 2014), para 9, available at https://www.whitehouse.gov/the-press-office/2014/05/27/statement-president-afghanistan.

with a direct threat (including support from U.S. combat aircraft and drones) (Mazzetti & Schmitt, 2014; DoD, July 12, 2016).[172]

Similar to the future of U.S./NATO relations, the level of amity and engagement between the current National Unity Government of Afghanistan and the incoming Trump administration remains unknown at the time of writing. In his testimony before the Senate Armed Services Committee, General Nicholson testified "We have a shortfall of a few thousand," in relation to the 8,448 U.S. troops (and 26,000 private contractors) currently deployed (February 9, 2017). Troop density ratio's notwithstanding, increased boots on the ground is not a strategy; previous surges in Afghanistan and Iraq COIN campaigns were part of a broader strategic shift.[173] Once again the U.S. is faced with the reality that was articulated by Major General Jim Molan who wrote that the number of troops in Afghanistan "will only become decisive when there is unity of effort" (2009: 15).

An important aspect of the transition to full Afghan control is security related infrastructure, and again defence diplomacy plays an important role from concept to creation. The U.S. military has also built five ANA bases across the country and U.S. funds were used to construct a new Defense Ministry headquarters in Kabul. It has also developed a network of military bases throughout the region with selected coalition partners which deliver strategic political and military benefits in the short to long-term for both the U.S. and the HN. Dos Santos Lersch & Simao Satri found that from "the onset of the 'War on Terrorism,' a rapid increase in the number and geographical spread of U.S. military bases commenced" (2014: 99–100).[174] When the ISAF combat

172 This caveat has enabled U.S. military personnel to adapt to increased threat levels by "anticipating battlefield dynamics and ... deploy and employ their forces together [with the ANDSF] in a way that stops a situation from deteriorating; interrupts an enemy in the early stages of planning and formulating an attack."

173 Most density recommendations fall within a range of 25–20 soldiers per 1000 residents in an area of operations based on historical data. However, the success of the 2007/8 'surge' in Iraq was in part due to the 28/1000 ratio according to General David Petraeus. For more information see: John McGrath, 'Boots on the Ground: Troop Density in Contingency Operations', *Global War on Terrorism Occasional Paper 16*, (Fort Leavenworth, Kansas: Combat Studies Institute Press, 2006), pp. 1–212.

174 In 1990, prior to the Gulf War, the United States had no bases in South Asia and only 10% as many in the Middle East/Africa as in 1947. In 2016, Afghanistan has a number of foreign military bases in its territory with the U.S. currently maintaining eleven installations. Although other Western powers, such as the UK (Camp Bastion) and Germany (Camp Holland) have military facilities in the region, the majority fall under the auspices of NATO and ISAF.

mission ended in 2014, ISAF turned over the vast majority of the about 800 bases to the ANDSF. Military bases signal U.S. intentions by directing funds to infrastructure projects as well as signally long-term commitments to the region. However, non-verbal signalling must be supported by dialogue because signals can be misread (Cohen, 1987).[175] For example, as a result of U.S. military bases in Afghanistan, Pakistan, and Central Asia, regional powers Russia, Iran and China may view the U.S. presence as a threat to their security. When South Asian bases are combined with U.S. bases to the east in Japan, to the south-east in South Korea, military installations in the Persian Gulf as well as Western encroachment from NATO, the U.S. military apparatus which provides a level of security for the U.S., threatens to encircle global rivals thereby creating insecurity for its partners (Beehner, 2005).[176]

Similarly, the outcomes for HN partners are many and varied, covering the political, military and economic spectrum, both material and psychological. Perceptions are critically import domestically and nowhere is this more evident than in Afghanistan. In a country where "the only direct experience the people have with the government is through the Afghan police and the army" the critical role of defence diplomacy oriented mentoring as well as train and equip programs cannot be overestimated (Qurban-Ali, 2014 16). Additionally, an 'immediate' internal and external HN benefit comes from identifying itself as part of the U.S. strategic defence orbit, sending a signal that it has the potential to 'punch above its weight.' Because psychological based deterrents are formed by interactions over time, any improvements in internal confidence and external perceptions are important. From a realist perspective, conflicts occur as a result of a shift in power and the display or presence of relative strength, whereas in psychological terms, it is the perception of power, rather than the actual possession of power. Defence diplomacy bridges the two by inducing tangible relationship and capacity building measures to support perceptions formed through external observations. For example, defence diplomacy initiatives which prioritize "the development, acquisition and potential

175 Cohen examines the importance of non-verbal signalling, stating that although primarily as an exercise in communication, diplomacy consists of other "discrete activities" such as information, clarifying intentions, and engendering goodwill," p. 1. Language is obviously the most effective method of engagement; however, other "extra-linguistic forms of communication" have been incorporated into what Cohen labels the "language of diplomacy," p. 1.

176 In an attempt to offset U.S. intentions, the Shanghai Cooperation Organization (SCO), a regional security body (whose members include China, Russia, Kazakhstan, Kyrgyzstan, Tajikistan, and Uzbekistan) issued a declaration in 2005 calling for the United States to set a timeline for its withdrawal of military forces from the region.

deployment of any weapon system and/or military force" send important diplomatic signals in time of peace as well as during protracted conflict such as the Long War according to Dorman & Uttley (2016: 202). The outcomes of these programs have the potential to balance the political aspirations of Coalition partners (including the HN) with their military capabilities.

The ScanEagle UAV program is an example of a project generated through the process of defence diplomacy producing mutually beneficial systemic, operational and economic outcomes; outcomes which underpin the process. The UAV program emphasises important but underrated results of this type of military assistance military, including sales and technology transfers, contributing to not only improved interoperability (military) and dialogue (diplomacy), but also deliver expressly commercial objectives (economic). The ScanEagle UAV delivers new intelligence gathering capabilities to the ANDSF. The AFDSF is now able to see enemy movements and can visualize enemy tactics which will reduce the reliance on U.S. and NATO airborne and in situ intelligence assets. The ANA led the construction efforts on multiple operational, storage and launch sites across Afghanistan, while the ANA Engineering School will provide ongoing maintenance. The ANDSF anticipates having full control of the project by 2018 and selected ANA personnel have attended a month-long training seminar in the U.S. to familiarise themselves with ScanEagle systems.

This example demonstrates allied defence and security exports support the domestic economies of both the exporter and import nation. Defence and security oriented exports simultaneously enhance and sustain training and capacity building initiatives while supporting overall national security objectives. They generate revenue as well as meeting the commercial interest component of foreign assistance programs by "promoting U.S. exports, creating new customers for U.S. products or by improving the global economic environment in which U.S. companies compete" (Tarnoff & Lawson, 2016: 4). The ScanEagle program provides a direct connection between the multi-national manufacturer (Boeing) and the Afghan state. With Afghan defence expenditure growing at 18.5% over the last four years, from US$0.9 billion in 2011 to US$1.8 billion in 2015, expanding to US$3.4 billion in 2020 these commercial relationships are an important component of the U.S. Long War strategy. The ScanEagle project is another incremental step towards a complete transition of national security to the ANDSF and provides an example of the political, security and economic benefits delivered through the process of defence diplomacy.

While scholars such as Sharp & Wiseman and Constantinou & Opondo suggest the equalization of diplomacy, defence and development in U.S. foreign policy should be welcomed, others have criticised U.S. development assistance for prioritising the winning of 'hearts and minds' of people abroad and directed by political or military interests; rather than by universal goals such as poverty reduction (Schirch and Kishbaugh, 2006). Although such concerns may be justified, former member of the Canadian military emphasises that "the defence, diplomacy and development (3D's) approach to operations in Afghanistan aligns with good theoretical COIN practices" (Conliffe, 2009: 100). Such declarations are not new or untested, with COIN scholars and practitioners from the "Clausewitz of COIN" David Galula, to Frank Kitson and John Nagl, and the architects of *U.S. Counterinsurgency Field Manuel FM 3-24*, Frank Hoffman and David Killcullen all recognising an increasing interdependence between the 3D's and COIN.[177] Given the influence of these SME's on senior Bush administration officials and that the 3D's have been present in U.S. foreign policy in same shape or form since the post-WWII Marshall Plan, it's not surprising that the President released the U.S. *3D Security Framework* in 2006.

General Anthony Zinni testified in 2008 that if the U.S. wanted to continue to positively influence world events "it must strategically balance all three aspects of its power–defense, diplomacy, and development" (March 5, 2008). In response to this line of thinking, President Obama reworked Bush's framework in 2009 with former Secretary of State Clinton articulating the revised 3D strategy declaring that "the foreign policy of the United States is built on the three Ds: defense, diplomacy, and development" (April 30, 2009).[178] The *3D Planning Guide: Diplomacy, Development and Defense* identifies the 3D's as "the three pillars that provide the foundation for promoting and protecting U.S. national security interests abroad" through enhanced cooperation and collaboration

177 David Galula, *Counterinsurgency Warfare: Theory and Practice*, (New York: Frederick A. Praeger, 1964), pp. 1–118. Galula, who wrote what many consider to be the best book on COIN claims that the military aspect of COIN is only 20% of the strategy, the remaining 80% being political, economic, information operations, p. 66; Frank Kitson, Low Intensity Operation: Subversion, Insurgency, Peace-keeping, (London: Faber & Faber, 1971), pp. 1–112; Frank G. Hoffman, Neo-Classical Counterinsurgency, Parameters, Summer Issue (2007), pp. 1–17; David Kilcullen, 'Three Pillars of Counterinsurgency', *U.S. Government Counterinsurgency Conference*, (Washington D.C., Office of the Coordinator for Counterterrorism, U.S. Dept. of State, 2006), pp. 1–8; U.S. Army *Field Manual 3-24/Marine Corps Warfighting Publication 3-33.5, Counterinsurgency*, (Washington D.C.: Department of the Army, December 2006). Hoffman noted that contemporary COIN "highlighted an increased requirement for discriminate force in operations to remove irreconcilable extremists.... in an increasingly complex strategic environment," pp. 12–13.

178 Hilary Clinton, 'Remarks to Department Employees at Welcome Event', *U.S. Department of State*, (Washington, D.C. January 22, 2009), Secretary Clinton labelled the 3D's as "the three legs to the stool of U.S. foreign policy."

internally between the departments of State and Defence and USAID as well as externally with international partners (U.S.G., 2012: 8). The issue for the U.S. is how to replicate the interagency domestic coordination prioritized by the *3D Planning Guide* into its interactions with international partners.

To facilitate the transition from the whiteboard to practice State and DoD have invested in the skills necessary to engage in with like-minded transnational stakeholders to secure its interests in the Long War. Deputy Assistant Secretary Kelly declared in 2014 that "the current level of cooperation between State and Defense is truly unprecedented. We are seeing more interaction, more coordinated engagements, more personnel exchanges than ever before" (April 17 2014). Combining the three sectors consolidates U.S. power. Finney concludes that "stabilizing a country or region requires an integrated effort of all the actors involved in defence diplomacy, and development" (2010: 3). The following section tests Finney's conclusion by examining how the 3D's been utilised in Afghanistan during the Long War to demonstrate how the troika reinforces both the process and practice of defence diplomacy in the Long War.

Diplomacy, Defence and Development: 3D's in the Long War

> *Gone are the days when only the U.S. Agency for International Development 'does development' while the military only fights battles. Soldiers, diplomats, USAID ... are all partners in rebuilding infrastructure and shaping the political environment ... and achieving U.S. foreign policy goals.*
>
> HUNT, 2010: PARA. 6

As the OEF bombing campaign began in early October 2001 President Bush proudly declared "the oppressed people of Afghanistan will know the generosity of America and its allies. As we strike military targets we'll also drop food, medicine, and supplies to the starving and suffering men, women, and children of Afghanistan" (Oct. 7, 2001). In tandem with a new approach to military engagement, the events of September 11 resulted in new aid programs, delivery mechanisms, and improved multi-level and multi-sector to address issues inter-related to international terrorism. The theory behind supplying aid in support of U.S. foreign policy since the end of WW II has consistently emphasised "modernisation, economic development, poverty reduction, humanitarian aid ... pacification and stability" (Kapstein & Kathuria, 2012: 2). The 2006 National Security Strategy affirms "development reinforces diplomacy and defense, reducing long-term threats to our national security by helping to build stable, prosperous, and peaceful societies" (2006: 33).[179] While U.S. National Security Advisory Council member Admiral James L. Loy testified that "the U.S. must fully utilize all three aspects of national power and international influence—defense, diplomacy, and development" (2013: 2). Kapstein and Kathuria emphasise that the complexity and resource intensive nature of COIN requires "the application of both military power and economic resources to combat the insurgents" (2012: 8). A 2016 CRS Report for Congress noted that since 9/11 U.S. policymakers have:

> frequently cast foreign assistance as a tool in U.S. counter-terrorism strategy, increasing aid to partner states in counter-terrorism efforts and funding the substantial reconstruction programs in Afghanistan and ... has been featured as a key element in U.S. national security strategy in both Bush and Obama Administration policy statements
>
> TARNOFF & LAWSON, 2016[180]

The U.S. provides military assistance to its allies, partners and cooperative developing countries in its battle against the global terrorism threat. These assistance packages have external security as well as domestic economic benefits for the U.S.[181] Military assistance accounted for about 28% (US$13.5 billion)

179 See also: Secretary of State Hillary Clinton, 'On Development in the 21st Century', Transcript of remarks delivered at the Center for Global Development, (January 6, 2010), available at http://www.cgdev.org/doc/2009/Clinton%20Transcript2.pdf Secretary Clinton spoke of equality between the 3D's and that they "must be mutually reinforcing."

180 See also: U.S. Government Accountability Office, *Foreign Assistance, GAO-17-316*, (Washington D.C.: U.S. Government Accountability Office, March 2017), This trend will continue into 2017 as the USG intends "to improve the lives and health of millions living in poverty, support democracy, enhance global security, and achieve other U.S. foreign policy goals" by allocating approximately US$35 billion for foreign assistance, p. 1.

181 Historically the U.S. Congress sought to enhance the domestic benefits of foreign aid by requiring that most U.S. foreign aid be used to procure U.S. goods and services—the "Buy America" provision, the Foreign Assistance Act of 1961 (P.L. 87-195, Sec. 604), this is sometimes called "tied aid." The United States joined other donor nations in committing to reduce tied aid in the Paris Declaration on Aid Effectiveness in March 2005; however, 37% of U.S. bilateral development assistance in 2013 was tied. A considerable amount of U.S. foreign assistance funds remain in the United States, through domestic procurement or the use of U.S. implementers, (Tarnoff & Lawson, 2016: 18); See also Edward Clay, Matthew Geddes, Luisa Natali and Dirk Willem de Velde, 'Thematic Study, The Developmental Effectiveness of Untied Aid: Evaluation of the Implementation of the Paris Declaration, Phase I Report', *Overseas Development Institute*, (Copenhagen: Ministry of Foreign Affairs, Printing Office, October 2008).

of total U.S. foreign aid expenditure in FY2015. State generates and administers three military assistance programs; the previously mentioned IMET which offers military training on a grant basis to foreign military officers and personnel, Foreign Military Financing (FMF) which is a grant program that enables governments to receive equipment and associated training from the U.S. government or to access equipment directly through U.S. commercial channels, and Peacekeeping funds (PKO) for non-U.N. peacekeeping operations. These State programs, and the accounts which fund them, are collectively called the Afghanistan Security Forces Fund (ASFF), and the ASFF is implemented by the DoD. Foreign assistance programs (the 2013 *U.S. Army Field Manual 3-57* labels these activities as Civil Affairs) are considered essential for establishing and maintaining positive relations and increasing international cooperation, contributing to increased economic opportunities at home, and enhanced national security.[182] Operational evidence of this is presented in *The Global War on Terror and U.S. Development Assistance: USAID allocation by country, 1998–2005* which detailed how CT oriented aid programs were prioritized early in the Long War yet the authors concluded (in 2005) "concerns there is a large and systematic diversion of U.S. foreign aid from fighting poverty to fighting the War on Terror do not so far appear to have been realized" (Moss, et al., 2005; Mekay, 2005).[183] Byman concludes that, basically, "when these programs work, they are far cheaper than deploying U.S. military forces" (2016: para. 2).

However, the efficacy off these programs combined with U.S. deficit blowouts have led to calls for a significant reduction in outreach funding, potentially restricting the ability of the U.S. to advance its international policy agendas. Congressional Budget Office (CBO, November, 2013) documents indicate that a reduction in foreign aid expenditure is one of the more popular budget saving measures of the USG. Other studies have reinforced the USG position, arguing that the results of U.S. Long War foreign assistance programs promoting growth and reducing poverty are simply ambiguous. For example, the previously mentioned McNerney et.al report which identified success rates varied

182 *U.S. Army Field Manual FM 3-57* lists six Civil Affairs functional areas: rule of law, economic stability, governance, public health and welfare, infrastructure, and public education and information. FM 3-57 notes that "all six functional are interrelated and that these activities may occur prior to, during, or subsequent to other military actions. They may also occur, if directed, in the absence of other military operations" pp. 1–2.

183 Data shows four main trends in aid flows. First, there has been an overall increase in real terms, with annual flows rising from about $5 billion in 1998 to a peak of about $8 billion in 2003, then dropping to $6.3 billion in 2005 (all figures in constant 1995 US$). This results in a post-9/11 total of $27.5 billion for the four years between 2002 and 2005, a 39 % increase over the $19.8 billion cumulatively spent between 1998 & 2001 (Mekay, 2005: 4).

widely in terms of both the region and the type of assistance provided. A 2014 RAND report on U.S. capacity building initiatives in Afghanistan since 2001 found that evaluating the effectiveness of current programs is difficult because of data limitations, lack of assessments and the long-time horizons for partnership efforts (Hanauer & Pezard, 2014). Similarly a U.S. government report released in late 2014 investigated restricting war-funding to activities related to war operations because of a "lack of evidence of success in previous similar programs, particularly in situations like the complex political-military environment in Syria and Iraq" (Belasco, 2014: ii). While a 2016 CRS report determined, "[I]n most cases, clear evidence of the success or failure of U.S. assistance programs is lacking, both at the program level and in the aggregate" (Lawson, 2016: 3).

Qualitative date suggests otherwise, with a 2017 report into U.S. security sector assistance (SSA)[184] detailing the more than US$250 billion the U.S. has spent building up foreign military and police U.S. since 9/11 hasn't always left the U.S. safer or its partners more stable and capable Jackson, 2017: 6). The report also revealed that 73% was allocated by the DoD, an 1147% increase since 2001, whereas allocation by State (although increasing by 201%) fell from 58% in 2001 to 26.5% in 2015 (2017: 33). Additionally, it identified USAID as "one of the least integrated agencies in the SSA realm yet it has expertise particularly relevant to defense institution building, monitoring and evaluation, and developmental approaches to programming" (2017: 26).[185] Similarly, a 2016 report commissioned by RAND investigated the U.S. Security Governance Initiative (SGI), a 'good governance' initiative which was launched in August 2014 across six African countries. Whilst serving as a preliminary assessment, researchers identified: "the lack of an overarching strategy; the complicated organizational architecture of U.S. security sector assistance programs, to include a lack of synchronization; inadequate systems for assessment, monitoring and evaluation; a restrictive set of legal authorities; budgetary uncertainty; and the DoD's disproportionately large role in administering security sector assistance" (Burns, et al., 2016: vi). An additional negative consequence of foreign assistance, and one which severely undermines the domestic legitimacy of fragile

184 The intention of SSA is to facilitate stability through better governance, i.e. helping "allies better fight terrorists, police territories they liberate from their clutches, defend their borders against enemies, and ensure the rule of law, and in doing so, diminish any need for U.S. intervention down the road" (Byman, 2016: para. 1).

185 The report recommends that "for priority SSR countries, or those within the "Internal Stability and Rule of Law Deficit" framework category, USAID should take a lead in developing the institution building component of the Security Sector Assistance plan," p. 27.

HN governments, is the impact on a nation's currency. A 2011 IMF report found that the Afghani (Afghanistan's currency) was 20 percent over its projected value; encouraging imports but stifling domestic growth (2011: 15). Research has also identified the negative legacy of foreign assistance programs can further weaken already fragile states (Kapstein & Kathuria, 2012).

An examination of U.S. aid and military assistance program in the AF/Pak region since 2001 exemplifies the difficult balance between ensuring U.S. national security, fulfilling international obligations, promoting democracy and creating sustainable development. To accommodate these objectives, over US$115 billion has been spent in what a RAND report labelled the most under-resourced reconstruction and stability operation in history (Dobbins, et al., 2005). Conversely, Theros & Kaldor argue that "how money is spent is more important than how much is spent" (2011: 46). Complicating the situation further is the fact that that some U.S. military partners prioritise the delivery of assistance "as a form of compensation when alliance expectations are substantial" (von Hlatky & Trisko Darden, 2015: 31).[186] This is not particular to Coalition efforts in Afghanistan and can be explained by the theory of band-wagoning which involves unequal exchange whereby states with lower capabilities make asymmetrical contributions and/or concessions to the dominant power and/or accepts a subordinate role (Walt, 1988: 282. Similarly, Kapstein and Kathuria question whether aid flows "substitute for a foreign military presence in dampening the insurgency" or simply lead to HN "rent-seeking and predatory insurgents?" (2015: 1). The authors question whether U.S. assistance "helped to build state legitimacy and strength in Afghanistan, and not just bolster state capacity to fight a war?" (2015: 2). These are important questions which need addressing. In doing so, most research into 3D's includes at least a rudimentary examination of the vanguard development initiatives implemented by the U.S. and their Coalition partners in Afghanistan: Provincial Reconstruction Teams (PRTS).[187]

186 The authors determine that "relatively weaker powers in a bilateral alliance can turn to non-military alliance contributions to compensate for their inability to contribute militarily and to preserve their value to the alliance by circumventing accusations of free-riding," p. 32.

187 Kilcullen (2016: 6–7) suggests that PRTs have often been treated as a panacea for civilian counterinsurgency. They are not. But careful analysis of why PRTs succeed in some areas and do less well in others can help tailor approaches for specific situations"; PRT's have also been labelled as Embedded Provincial Reconstruction Teams (EPRT) or village stability platforms (VSP's).

U.S. PRTs integrate civil-military capabilities through collaboration between the military, diplomatic and development agencies of the U.S. government (DoD, State & USAID). *National Security Presidential Directive 44* (December 2005) explicitly tasked State as the primary coordinator of U.S. post-conflict reconstruction efforts; however, as DoD is the lead agency in prosecuting the Long War, its influence in developing and actioning PRTs is significant.[188] According to *DoD Directive 3000.05 'Military Support for Stability, Security, Transition, and Reconstruction (SSTR) Operations,'* DoD's primary interests in PRTs are twofold. Firstly, stability operations are considered "a core U.S. military mission ... priority comparable to combat operations;" and secondly, DoD views PRTs as important COIN tools for "winning hearts and minds" as well as marginalizing insurgents and extremists. Theoretically, PRTs enable the Afghan authorities to establish legitimacy by consolidating the institutions and governance structures required to progressively establish good governance and the rule of law. In practice, advancing these interests requires the development of civic, economic and governance capacities—a particularly challenging task in unstable security environments.

A 2005 CRS Report for Congress supported both theory and practice, emphasising PRTs have "permitted U.S. forces to establish personal relationships with local Afghan leaders which some believe has helped to diminish insurgent influence in a numbers of regions" (Feickert, 2005: 9). PRTs debuted in the Afghan theatre in late 2002 and deploy civilian and military personnel to undertake the insurgency-relevant developmental work. This mix of personnel utilizes their individual diplomacy oriented skill-sets to engender long-lasting connections with the HN, and just as importantly within the Coalition itself.[189] The combination of military capability with civilian expertise has been viewed

188 Other USG agencies with less prominent PRT roles include the Department of Justice (DoJ), Department of Agriculture (USDA), and the US Army Corps of Engineers (ACE).

189 The program and objective of PRTs are developed and governed by the State but operate under military authority. PRTs are discussed at length in the following: Stewart Cowper-Coles, *Cables from Kabul: the inside story of the West's Afghanistan campaign.* (London: Harper Press, 2011); Robert Moelker, 'The Genesis of the "Dutch Approach" to Asymmetric Conflicts', *Armed Forces & Society, Vol. 40, no. 1,* (2014), pp. 96–117; Rietjens, S.J.H. 'Managing Civil-Military Cooperation: Experiences from the Dutch Provincial Reconstruction Team in Afghanistan', *Armed Forces & Society, Vol. 34, no. 2,* (2008), pp. 173–207; Vogelaar, A.L.W. & E.-H. Kramer, 'Mission Command in Dutch Peace Support Missions', *Armed Forces & Society, Vol. 30, no. 3,* (2004), pp. 409–431; Rem Korteweg, The Netherlands: To Fight, or Not to Fight? The Rise and Fall of a Small Power', in Gale A. Mattox & Stephen M. Grenier, (eds.), *Coalition Challenges in Afghanistan: The politic of Alliance,* (Stanford, CA: Stanford University Press, 2015), pp. 140–156.

as the most promising conduit for accelerating the development of civic, economic and governance capacities outside of secure zones (Kuwayama, 2008: 47). PRTs have also played a central role in the U.S. military's transition from containment to engagement in Afghanistan by not only engaging in daily operational liaisons but also "establishing bonds of effective collaboration and genuine community with host societies" (Henrikson, 2013: 277). Long War PRTs advance U.S. security objectives by supporting the stabilisation mission through the provision of security and reconstruction projects and when viewed collectively the outcomes of PRT projects should be a key criterion for U.S. strategic success (Cordesman, 2007: 8).[190]

Early U.S. PRTs usually operated in volatile areas, were led by a military commander, averaged approximately 80 personnel of which 3 to 5 were civilians and prioritised 'quick impact projects.' As the conflict environment evolved, so did the composition and mission of the PRTs. Civilian functional specialists and advisors (The Human Terrain System) appeared at the forefront of activities while civilian directors began to take over command duties from their military counterparts.[191] Additionally, USAID personnel have been integral part of the U.S. military mission, enhancing the capacity building operations of their uniformed kin. In the first 5 years U.S. PRTs finalised 469 projects, including the construction or rehabilitation of over 400 schools, 600 wells, and 170 health clinics, building community irrigation systems, roads were improved, small power systems were installed, as well as support for government capacity building, micro-finance, job placement, gender-related and media projects (USAID, 2007).[192] Beyond the recognised stability and reconstruction projects, the outreach, engagement and relationships generated by PRTs make a

190 By the end of 2014, all NATO PRTs were phased out and their functions handed over to the GoIRA, traditional development actors, non-governmental organisations and the private sector.

191 All U.S. Government COIN strategies, plans, programs, and activities are undertaken in support of the affected government and managed through the U.S. Mission's Country Team, led by the Chief of Mission (COM) in coordination with State, primarily through the Bureau of Political-Military Affairs and the Office of the Coordinator for Reconstruction and Stabilization (U.S.G., January 2009: 30, 51); See also Sebastiaan Rietjens, Joseph Soeters & Paul C. van Fenema, 'Learning from Afghanistan: Towards a compass for civil-military coordination', *Small Wars & Insurgencies, Vol. 24, no. 2*, (2013), pp. 257–277; Christopher Sims, *The Human Terrain System: Operationally Relevant Social Science Research in Iraq and Afghanistan*, (Carlisle Barracks, PA: Strategic Studies Institute/U.S. Army War College, 2016).

192 For current allocation and delivery agencies see: *U.S. Foreign Aid by Country*, USAID, available at https://explorer.usaid.gov/cd/AFG (Last accessed January 2, 2017).

positive contribution to the U.S. effort in Afghanistan. Reconstruction efforts such as the program to rebuild the Mausolea Shahzada Abdullah and Shahzada Qasim in Herat are examples of strategic diplomatic/cultural engagement. The two important cultural sites were restored with local Afghan workmanship, ANSDF/U.S. military protection and State/DoD funding in collaboration with the Afghan Ministry of Information and Culture.[193]

Current JCOS, General Dunford presented the objective of U.S. multi-level civil-military engagement in the *2013 Civil-Military Framework*, highlighting that in pursuit of U.S. foreign policy in Afghanistan "there will be challenges, even as progress continues. Civil-military teamwork and coordination will help us overcome these challenges, while supporting our Afghan partners as they take ownership of their future." These collaborative efforts will assist in the creation of "credible and capable district governments" across the operating environment "underwritten by effective, indigenous security forces" (Lushenko & Hardy, 2016: 120). For example, State has developed and redeveloped its Civilian Response Corps which provide a pool of civilian specialists and experts in reconstruction and stabilization.[194] The *U.S. Government's Counterinsurgency Guide* states these rapid reaction teams "may help to address the causes of unrest before the crisis escalates and limits political alternatives to the use of force" (2009: 31). Another example of the improved civil-military nexus manifests in an arm of DoD, called the Task Force for Business and Stability Operations (TFBSO), which operates with a mandate to facilitate additional private investment in Afghanistan.

---

193 In October 2013, a Federal Assistance Award was made by State to Afghanistan Cultural Heritage Consulting Organisation (ACHCO) to ensure the mausolea conservation. More details available at http://afghanculturalheritage.org/7.html (Last accessed December 2, 2017).

194 See Coordinator for Reconstruction & Stabilization, 'Preventing & Responding to Conflict: A New Approach', U.S. Department of State, (2009). Dan E. Stigall, 'The Thickest Grey: Assessing the Status of the Civilian Response Corps Under the Law of International Armed Conflict and the U.S. Approach to Targeting Civilians', *American University International Law Review 25, No. 5*, (2010), pp. 885–914; Nina, M,. Sefarino, Peacekeeping/ Stabilization and Conflict Transitions: Background and Congressional Action on the Civilian Response/Reserve Corps and other Civilian Stabilization and Reconstruction Capabilities', CRS Report for Congress, (Washington D.C., Congressional Research Service, October2, 2012); Robert Lamb, Kathryn Mixon & Joy Aoun, Rethinking Civilian Stabilization and Reconstruction', *A Report of the CSIS Program on Crisis, Conflict, and Cooperation*, Center for Strategic and International Studies, (Lanham, MD: Rowman & Littlefield, 2013), pp. 1–56.

The objective of U.S. Afghan policy is to facilitate the establishment of a secure, self-sustainable Afghanistan by building political institutions and encourage economic development. However, similar to other U.S. development initiatives, the rate of progress for PRTs in achieving this objective is difficult to ascertain. In stabilisation efforts "there is a fine line between military operation and politics as everything is related-everything is connected" (Hunt, 2010: para. 11). Do tactical successes mask limited governance and/or development? For example, by 2011, troop reductions were being tabled because the 'surge' was appearing to have worked yet the GoIRA "relied upon foreign aid for 100 percent of its development budget and 45 percent of its operating budget" (Kapstein & Kathuria, 2010: 10). A CRS Report for Congress released in November 2016 determines Afghanistan will remain dependent on foreign aid for many years and the outgoing administration "requested about US$4.67 billion for FY2017, of which US$3.5 billion is for the ANDSF" (Kratzman, 2016).[195] Are these ongoing budgetary commitments an indication that PRTs have under-delivered? Are expectations unrealistic to begin with, as research indicates even without the insurgency that erupted after the fall of the Taliban government "the challenge of rebuilding the country from its 2001 base would have proved overwhelming?" (Kapstein & Kathuria, 2012: 9).[196]

However, some investigations by stakeholders reveal criticism of PRTs is warranted. Before reviewing these negative assessments, the paper poses two questions. Firstly, are these issues structural? After all, both civilian and military personnel are "dedicated to mission success, willing to sacrifice their lives to serve their country" (Hunt, 2010: para.4). Secondly, are these problems inevitable when "two very different cultures are striving to work together in a complex and challenging environment?" (Ibid.: Para. 4). A 2008 report from the Woodrow Wilson School of Public & International Affairs identified:

> a lack an overarching strategy, a set of common objectives, and a common concept of operation and organizational structure. Metrics to

195 Through the end of FY2014, the U.S. provided about $100 billion to Afghanistan since the fall of the Taliban, of which about 60% has been to equip and train the ANDSF. About $5.7 billion was being provided in FY2015, including $4.1 billion for the ANDSF. For FY2016, the United States is providing $5.3 billion, including $3.8 billion for the ANDSF.

196 A 2008 Asian Development Bank report revealed "War and civil conflict resulted in the deaths of over 1 million Afghans between 1978 and the end of 2001, with a further 1 million left orphaned or disabled. Up to one third of the population became refugees ... most of Afghanistan's basic infrastructure was destroyed ... The education of an entire generation of young Afghans was disrupted," (2008: 1).

> assess the success and impact of current PRT models are also missing from national PRT strategies ... The importance of personalities, donor countries' political caveats, and imbalances in program funding have also negatively affected PRT performance
>
> ABBASZADEH, 2008: 5

Several studies identified flaws in the leadership structure of U.S. PRTs. Despite each PRT having a formal organisational structure and a clearly defined leader, "these leaders do not exert command authority over the activities of other agencies' staff members" leading to "incoherence in the planning process" (Kuwayama, 2008: 50). PRT security and stability operations, such as patrolling, monitoring, influence, and mediation efforts are more difficult for researchers to assess as comprehensive data on these combined activities is not readily available. This undermines PRT effectiveness as a deteriorating security situation will directly impact the delivery of PRT projects throughout the country.[197] Moreover, even when projects are completed, there are second and third order consequences which must be considered in evaluating the role of PRTs Lt. General Daniel Bolger, who led troops in both Iraq and Afghanistan COIN operations, states emphatically that measuring success by how much U.S. led stability operations improve the situation in Afghanistan ignores the reality that every well we dig, school we build of mayor we train is another well not dug, school not built or person not trained by the local government which means we're undermining the people" whom the U.S. must rely upon if and when the majority of coalition troops leave Afghanistan (Bolger & Nagl, February 13, 2015). Bolger was perhaps recalling the advice of T.E. Lawrence who wrote "Do not try to do too much with your own hands. Better the (HN) do it tolerably than you do it perfectly."

U.S. partners in Afghanistan have delivered similar criticism of PRTs. The Norwegian government recently released the *Godal Report* (*June 2016*) which found "the Norwegian armed forces were not in favour of engaging in a PRT, as it was deemed to be an overly extensive and risky commitment ... the Norwegian government considered such participation an unavoidable consequence of Norway's NATO membership" (Wilkins, August 23, 2016). While Lushenko and Hardy present a practical assessment of PRT operations in Panjwai District, describing how road building were prioritised by the benefit to military operations rather than the needs of the local civilian population

197 For example Killcullen claims that PRTs have not been able to complete any projects in Eastern Afghanistan, since 2013 as a result of adverse security conditions (Kilcullen, 2016: 171).

(2016: 119). The author's personal experience in Panjwai led them to claim that "outreach programs were pursued more to co-opt the locals to rat-out insurgents rather than persuade them by fostering trust" (Ibid.: 119). Rietjens, et.al acknowledge that "today's crisis operations demand that political, economic, developmental as well as security factors have to be addressed simultaneously ... however, coordination within and between civil-military networks, characterized as multi-actor and multi-level, does not come automatically" (2013: 257). For example, Major General James P. Hunt reveals civilian input into creating PRT initiatives was limited, with embassy staff "not part of the process that led to the plan and weren't asked specifically what support it needed" (2010: 3). Major General Hunt, who facilitated cooperation and integration at the tactical and operational level with interagency and partner organisations, found that the lack of State influence in the preliminary development stages resulted in both military and civilian personnel "spending staff hours they simply don't have to make significant changes to the plan" (Ibid.: 2–3).

The PRT Ninewa(h), Iraq is often presented as an exemplary of civil/military cooperation; however, there is little evidence available which indicates that this 'successful' model was replicated elsewhere. While the Ninewa(h) example highlights the potential of defence diplomacy to improve inter and intra-operability, adequate transfer of knowledge is necessary to transform a tactical anomaly into an operational norm. Another question worth examining is whether PRTs have been undermined by an absence of Muslim members of Coalition security forces? For example, the Soviets recruited large numbers of Muslim soldiers from Central Asia for their conflict with the Mujahideen (Pomper, 2005). Although the Coalition did have some success with troops from the UAE and Jordan who connected with members of the Afghan civilian population on shared religious beliefs, the presence of large number of foreign (non-Muslim) troops continues to undermine the legitimacy of an already limited central government. Finally, Miller concludes that although U.S material power (its wealth and its military) remain unrivalled, "the U.S. has underinvested in its tools of reconstruction and stability for decades (2016: 18). Could *this* be a reason PRTs underperformed in progressing U.S. strategic objectives?

Similarly, opinions from the 'traditional' diplomatic community on the effective deployment of the PRT's and the 3D's are mixed. When launching the U.S. diplomatic effort in early 2011, Secretary Clinton called for a "diplomatic surge to match the military and civilian efforts to try to catalyze and shape a political end to years of war" (February 18, 2011).[198] An additional 3000 civilian

198 Sec Clinton also spoke of "the civilian surge underway in Afghanistan, which had brought thousands of courageous Americans from many U.S. government agencies, as well as

government personnel would provide a 400% increase to U.S. Foreign Service staff (Erickson, et al.). She also spoke of the role the military would play in the 'surge,' emphasising without "the heroic effort of U.S. forces, joined by many allies, friends and partners, there was no chance of pursuing a diplomatic end to 30 years of conflict" (February 18, 2011). The Secretary's observations are underpinned by contemporary COIN doctrine which situates the military's contribution within a unified & comprehensive approach to establish conditions conducive to security and stabilisation improvements.[199]

Ambassador Mark Grossman served as the U.S. special representative for Afghanistan and Pakistan (SRAP) from 2011 to 2012, taking over the role after the untimely death of the original representative, Richard Holbrooke. During his tenure as SPAR, Grossman operationalised the U.S. diplomatic effort, overseeing a comprehensive"diplomatic campaign" which would require simultaneous, coordinated action by the SRAP team to connect the military effort with the instruments of non-military power in South and Central Asia, including official development assistance, involvement of the private sector, support for civil society, and the use of both bilateral and multilateral diplomacy (2014: 25). Grossman emphasised America's need to maintain alliances and create new coalitions in order to successfully navigate a security environment which is "defined by the need to recognize the overriding reality of simultaneity: the political, economic, military, cultural, humanitarian and media spheres have merged," requiring stakeholders to generate policies "as multifaceted as the challenges we face" (Ibid., p. 23). Grossman outlined "a synthesis of traditional diplomacy and a diplomacy of the future" which prioritised the "need to use and respond to simultaneity as a key component of every future diplomatic plan," within a whole-of-government framework to respond to today's challenges (Ibid., p. 26). The Ambassador believes "a compelling aspect of 21st-century diplomacy: acting as a "whole of government" on opportunities and challenges simultaneously ... to face tomorrow's challenges or the return of yesterdays" (Ibid., p. 24).

Bill Bent a U.S. Foreign Service Officer (FSO) working in Afghanistan claims the "adage, that soldiering is 99 percent boredom and 1 percent sheer

---

international and Afghan civilians, to promote economic development, good governance, the power of civil society ..."

199 NATO's Allied Joint Doctrine for Counterinsurgency notes that the aim of such activity is to foster HN government capacity and legitimacy, build human security and stimulate economic activity. Tasks that may fall to the military include: providing security for the population, restoration of essential services, support to economic and infrastructure development, establishment of interim governance and security of communication, p. 3.

terror, applies equally well" to those engaging in "expeditionary diplomacy" in Afghanistan (2014: 46). Generally "movements outside the compound are limited to "mission-essential" trips; however, officers from the senior leadership down to entry level are able to travel to meetings in Kabul or field locations in Herat, Mazar-e-Sharif, Bagram and Kandahar" (Ibid.: 47).[200] Bent laments the inability of the FSO's to travel safely and regularly outside the wire which undermines their "ability to develop deep, ongoing relationships with our contacts ... meaning that we are not able to call upon close relationships to subtly shape issues as our colleagues serving in other countries can" (Ibid.: 47). Bent's comments reflect NATO's Allied Joint Doctrine for COIN which notes while "civil authorities should normally have the lead for delivering internal security and stabilisation, the lack of a permissive environment may require military forces to contribute more widely to security and capacity-building tasks. As a result the military contribution may dominate the early phases of a campaign during the contest to deliver a favourable security environment that protects the population" (2011: 1–3). Those within the embassy comprehend the current threat landscape faced by the U.S. require "policies that press new ideas and simultaneously bring to bear all the elements of national power while remaining rooted in our values and philosophy" (Grossman, 2014: 26).

Following extensive interviews, Shoon Murray determined that while the combat commander had increased their contact with the higher levels of both HN and partner governments, "it was the ambassador who had the deeper day-to-day relationships with officials in the country" (2011: 2). While other senior FSO's perceived the civil/military relationship as largely favourable, describing it "as cooperative, not as competitive or displacing" (Belote, 2004). Shepard Cowper-Coles, Britain's former Ambassador to Afghanistan and later the UK's SRAP, recalled the vital and complimentary relationship between military personnel and his foreign services colleagues; however, he identified institutional limitations of the U.S. effort. Cowper-Coles noted that although U.S. Ambassador Bill Woods "saw more of President Karzai than all other foreigners put together," the "vigorous American tradition of inter-agency warfare" means that "neither the Pentagon nor the CIA respects the State Department, or accepts its primacy in Foreign Affairs (2011: 159, 283). Consequently, entrenched institutional 'silo's leave the ambassador and his staff competing with military personnel who "increasingly wield more resources with a regional engagement agenda" (2011: 3). For example, a 2006 U.S. Senate report recommended all

200 Bent claims that this security situation has led to the development of "creative ways" to successfully conduct outreach such as "diplomacy via social media and hosting events and meetings on the embassy grounds.

ambassadors should pursue a MOU whereby "the Ambassador's authority over military activities was made clear" (U.S. Senate Report: 11).[201] The same report revealed an unnamed ambassador complaining that "his effectiveness in representing the United States to foreign officials was beginning to wane, as more resources are directed to special operations forces and intelligence ... Foreign officials are 'following the money' in terms of determining which relationships to emphasize" (Ibid.: 12).

While prioritising outcomes rather than the theory which underpins the process or the process itself, the preceding evaluations are an important contribution to the discussion. Additionally, the commentary from scholars, military practitioners and members of the broader diplomatic community add an additional layer of understanding to the multidimensional puzzle that is the Long War in Afghanistan.[202] The *Quadrennial Diplomacy and Development Review* re-affirmed, "American diplomacy and development are crucial to ensuring that this century will be defined by the opportunities rather than the threats" (2015: 8). Yet how can the U.S. determine ROI when creating opportunities? Have the billions of dollars in assistance provided throughout the Long War improved the security of the U.S. homeland? The following section summarises assessments produced using a variety of metrics by both academics and U.S. government departments including the *Special Inspector General for Afghanistan Reconstruction* (SIGAR) quarterly report to U.S. Congress, the annual *Enhancing Security and Stability in Afghanistan,* various *Government Accountability Office* assessments as well as reporting required under Sections 1212–1226 of the FY2013 *National Defense Authorization Act.*[203] This aim of the section is to discuss whether defence diplomacy delivers upon its theoretical promise for the U.S., its Coalition partners as well as the HN. In keeping with the defence oriented language at the core of this paper this final section also serves as an AAR or 'After Action Review'; assessing strategic progress,

201 The report recommended that State "should pursue a more systemic solution offered by a global memorandum of agreement between the Secretaries of State and Defense."

202 Their insight while valuable comes with a caveat; their experiences are individual. Just as in the Indian parable of the blind men and the elephant where each blind man feels and describes a different part of the elephant, their individual impressions, while true, do not accurately describe the elephant in its totality.

203 Congress created SIGAR to provide independent and objective oversight of Afghanistan reconstruction projects and activities. Under the authority of Section 1229 of the National Defense Authorization Act for Fiscal Year 2008 (P.L. 110–181), SIGAR conducts audits and investigations to: 1) promote efficiency and effectiveness of reconstruction programs and 2) detect and prevent waste, fraud, and abuse.

identifying areas which should be sustained as well as areas which can be improved in order to achieve strategic/policy objectives.[204]

Long War Defence Diplomacy: Outcomes?

> *the results of war are never final*
>
> VON CLAUSEWITZ, 1997: 80

Generating an assessment of the efficacy of defence diplomacy requires comprehensive analysis, including a mix of tangible material indicators as well as subjective measures such as the perception of those inside and outside the process. The literature examined during this research focused on the relationships between the U.S. and the various NATO and non-NATO members of the Coalition, the stability and reconstruction initiatives associated with the U.S. COIN strategy as well as the U.S. CT campaign; three separate but interdependent components of the Long War. The various objectives to which 'progress' has been measured against have been presented throughout the paper and can be summarised as using U.S. "diplomacy and leadership, backed by a strong military" to build a strong Coalition of *capable* allies and partner nations to confront a common threat, maintain territorial integrity and support region stability (U.S.G., 2015). Have these objectives been met and what has been the role (positive or negative) of defence diplomacy. Considering that defence diplomacy, in accordance with the fundamentals of diplomacy, should not be not a 'zero-sum' game, the discussion organically shifts to calculating whether U.S. partners in Afghanistan have benefited from their engagement since 2001, thus advancing the process of defence diplomacy. The narrowly focused practical summaries from an Australian, British, Canadian, Indian and Afghan perspective were outlined previously therefore the aperture widens to view the impact of the Long War on the mechanism of defence diplomacy.

This broader evaluation is helped by looking at some fundamentals of international relations. For example, do European states in particular, limit or even undermine their strategic and/or operational future by committing wholesale acquiescence to U.S. military doctrine, command and control, reconnaissance and intelligence? Not according to King who found that European states prioritised operations in the Afghan theatre "in order to cement their links to the U.S." (2011: 78). Scholars have determined that the strategic culture of an

---

204 An AAR has four key questions: "What were our intended results? What were our actual results? What caused our results? And what will we sustain or improve?" US Army, 2014: 207–214).

individual state is an independent variable and plays a significant role,[205] while others apply a collective, realist explanation, such as a need to prevent prominent European states from dominating European security aspirations.[206] At its most basic level, a significant measurable outcome of military to military engagement with the U.S. is what Art refers to as "swagger" Art, 1980:17–18). Research reveals that states signal their intentions, justify and develop their identity as well as legitimating their defence/security apparatus by "acquiring certain military capabilities, while ignoring others" (Angstrom & Honig, 2012: 670).

Scholars Claudia Seymour (2003) and Kenneth Payne (2014) have identified and evaluated the role of emotion in the resolution of conflicts and this paper suggests emotion certainly influences the decision of partners to both commit to and remain in the fight. For example, Rasmussen found that post-9/11, the Danish government "made activism the emblem of its foreign policy and equated activism with a close alliance with the U.S." which was a definite "break with the passive appeasement policy' that supposedly had characterized Danish foreign policy for most of the twentieth century" (2005: 81).[207] Additional research finds the Coalition "has been plagued by caveats:

205 For example: Jan Angstrom & Jan Willem Honig (2012: 668); Kilcullen articulates how the strategic culture of Australia is shaped by "several enduring circumstances" such a population size and geography, (2007: 49).

206 For examples of the different approaches to engagement with the U.S. see: Vogelaar, A. L. W. & E.-H. Kramer. 'Mission Command in Dutch Peace Support Missions', *Armed Forces & Society, Vol. 30, no. 3*, (2004), pp. 409–431; Fawn R. Alliance Behaviour, the Absentee Liberator and the Influence of Soft Power: Post-communist State Positions over the Iraq War in 2003', *Cambridge Review of International Affairs, Vol. 19, no. 3* (September 2006), pp. 465–480; Rietjens, S. J. H. 'Managing Civil-Military Cooperation: Experiences from the Dutch Provincial Reconstruction Team in Afghanistan', *Armed Forces & Society, Vol. 34, no. 2*, (2008), pp. 173–207; Kilcullen, D. *The Accidental Guerrilla: Fighting Small Wars in the Midst of a Big One*, (New York: Oxford University Press, 2009); Cowper-Coles, S. *Cables from Kabul: the inside story of the West's Afghanistan campaign*, (London: Harper Press, 2011); Bailes, A. J. K. & B. Thorhallsson 'Instrumentalzing the European Union in Small State Strategies', *Journal of European Integration, Vol. 35, no. 2*, (2013), pp. 99–115; Moelker, R. 'The Genesis of the "Dutch Approach" to Asymmetric Conflicts', *Armed Forces & Society, Vol. 40, no. 1*, (2014), pp. 96–117.

207 Rasmussen determines that Danish strategic culture has been shaped by 3 external 'shocks' since World War II which unhinged discourse from practice and set Danish defence policy on a new course. "The first shock occurred when Denmark joined NATO and adopted the strategic practice of deterrence and the strategies, doctrines, operational principles, command and control structures—even uniforms—developed by the Alliance. The second shock occurred with the 'second Cold War', when the lack of agree-

restrictions on what Coalition militaries can and cannot do ... diminished the alliance's overall effectiveness and created resentment within the coalition" (Saideman & Auerswald, 2012: 67). Similarly some scholars have examined the commitment and reliability variations of democracies (Tago, 2009; Kreps, 2010). While in theory, defence diplomacy has the capacity to mitigate domestic obligations and restrictions by providing regional and/or global incentives; further scholarship reveals it delivers on its theoretical promise. Tago finds that states which become part of U.S.-led coalition in Iraq, earned:

> a reputation as a loyal ally of the U.S.... a crucial diplomatic asset and strong incentive for a state to remain in the coalition ... However, in the deadlocked and prolonged operation in Iraq, most partner states would like to accelerate, and many actually have, the withdrawal of troops from Iraq, even though an early departure could seriously harm their reputation as a good ally.
>
> TAGO, 2009: 220

Military aid/assistance has been a central pillar of the U.S. Long War strategy. Beyond the financial component, how has defence diplomacy supported U.S. military assistance? Since the launch of the 'Global War on Terror' the Pentagon has extended military aid, through programs such as the Counterterrorism Partnership Fund and the European Reassurance Initiative, to Pakistan, the Philippines, Turkey, Georgia, Djibouti, Ethiopia, Nigeria, Oman, Yemen, Uzbekistan, and Columbia, and numerous European states, to facilitate co-operation, essentially encouraging and rewarding those who take up the fight against international terrorism (Sullivan, et al., 2011: 276). This concept is neither new nor unique. George Keenen enthused in 1947 "When you have a government which has the will, the men, and the efficiency to operate, and when arms are the elements that are lacking, I certainly feel that that is something we can do ..." (Harlow & Maerz, 1991: 309). Numerous studies have examined the benefits of military aid programs in the Long War including Sullivan et.al which observed U.S military aid through three theoretical lenses; 'arms for influence, the lonely superpower and reverse leverage.' Each of the three models identified reasons why the U.S has leveraged military aid in the Long War (2011: 279–282). Conversely, Cordesman claims that this type of metric "is useless in counterinsurgency and nation building ... particularly true in the case

ment within the Alliance about deterrence provided new discursive possibilities. The third shock occurred after the end of the Cold War when globalization set a new agenda for the Danish armed forces," p. 83.

of Afghanistan and Iraq, where regional and local differences are critical, and coalition partners take different approaches to fighting and aid" (2007: 29). Overall, the strategy of providing economic and political incentives creates unintended consequences due to "the complexities of U.S. interventions in another country's military whose goals, operating practices, and political constrains" (Belasco, 2014: 4).

Sullivan et.al hypothesised "States that the U.S. believes are critical to its security interests will be more likely to receive military aid but less likely to increase their cooperation with the United States as the amount of aid they receive increases" (2011: 282). Similarly, Hanauer & Pezard identified the difficulty of ensuring the goals of the U.S. and partner nations are compatible, particularly when the U.S. has parallel involvement with insurgency groups or non-state actors within HN territory (2014: 2–3). Moreover, the U.S. faces domestic and international criticism for providing arms and funding for a political/military apparatus in states which are complicit in the enduring threat from the Taliban, al Qa'ida and other violent non-state actors (Cottey & Forster, 2004; Nolan, 2009).[208] The Sullivan et.al study identified parallel domestic pressures on the recipient nation which resulted in some nations becoming less cooperative as U.S. military assistance increased. Moreover, recipient nations may be either less overtly cooperative with the U.S. to counter any perception that their foreign policy is dictated by a foreign power as dependence on U.S. military aid increased, or, "high value" recipient nations will increasingly exploit the U.S. as it becomes dependent on them for U.S. security (Sullivan, et al., 2011: 287,289). Their research concluded that "U.S. military aid is less able to buy better behaviour from states with which the U.S. has formal security ties—perhaps because the U.S. is not likely to decrease military aid when allies are uncooperative" (Ibid.: 289).[209] However, Claudia Seymour identifies the legacy of shared experience whereby "previous wars fought, previous aggressions committed, or previous actions ... a history of domination of one party over the other" influences trust building and cooperation (2003: para. 4).

208 Nolan identifies a "tendency to engage other countries simply a conduit for U.S. realpolitik, moreover, continues to influence current policy ... the deepening reliance of the U.S. on potentially unstable authoritarian regimes in the Middle East and in Central and South Asia" in the long war. p. xii.

209 The study found that "states receiving military aid from the U.S. exhibit lower levels of cooperation than states that do not receive military aid, (ii) in the population of all states, higher levels of military aid appear to produce more defiant behaviour, and (iii) the U.S. does not punish defiance with reductions in aid or reward greater cooperation with increases in military aid," p. 290.

This is where the process of defence diplomacy can overcome external/internal dynamics by using the foundation of past experience to foster cooperation in the near or long-term.

The complexity of the Afghan theatre in the Long War dictates that assessments of the process must also consider U.S relationships with Coalition states on Afghanistan's periphery such as Pakistan, Iran, Russian and several Central Asian states.[210] Pakistan is often criticised for its parallel overt and covert actions which both help and hinder U.S. progress in the Long War. However, Zaidi explains "the lack of trust didn't start following 9/11; Pakistan's relationship with the United States has a tortured history" (2011: 1).[211] The relationship waxed and waned through the 1960s and 1970s, but it became an indispensable partner when the Soviets invaded Afghanistan in 1979. During their surreptitious intervention in Afghanistan throughout the 1980's U.S. defence diplomacy was expressed through bilateral engagements with Pakistan. However, the relationship deteriorated during the 1990's and sanctions were applied as Pakistan crossed the nuclear threshold. Incorporated into the sanctions regime was the Pressler Amendment which limited the ability of Pakistani defence personnel to travel to the U.S. for training, a shift in U.S. foreign policy which deeply military to military relations. The IMET program was significantly reduced which led to a diminished understanding between Pakistani and U.S. forces. Pakistan's mid-low-level officers no longer looked westward and the U.S. "lost the opportunity to appreciate and understand the ethos, capabilities, orientation, and competence of the Pakistani military" (Fair, 2004: 12).[212]

This disconnect would subvert U.S. strategic planning in the aftermath of 9/11 when "Pakistan was made a major non-NATO ally and given huge amount of military and economic assistance" (Mahapatra, 2011: 41). On September 13 2001, Pakistani President Musharraf announced his country would take a 'principled stand' by joining the U.S.-led counterterrorism Coalition by severing diplomatic relations with the Taliban and deploying almost 150,000 troops along the Afghan-Pakistan border, as well as providing critical logistical support

210 Pakistan, Iran, Russian, Tajikistan, Turkmenistan, Kyrgyzstan and China were all foundation members of Operation Enduring Freedom.

211 See also Richard Grimmett, 'U.S. arms sales to Pakistan', *CRS Report for Congress RS 22757*, (Washington D.C.: Congressional Research Service, August 24, 2009).

212 The author explains that "fortunately for OEF and the war on terrorism, the senior leadership of both the militaries likely had maintained fairly robust ties dating back to the period of the Soviet invasion of Afghanistan when security cooperation had been strong." Interestingly, India's IMET budget doubled between 1995 and 1998 but was reduced after India advanced its own nuclear program.

and conducting military offensives against Al Qa'ida and the Taliban in border tribal areas. Despite Musharraf's commitment, support among the Pakistani military was not absolute and SECDEF Mattis vividly recalls the looks of suspicion of the current generation of Pakistani military officers when he arrived in Afghanistan during the Long War's embryonic stages (March 20, 2014).[213] A U.S. Congressional Research Service report released in 2016 reveals total 'overt' aid to Pakistan since 2002 totals more US$33 billion (Tarnoff & Lawson, 2016).[214] Although that number is high it needs to be viewed in context of the US$1.7 trillion for activities and operations in support of U.S. response to the 9/11 attacks allocated to DoD, State and USAID (Epstein & Williams, 2016; U.S. GOA, January 2017).

Any gains in Afghan security will not be sustainable without the cooperation of Pakistan yet analysts question its commitment to Afghan stability. One theory is that "Pakistan sees Afghanistan as potentially providing it with strategic depth against India" (Katzman, 2016: 42). Despite its status as a key partner in the Long War, Zaidi claims "the relationship has been so fraught with cross-purposes and doublespeak that the real purpose of U.S. aid to Pakistan in the post-9/11 era is no longer clear" (Zaidi, 2011: 3). Moreover, the death of al Qa'ida founder Usama bin Laden in May 2011 confirmed that he enjoyed a lengthy and relatively comfortable refuge inside Pakistan. This revelation led to intensive U.S. government scrutiny of the bilateral relationship, with the legislative branches of government openly questioning the wisdom of providing significant U.S. foreign aid to a nation that may not have the intent and/or capacity to be an effective U.S. partner (Kronstadt, 2015). In May 2016, the U.S. House of Representatives voted 277 to 147 in favour of a defence policy bill which increased restrictions on military aid for Pakistan unless certain

---

213 For information see: *The Pressler Amendment And Pakistan's Nuclear Weapons Program*, Pakistan Defence Department, (December 11, 2009), available at https://defence.pk/pdf/threads/the-pressler-amendment-and-pakistans-nuclear-weapons-program.41174/ (Last accessed February 3, 2017).

214 See also: Kronstadt, K. A. 'Pakistan-U.S. Relations: Issues for the 114th Congress', *CRS Report for Congress R44034*, (Washington D.C.: Congressional Research Service, May 14, 2015). Kronstadt reports that Congress began appropriating billions of dollars to reimburse Pakistan and other nations for their operational and logistical support of U.S.-led CT operations in FY 2002. "These "coalition support funds" (CSF) have accounted for roughly half of overt U.S. financial transfers to Pakistan since 2001, or about $13 billion to date," p. 14.

anti-terror conditions are met.[215] However, Kronstadt revealed that since the re-evaluation began in 2011, the (Obama) "administration has exercised authority granted by Congress to waive those conditions in the interests of national security" (2015: 1). Applying punitive measures for non-compliance may be influenced by Pakistani government figures which indicate more than 50,000 civilians and security personnel have been killed in the Long War since 2001, as well as spending almost US$80 billion (roughly one-third of the nation's current GDP).[216] Ambassador Crocker, who has represented U.S. interests on both sides of the Durand Line summarises the "very complex and often difficult relationship with Pakistan" thusly:

> We both need to take a deep breath and commit ourselves to a strategic partnership over the long run. The Pakistanis continue to fear we're going to just pull out of the area as we did after the Soviet withdrawal at the beginning of the 1990s and leave them with an unsustainable mess in Afghanistan at a time when they're fighting an insurgency or insurgencies on their own territory.
>
> 2013: 105

State's *Annual Report on Assistance Related to International Terrorism Fiscal Year 2016* outlines how State's security assistance strengthens non-military efforts, partnerships, and capacity with Afghanistan neighbours to address evolving terrorism challenges. State directs CT capacity-building assistance to partner nations throughout Asia, prioritising aviation and border security, CT oriented legal frameworks and law enforcement, as well as enhancing information sharing (UNSCR 2178) through greater INTERPOL connectivity. In Pakistan and Bangladesh for example, State supports police and border security training, including support for the new Dhaka-based Counterterrorism and Transnational Crime Unit. More broadly State's Antiterrorism Assistance Programs included "525 courses, workshops, and technical consultations involving 10,455 participants from 50 countries" (State, 2017: 4). These examples provide a snapshot of the regional engagement which allows "State to

215 The House of Rep's expressed frustration over what they term Islamabad's failure to crack down on the Haqqani network, a militant group which lawmakers see as a major threat to US forces in Afghanistan. The Bill will block US$450 million in aid to Islamabad unless it does more to disrupt the group.

216 See the South Asian Intelligence Review for briefings, statistics, assessments and official documentation, available at http://www.satp.org/ (Last accessed January 10, 2017).

significantly expand efforts with key countries and elevate the civilian dimensions of counterterrorism" (Ibid.: 1). They also demonstrate that State is highly active and more prominent in shaping regional initiatives and providing parallel support for defence oriented engagement in the USG's regional strategy to promote CT cooperation and best practices.

Across the region, the U.S. has encouraged Afghanistan's neighbours to support a stable and economically viable state. To this end, the U.S. received 'formal' non-interference pledges from Afghanistan's neighbours through the 'Istanbul Declaration' and 'Bonn Statement' in 2011. In June 2012, Afghanistan hosted 14 regional countries and 11 regional and international organizations at the 'Heart of Asia' ministerial conference, where all agreed to broaden cooperation and exchanges such as jointly fighting terrorism, develop joint plans for disaster management and pursue economic development (Participating were Afghanistan, Azerbaijan, China, India, Iran, Kazakhstan, Kyrgyzstan, Pakistan, Russia, Saudi Arabia, Tajikistan, Turkey, Turkmenistan, UAE, and Uzbekistan). U.S. officials have also sought to enlist both regional and greater international support for Afghanistan through the 50-plus nation International Contact Group. Another effort, the Regional Economic Cooperation Conference on Afghanistan, was launched in 2005. Turkey and UNAMA co-chair a 'Regional Working Group' initiative, while UNAMA also leads a 'Kabul Silk Road' initiative to promote regional cooperation on Afghanistan. Interestingly, summit meetings between Iran, Afghanistan, and Pakistan which had been ongoing since 2007 ended in mid-2012 after Afghanistan signed the SPA with the U.S., which Iran strongly opposed. Meanwhile Russia has assembled several quadrilateral summits among it, Pakistan, Afghanistan, and Tajikistan. Congress provided US$150 million in FY2014 to promote Afghanistan's links within its region with the Economic Support Funds appropriating additional funding for programs in South and Central Asia to expand linkages between Afghanistan and countries in the region (Katzman, 2016: 42).[217]

However, regional countries, such as China, Pakistan, Iran, Russia and the Central Asian republics, have their own interests in a stable Afghanistan. Exemplified by the breakdown in Iranian dialogue demonstrates, balancing the interests of these regional actors whilst achieving U.S. strategic security objectives presents another challenge for U.S. defence diplomacy. This problem further manifests itself in the Quadrilateral Coordination Group (QCG) (consisting of Afghanistan, Pakistan, the United States, and China) which was formulated to advance the peace process and facilitate direct talks with the

217 For a list of Regional Facilities Used for Operations in, and Supply Lines to Afghanistan, available at https://fas.org/sgp/crs/row/RL30588.pdf (Last accessed January 2, 2017).

Taliban. The success of the QCG is hampered by both an inability to coerce the Taliban to the negotiating table but more importantly intrinsic mistrust between QCG members. Issues with Long War military cooperation identified between QGC participants at a bilateral level are exacerbated in the multilateral forum, with pejorative claims and counterclaims at the political/diplomatic level destabilising the alliance (Kousary, July 8, 2016). These challenges will need to be overcome so that its neighbours can be encouraged to "reach a diplomatic solution that respects both Afghanistan's sovereignty and each country's geopolitical concerns" (Qurban-Ali, 2014: 14). U.S. diplomacy is necessary to explain U.S. Afghan intentions. The longer the U.S. and the Coalition stays in Afghanistan and the more opaque its objectives, the more regional actors such as Russia, China, Pakistan and Iran, will view the U.S. presence through a purely geostrategic lens.[218] This situation is not unique and remains at the core of effective strategic/security planning.[219]

How does one measure the role of defence diplomacy in U.S. stabilization programs, development initiatives, train & equip missions and regional CT efforts in the Long War? The previous paragraphs demonstrate that locating progress on the continuum of 'success' is complicated. As is the norm in insurgencies, U.S. "tactical victories become irrelevant unless the GoIRA succeed in uniting Afghans, creates effective governance, provides key services, and develops the economy" (Cordesman, 2007: 4). Others emphasise that "the U.S. is very good at fighting long wars with short-term strategies" (Green, September 22, 2016). Five years into the Long War Lt. Col. Combs wrote "our ability to assess strategy implementation begins with strategy formulation. Communicating specific strategic objectives precisely and unambiguously fosters clarity in the determination of strategic and operational effects" (2006: 13). After almost a decade of combat in Afghanistan, Tara McCormack acknowledged that, although the Obama administration claimed Afghanistan was a 'war of necessity rather than choice,' the campaign suffered from a striking lack of strategy both in terms of short and long-term goals (2011: 67). Today, there seems to be divergence between the long and short term objectives of the U.S. and "hope" remains neither "a course of action" nor a solid platform from which to build a successful political/military strategy (Smith, 2000). Moreover, as L'Estrange points out, defence diplomacy and international engagement can only support

218 Bjola confirms that "diplomatic opacity hinders joint problem-solving and decision-making" (2013: 16).

219 Buzan, Waever and de Wilde (1998) demonstrate how regional disaggregation simplifies and clarifies while a comprehensive understanding can only be achieved by "reassembling the parts to see how they relate to each other," p. 8.

a coherent, appropriately calibrated and implemented force structure planning; "focusing on the former cannot compensate for deficiencies in relation to the latter" (2013: 28).

Such is the uncertainty about what victory in Afghanistan might actually mean for the U.S., even the inaugural U.S. SRAP could not say what it would be. Richard Holbrooke professed "we'll know it when we see it." Holbrooke's announcement was somewhat surprising considering the campaign was (at the time) in its eighth year, had cost billions of dollars, resulted in thousands of deaths and was supposed to be addressing a major threat to the West (McCormack, 2011: 69). Lt. General H. R. McMaster indicated that the U.S. will never achieve a clear-cut victory whereby "the enemy acts as a passive recipient of your military prowess" and relents (May 4, 2016). While U.S. Senate Armed Services Committee Chairman John McCain, declared that "the Obama administration focused more about measuring troop levels than measuring success. ... instead of trying to win, we settled for just trying not to lose" (2017: para. 3). Therefore, if victory in Afghanistan seems a vague concept, what is the most appropriate metric to identify success or failure, progress or stagnation? Inconclusive assessments by scholars, practitioners and policy makers identify this as is an area which requires greater focus, whether in terms of more accurate metrics, more comprehensive reporting or a combination of both.

The Government Performance and Results Act (GPRA-2010) requires agencies to set goals and objectives for their performance, and to measure progress against these goals and objectives. However, research reveals that the "tools, models, and even the methodologies for assessing success are biased toward measuring physical effects on near-peer forces, played out over the days or months of a maneuver and attrition campaign" (Clancy & Crossett, 2007: 88). Moreover, identifying an accurate universal metric has been a perennial problem when examining the success and/or failure of war and/or diplomacy more broadly.[220] For example, how do we measure our ability to deter or compel

220 Recent research has progressed towards accurately assessing the outcome of public diplomacy, see: Lisa Tam & Jeong-Nam, 'Conceptualising and measuring relationship as public diplomacy outcome: development of the Relationship Assessment of Diplomatic Interaction Outcome (RADIO) scale', *Communication Research and Practice*, (2016), pp. 1–19; Wallin, M. 'Tara Sonenshine on measuring the effectiveness of public diplomacy', *American Security Project*, (2012); Brown, Robin. "Measurement and Evaluation in Public Diplomacy," Public Diplomacy, Networks, and Influence, (March 31, 2011); Pahlavi, Pierre C., 'Evaluating Public Diplomacy Programmes', *The Hague Journal of Diplomacy, Vol. 2, no. 3*," (2007), pp. 255–81; Ted Kniker, 'The Program Assessment Rating Tool (PART): What

an insurgent group from conducting operation? As Crenshaw points out, we "must usually infer compliance from the absence of over non-compliance" (2003: 316). Put simply, we only know it's working until it doesn't. The issue of metrics is an important area of research and discussion; however, for the purposes of brevity the following three paragraphs outline 'some' of the issues of measuring outcomes.

This paper suggests that the spectrum of defence diplomacy (breadth, depth and outcomes) should be integrated into current conflict metrics, providing better qualitative measures of progress, and more realistic and transparent indications of the extent to which the U.S. and their alliance partners are 'succeeding' in the Long War. Additionally, as this paper supports defence diplomacy's role in the Long War it's also useful to view it, and therefore measure it through the lens of CT. At a tactical level, a CT effort can be said to be effective if it achieves its intended tactical outcome without negatively impacting other tactics within the current CT strategy. Another primary indicator of tactical effectiveness is whether said tactic is accepted as legitimate by an external audience. For this study a tactic is legitimate, therefore classified as effective, if both domestic and foreign publics maintain the view that the tactic is proportionate and justified, its tactical outcomes are achievable and that progress towards those outcomes is being made. Therefore, again, from a theoretical perspective, defence diplomacy would be classified as effective. Despite this theoretical clarification, at a practical level, the pace of developing sustainable indicators to measure the effectiveness of CT in the Long War has been glacial with assessments lacking substance and clarity.[221] After fifteen years of assessing progress in the Long War, analysts are yet to formulate a "generally accepted definition or framework of CT effectiveness" (van Um & Pisoiu, 2014: 235). Adams et al. maintain that "the most salient feature about contemporary evaluations of CT tactics is how few there are, despite the central role they must play in preventing terrorism" (2011, 41). The *U.S Government*

PARTs Help and What PARTs Don't', *American Evaluation Association Public Issues Forum: Edited Proceedings*, (November 2, 2006), pp. 17–22.

221 Scholars have written extensively on the limit of current CT metrics, for example: Reifler, J., Gelpi, C. & Feaver, P. 'Success Matters: Casualty Sensitivity and the War in Iraq', *Project Muse*, (Gorgetown University Press, Winter 2006); Lum, C., Kennedy, L. & Sherley, A., 'The Effectiveness of Counter-Terrorism Strategies', *Campbell Systematic Reviews*, (The Campbell Collaboration, 2006); Van Dongen, T. 'Break it Down: An Alternative Approach to Measuring Effectiveness in Counterterrorism', *Economics of Security Working Paper 23*, (Berlin, Economics of Security, 2009); Dubik, J. 'Winning Battles, Losing Wars. Army', *ARMY, The Magazine of the Association of the Unites States Army, Vol. 64.*

Performance and Results Act requires that standards and performance measures are created for all state and federal agencies; however, this act does not cover CT operations.

However, inbuilt accountability mechanisms to calculate ROI's and measure and evaluate the operational and tactical implementation, outcomes, impact and cost-benefit/cost-effectiveness do exist in USG departments such as the DoD, State, USAID, as well as the Government Accountability Office (GOA). For example, the GOA, the audit, evaluation, and investigative arm of Congress, produces a monthly *Costs of War* document, annual reports and mission specific assessments. In a report into U.S. foreign assistance, the GOA emphasised "the importance of evaluation, and the Foreign Aid Transparency and Accountability Act of 2016 requires the President to establish guidelines for conducting evaluations" (2017: 2). The DoD recently released its latest mechanism for measuring effectiveness releasing the Assessment, Monitoring, and Evaluation Policy (AME). The nascent policy aims to ensure "security cooperation programs will be based on clearly defined of the anticipated outcomes, a set of "specific, measurable, achievable, relevant/results-oriented, and time-bound objectives," and a theory of change that explains why and how the outcomes are to be achieved (DoD, January 13, 2017, 15).

Cordesman critiques Long War assessments which focus on "inputs: cost, number of troops, aid and military activity levels" for not attempting to measure requirements, "whether requirements are being met, and whether the end result is winning or losing" (2007: 3). Similarly, the GOA found that reporting is not and end in of itself, recommending that the agencies involved in U.S. foreign assistance should "develop a plan to improve the quality of its evaluations (and) improve their procedures and planning for disseminating evaluation reports" (2017: 2). Moreover, even when official data is presented, investigations often reveal it is either incomplete or ambiguous. Focusing on that which is measurable has several possible drawbacks. First, the measures in question may be irrelevant to strategic success. Second, regardless of a particular measure's significance, the fact that it's being measured often causes a disproportionate amount of emphasis to be placed upon it. In other words, 'what gets measured gets measured.' Another problem occurs when determining timeframes for measuring short-term behavioural changes. Finally, most strategic endeavours, including defence diplomacy, have some form of tangible output which is usually conducive to measurement, but numbers alone do not always reflect reality. 'Real' effectiveness often lies in the intangibles, with critical measures more likely to be 'process-related' rather than tangible, progress-related. Thus, discussion returns to the defence diplomacy being assessed through the delivery of expected outcomes rather than on the theory behind the process and the processes self-sustaining qualities.

Conclusion

For more than 13 years our nation has been at war in Afghanistan. Now our combat mission is ending and the longest war in American history is coming to a responsible conclusion.

OBAMA, DECEMBER 28, 2014

Given that defence diplomacy's origins lie in classic military doctrine extant for centuries, the concept was somewhat marginalised as a by-product rather than an enabler of military relations. The outcomes of two World Wars and a rise in the number of sovereign nations from 77 to 193 in the 20th century increased the pace and scope of military engagement, more so as the 1990s delivered a new era in international affairs. Momentum increased in the new millennium with complex, multi-layered interdependent networks developing alongside non-traditional threats to national security. This situation is the motivation and justification for a review, or more fittingly, an updated interpretation of defence diplomacy.

In support of its hypotheses, the paper has presented defence diplomacy as a dynamic, continuous and understated process for building and managing existing relationships; a mechanism which prioritizes dialogue, transparency and cooperation. It determines that defence diplomacy addresses common or collective interests by "mobilizing dynamic partnerships to confront new interconnected challenges" (QDDR, 2015: 8). The paper has also examined the theoretical foundation which supports defence diplomacy as process which reduces tension, provides positive signals to others, institutionalizes accountability in the armed forces of partners, increases transparency and builds confidence, changes perceptions and aligns short-term priorities with long-term interests. Arguments for and against defence diplomacy in theory and practice have been provided in an effort to offer a balanced preliminary assessment. The study identifies the potential for defence diplomacy to deliver long-term systemic and operational benefits when the military, the most powerful institution of the state, integrates diplomacy in pursuit of foreign policy objectives. If managed properly, it can be an invaluable process of statecraft, by bringing to bear the manifold dimensions of both soft and hard power on any given security issue. Defence diplomacy generates what the U.S. Army terms 'comprehensive deterrence,' the outcome of a whole-of-government approach protects U.S. interests by "preventing an adversary's action through the existence of credible physical, cognitive and moral threats by raising the perceived benefit of action to an unacceptable risk level" (U.S. Army, 2015, 10).

The dominant feature of the process, evident in each of benefits outlined above is its ability to build and maintain relationships. The paper affirms that defence diplomacy creates "a common foundation between the U.S. and its partners" through military training and education programs, hosting regional conferences, and other activities which enhance strategic and operational capabilities Reveron, 2014: 67). The benefits of security cooperation are reciprocal as the U.S. learns and adapts through engagement to create a more universal doctrine/approach to COIN. Thus the benefits of a universal doctrine can be articulated and implemented at both the joint and combined level. The purpose of Joint doctrine is to enhance the operational effective of U.S. forces. It represents what is being taught, believed, and advocated as what is right. It also provides the national position for multinational doctrine and serves as the basis for multinational and interagency coordination; where as a multinational doctrine provides the "Fundamental principles that guide the employment of forces of two or more nations in coordinated action towards a common objective" (DoD, 2016: 125). A bi-product of this coordination and an import future outcome of defence diplomacy oriented engagement would be the development of unified 'Mission Rehearsal Exercises' to certify force readiness for combined operations.

It is perhaps inevitable that "the ebb and flow of military priorities", fighting todays enemy while preparing for tomorrows, undermines the ability to internalize "key lessons learned from recent military experience" (Berg, 2017: para. 2). However, Farrell and Rynning find that the lessons learned from NATO's role in Afghanistan supports its transformation into a 21st century force capable of "generating deployable forces able to operate alongside the U.S. military in serving NATO's new global security role and missions" (2010: 674). Focusing on NATO capability short-falls obscures the fact that the U.S. is learning its own lessons from the Long War. Scholars assert that the U.S. is "leaning more heavily or frequently on its armed forces" and the Long War has exacerbated the situation (CSIS, 2000: xvi). As a result, the entire U.S. defence institution is undergoing changes from a departmental to personnel level. Palazzo highlights that in the last decade "members of the U.S. military and defence communities have participated in a robust, vibrant, sometimes painful but ultimately healthy debate over the changing character of war and the organisation, equipment and doctrine that the US Army requires to meet the challenges of future conflict" (2012: 5). Nor is transformation a finite process, as SECDEF Rumsfeld declared "you go to war with the Army you have. They're not the Army you might want or wish to have at a later time" (Quoted in Ricks, December 9, 2004).[222]

FM 3–0 states that establishing a sustainable integrated command structure is probably most effective when partners are similar in culture, doctrine, training, and equipment, or if extensive cooperative experience exists" (2001: 2–54). Is this desired end-state reflected in reality? While scholars acknowledge that the U.S. has "been at the forefront of the learning and adapting to the challenges of COIN" in Afghanistan, they regret "many important lessons from operations never get institutionalised in new doctrine, training, equipment and organisational structures" (Farrell & Rynning, 2010: 688). Moreover, while there is a measurable 'gap' between the U.S and its alliance partners which needs to be addressed, maintaining a minimum 2% of GDP on military spending will not spontaneously stabilise a dynamic conflict environment or generate a consistent COIN strategy. Likewise, "as U.S strategy has vacillated between CT and COIN, NATO has been unable to serve as a correcting, stabilising mechanism" (Ibid.: 694). However, this paper asserts that the transfer of technology, increased military equipment sales, strategic and tactical knowledge sharing, cooperation and integration generated through defence diplomacy will enhance the unilateral and multilateral capacity of the U.S. to "retool on the fly" in the Long War (Ibid.: 394).[223] Farrell supports this proposition, claiming that adaptation, even when explorative, "is easier for a military to contemplate and undertake than innovation because it does not require institutional change" (2010: 527).[224] Additionally, it's important to recognise the impact of the learning experience on the HN through multi-level interaction generated by defence diplomacy. The paper finds that intra-Coalition learning facilitates a thorough understanding of the strategic and operational imperative's which allows policy makers and practitioners to adapt and respond to the dynamics of irregular warfare.

The Air & Space Power Mentoring Guide states that a contemporary campaign involves both the "employment of military forces in a series of related military operations to accomplish a common objective in a given time and

222 For more on this concept see: Bonds, T. *Limiting Regret: Building the Army We Will Need-An Update*, (Santa Monica, CA: RAND Corporation, 2017).

223 For more detail see: Philipp Rotmann, David Tohn & Jaron Wharton, 'Learning Under Fire: Progress and Dissent in the US Military', *Survival, Vol. 5, no. 4*, (2009), pp. 31–48.

224 For more detail see: Catignani, S. 'Getting COIN' at the Tactical Level in Afghanistan: Reassessing Counter-Insurgency Adaptation in the British Army', *Journal of Strategic Studies, Vol. 3, no. 4*, (2011).

space" as well as "a series of related military, economic and political operations to accomplish a common objective in a given time and space" (1997: 2). The second part of the definition accurately reflects the shift from 'conventional' to 'unconventional' or irregular warfare. Based on this definition, this study concludes: defence diplomacy not only contributes to the success of a COIN campaign in the 21st century; it is central to it. Combined operations can overcome the funding constraints of individual states as well as providing a platform for partners to develop, test, evaluate and recalibrate a universal CT/COIN strategy. Although it is extremely difficult to implement strategic, operational and tactical change in the midst of a war, this paper argues the task is made easier through shared experience facilitated by defence diplomacy. In an "era of persistent conflict" this paper recommends defence diplomacy should continue to be utilised in the Long War as well as in future CT/COIN operations (U.S. Army TRADOC, 2009: 5).

Moreover, war is difficult to plan and even more difficult to predict and map in 21st century irregular conflicts exacerbated by the complexity and dynamism of human interactions.[225] Clausewitz states that "no other human activity is so continuously or universally bound up with chance" than war, with chance being a significant factor in points of friction transitioning from war on paper and war in reality (1997: 85). Diplomacy is the 'salve' that soothes points of friction and greases the wheels of international relations. U.S. defence diplomacy prioritises the "building of cohesive teams by establishing relations built upon trust, rapport, equality and reciprocity" (U.S. Army, 2012: 1). Willard concludes that these efforts "establish the military as an essential player in not only the realm of defence related activities, but also in the realm of diplomacy ..." (2014: 58).

Reflecting upon U.S. efforts in Long War "the costs seem clear, painful and excessive," the gains appear tenuous, while "the benefits are unclear or still

225 SECDEF Mattis declared that you cannot send military personnel "into a theatre and expect them to have a positive impact unless they are historically, culturally, linguistically & religiously" aware of the operating environment. The U.S. Armed Forces developed the Joint Concept for Integrated Campaigning (JCIC) and the Human Aspects of Military Operations (HAMO) to bridge the intersection of land, cyber and human elements, and how the increasing speed of human interactions is a driving factor in current events around the world. Prioritising the 'human elements' helps the U.S. achieve its campaign objectives in the uncertain and gray conditions between peace and war; See for example *Joint Concept for Human Aspects of Military Operations* (*JC-HAMO*), Joint Chiefs of Staff, (Washington D.C., October 19, 2016); See also Christopher Sims, The Human Terrain System: Operationally Relevant Social Science Research In Iraq And Afghanistan, (Carlisle, PA: Army War College Press, Strategic Studies Institute, 2016).

beyond the horizon" (Hooker & Collins, 2015: 403). The U.S. are engaged in a political and military war of attrition with an array of insurgents in Afghanistan therefore positive progression facilitated by defence diplomacy need to be identified in order to sustain widespread domestic and international support for the Coalition and to encourage ongoing government commitment to military to military cooperation. For example, Reveron believes the decades of inter-military engagement by U.S. forces enabled it to operate "with fifty partners who often could provide capabilities that the U.S. forces could not" (Reveron, 2016: xii). Although mistakes have been made, "hard lessons have been learned" and new programs are closer to "finding the balance between U.S. national interests and partners national interests" (Ibid.: xiv). To achieve this balance "U.S. military officers build relationships, promote human rights, encourage military professionalization, mentor military officers in developing countries throughout the world and seek to change perceptions and encourage participation in the process. One must remember that it's difficult to professionalize another country's military. The ANA has been built 'from scratch', an effort General Petraeus labelled "a huge undertaking, and there is nothing easy about it" (Testimony, March 5, 2011). Similarly, Reveron emphasises the importance of not viewing the failure of the ANA as "our failure" and stakeholders should be mindful of reconciling ambition with results (2016: xiii).

Major General Jim Molan wrote that "Afghanistan's worth doing, even badly" (August 10, 2009). Similarly, Vanda Felbab-Brown testified that "U.S. engagement in Afghanistan, including our deployment of adequate military force, still advances key U.S. interests" beyond its COIN/CT objectives, "other U.S. interests and values still call for a judicious continuation of U.S. military, political, diplomatic, and economic efforts in Afghanistan" (2017: para. 8). In this regard, the central hypothesis of this paper can be articulated accordingly: can the benefits of defence diplomacy overcome the potential failure to achieve U.S. strategic objectives; this paper argues yes. Defence diplomacy contributes to the U.S. militaries 'strategic solvency', serving as a means of generating a widely disseminated (and hopefully amenable) "intellectual framework from which state's decide what capability's to acquire, how to allocate finite resources across competing priorities" and importantly when and how to respond to coalition/national interests. Furthermore, it determines the structural buttressing of the mechanism through 15 years of the Long War will overcome a mix of operational gains and strategic losses. Establishing coalitions in the 21st century requires a mix of military partners selected independently to address security issues in their region to augment U.S. defence capabilities, drive Coalition operations and support the U.S. strategic objective of global peace and stability along with "long-time allies, friends and partners (who) request U.S. assistance for training, equipment and professionalization" (Reveron, 2014: 66). Mattox proclaims "the end results of Coalition efforts in Afghanistan since 2001 have proved broadly positive in terms of cooperation ... the collaboration of politically and culturally diverse nations ... set new standards for alliance operations within a Coalition from which much can be learned" (2015: 288).[226]

The paper determines that U.S. defence diplomacy has achieved its technical objective of forming and sustaining its Long War Coalition, providing as a structured yet dynamic progressing a goal of a unified effort in the Afghan theatre. It also finds that defence diplomacy oriented programs have not negatively impacted on U.S. Long War strategy; therefore it can be considered to be a successful from a CT perspective. Similarly, it demonstrates that the short-falls, mis-steps and weaknesses in Coalition efforts in Afghanistan have been, and continue to be mitigated by defence diplomacy oriented engagement. Whether deploying a population or enemy-centric COIN model, or a combination of both, defence diplomacy corals the political and military objectives of various coalition partners to generate a combined doctrine, adequate burden sharing, effective communication as well as a heightened degree of transparency and trust required to deliver its strategic objectives. Moreover, the relationships built and maintained through U.S. defence diplomacy since 2001 have created a parallel national security support network which compliments, and at times compensates, an explicit U.S. security umbrella. In conclusion, the paper finds that U.S. military outreach across the political/military spectrum in the Long War has yielded no negative effects thereby enhancing the efficacy of defence diplomacy. Through the process, the U.S. has built, stabilised and maintained relationships around the world which both supported and progressed U.S. efforts in the Long War. Identifying the utility and centrality of defence diplomacy helps us to better understand the past, address today's crises, as well as mitigate long-term threats or prepare for future conflicts.

Acknowledgments

The author would like to thank all who have contributed to this research project. Special thanks go to Dr Stuart Murray (Bond University) and Professor Ian Hall (Griffith University) for their assistance during this study's conceptualisation

226 The Afghan Coalition brought together nations from all corners of the globe such as El Salvador, the UAE, New Zealand, Slovakia & Ethiopia.

as well as to the anonymous review panel for the comments and support. Moreover, the insight, opinions and candid commentary of 'warrior diplomats' from the Australian and U.S. Armed Forces has been indispensable.

Bibliography

2012 Defense Strategic Guidance, *Sustaining U.S. Global Leadership: Priorities for 21st Century Defense.*

A Report to the National Security Council—NSC 68', *President's Secretary's File, Truman Papers*, (April 12, 1950), available at https://www.trumanlibrary.org/whistlestop/study_collections/coldwar/documents/pdf/10-1.pdf (Last accessed December 24, 2016).

'American Military Culture in the Twenty-First Century', *A Report of the CSIS International Security Program*, (Washington D.C.: The Center for Strategic and International Studies Press, February 2000).

ANA Graduating Class Field Exercise and Parade', Australian Government Department of Defence, (March 28, 2017), available at http://video.defence.gov.au/play/5065 (Last accessed April 4, 2016).

Annual Report 2003–04, Ministry of Defence, (Government of India, 2004), available at http://www.mod.nic.in/.

Abbaszadeh, N., Mark Crow, Marianne El-Khoury, Jonathan Gandomi, David Kuwayama, Christopher MacPherson, Meghan Nutting, Nealin Parker, Taya Weiss, Provincial Reconstruction Teams: Lessons and Recommendations, Woodrow Wilson School of Public & International Affairs, (January 2008), pp. 1–56.

Adams, G. & Murray, S. *Mission Creep: The Militarization of US Foreign Policy*, (Washington D.C.: Gorgetown University Press, 2014).

Adams, G. & Richard Sokolsky Governance and Security Sector Reform: The Missing Link—Part II, Lawfare, (July 19, 2015).

Adams, N., Nordaus, T. & Shellenberger, M. 'Counterterrorism Since 9/11: Evaluating The Efficacy Of Controversial Tactics', *The Science Of Security*, (Oakland CA: The Breakthrough Institute, 2011).

Adamson, F. 'Australia in the World: How our Diplomatic Partners See Us', Speech Secretary of the Department of Foreign Affairs and Trade Frances Adamson, Australian Institute of International Affairs, ACT branch Annual dinner, (Canberra, March 15, 2017).

Asian Development Bank, *Afghanistan: Country Partnership Strategy-2009–2013*, (2008).

American, British, Canadian, Australian and New Zealand (ABCA), *Armies Coalition Operations Handbook* (4th ed.), (2008).

Amnesty International, *Unmatched Power, Unmet Principles: The Human Rights Dimensions of US Training of Foreign Military and Police Forces*, (Amnesty International USA Publications, 2002), available at http://www.amnestyusa.org/pdfs/msp.pdf (Last accessed December 12, 2016).

Anderson G. W. & Connie Veillette, 'Soldiers in Sandals', in Gordon Adams & Shoon Murray (eds.), *The Militarization of US Foreign Policy*, (Washington D.C.: Georgetown University Press, 2014).

Angstrom, J. & Honig, J. W. 'Regaining Strategy: Small Powers, Strategic Culture, and Escalation in Afghanistan', *Journal of Strategic Studies, Vol. 35, no. 5*, (2012).

Arklay, T., Tiernan, A. & White, H. 'Advising Ministers—The Special Problem of Defence', *Australian Journal of Public Administration Vol. 70, no. 4*, (2011), pp. 365–376.

Armed Diplomacy: Two Centuries of American Campaigning, (Fort Leavenworth, Texas: Combat Services Institute Press, 2003), pp. 1–295.

Aron, R. 'Introduction', *Peace and War: A Theory of International Relations* (New Jersey: Transaction Publishers, 2003).

Art, R. 'To What Ends Military Power', *International Security, Vol. 4, no. 4*, (1980), pp. 17–18, available at http://www.columbia.edu/itc/sipa/S6800/courseworks/FourFuncForce.pdf (Last accessed December 2, 2016).

Art, R. & Patrick Cronin, *The United States and Coercive Diplomacy*, (Washington D.C.: United States institute of Peace Press, 2003).

Asia Foundation, *A survey of the Afghan people: Afghanistan in 2015*, (2015).

Aspin, L. *Report of the Bottom-Up Review*, Department of Defence, (October 1993).

Atkinson, C. 'Does Soft Power Matter? A Comparative Analysis of Student Exchange Programs 1980–2006', *Foreign Policy Analysis, Vol. 6*, (2010).

Auerswald, P. E., Duttweiler, C., & Garofano, 'Clinton's Foreign Policy: A Documentary Record', *Kluwer Law International*, (2003).

Australian Department of Defence, *RIMPAC 2016 Home*, available at http://www.defence.gov.au/Exercises/RIMPAC16/ (Last accessed February 1, 2017).

Australia's Regional Security, Ministerial Statement by Senator the Hon. Gareth Evans, QC, Minister for Foreign Affairs and Trade, Canberra, (December 1989).

Australian Government Department of Defence, 'Australia's Intentional Defence Engagement', *Defence White paper*, (Canberra: Australian Government, 2013).

Australian Government Department of Defence, *2016 Defence White paper*, (Canberra: Australian Government, 2016).

Ayson, R. & Pardesi, M. S. 'Asia's Diplomacy of Violence: China–US Coercion and Regional Order', Survival, Vol. 59, no. 2, (2017), pp. 85–124, DOI: 10.1080/00396338.2017.1302192.

Bacevich, A. (a) *The New American Militarism: How Americans Are Seduced by War*, (New York: Cornell University Press, 2016 update).

Bacevich, A. (b) 'Ending Endless Wars', *Foreign Affairs*, (August 2016) available at https://www.foreignaffairs.com/articles/united-states/2016-08-03/ending-endless-war (Last accessed December 10, 2016).

Bachmann, O. 'Civil–military relations in francophone Africa and the consequences of a mistaken analysis', *Small Wars & Insurgencies, Vol. 23, no. 3*, (2014), pp. 618–623.

Baldino, D. 'An Exercise in Management: Defence Engagement in the Indo-Pacific', *Security Challenges, Vol. 12, no. 1*, (2016).

Baldino, D. & Andrew Carr, 'Defence Diplomacy and the Australian defence force: smokescreen or strategy', *Australian Journal of International Affairs*, Vol. 7, no. 2, (2016).

Barkawi, T. 'Defence Diplomacy in North-South Relations', *International Journal: Canada's Journal of Global Policy Analysis, Vol. 66, no. 3*, (2011).

Barno, B. & Bensahel, N. 'The Military Is From Mars, Civilians Are From Venus: Avoiding Planetary Collisions In The Conference Room', War on the Rocks, (March 22, 2016), available at https://warontherocks.com/2016/03/the-military-is-from-mars-civilians-are-from-venus-avoiding-planetary-collisions-in-the-conference-room/ (Last accessed September 18, 2016).

Barrie, C. 'ADF not isolated from need for change.' *The Australian*, Defence Review, (18th June 1999).

Beehner, L. 'ASIA: U.S. Military Bases in Central Asia', *Council on Foreign Relations*, (2005), available at http://www.cfr.org/russia-and-central-asia/asia-us-military-bases-central-asia/p8440.

Belasco, A. 'The Cost of Iraq, Afghanistan, and Other Global War on Terror Operations Since 9/11', *CRS Report for Congress*, (Washington D.C.: Congressional Research Service, 2014).

Bell, S. R., K. Chad Clay & Carla Martinez Machain, 'The Effect of US Troop Deployments on Human Rights', *Journal of Conflict Resolution*, (2016), pp. 1–35.

Belote, H. D. 'Proconsuls, Pretenders or Professionals? The Political Role of the Regional Combatant Commanders', 23rd *Chairman of the Joint Chiefs of Staff Strategy Essay Competition*, (Zurich: Institute for National Security Studies, 2004).

Bensahel, N. *The Counterterror Coalitions: Cooperation with Europe, NATO, and the European Union*, (Santa Monica, CA: RAND Corporation, 2003).

Bent, B. 'Serving at Embassy Kabul', *The Foreign Service Journal*, (September 2014), pp. 46–50.

Bercuson, D. J., J. L. Granatstein & Nancy Pearson Mackie, 'Lessons Learned? What Canada Should Learn from Afghanistan', *Canadian Defence & Foreign Affairs Institute*, (Calgary, October 2011), pp. 1–53.

Berg, J. R. 'Building on Reconstruction: What We Have Learned and Where to Go Next', Small Wars Journal, (February 17, 2017) available at http://smallwarsjournal.com/topics/stabilizing%20activities (Last accessed February 18, 2017).

Berridge, G. R. *Diplomacy theory and practice* (4th ed.), (Basingstoke: Palgrave Macmillan, 2010).

Bjola, C. 'Understanding Enmity and Friendship in World Politics: The Case for a Diplomatic Approach', *The Hague Journal of Diplomacy, Vol. 8*, (2013), pp. 1–20.

Binnendijk, H. *Friends, Foes, and Future Directions: U.S. Partnerships in a Turbulent World*, (Santa Monica, CA: RAND Corporation, 2016).

Bisley, N. 'The Possibilities and Limits of Defence Diplomacy in Asia, in Defence Diplomacy: Is the game worth the candle? The Centre of Gravity Series (paper 17), (Canberra: Australian National University, 2014), pp. 12–14.

Bolger D. & John Nagl, Aftermath of Endless War-Why We Lost in Iraq and Afghanistan, *American Forum*, (published February 13, 2015), approx. 21:10 min, available at (Last accessed August 3, 2016).

Boot, Max. "Better a Stalemate Than Defeat in Afghanistan." *CFR.org*, (Council on Foreign Relations, February 23, 2017), available at http://www.cfr.org/afghanistan/better-stalemate-than-defeat-afghanistan/p38848?cid=soc-twitter-in-better_stalemate_than_defeat_afghanistan-030117.

Boutton, A. 'Of terrorism and revenue: Why foreign aid exacerbates terrorism in personalist regimes', *Conflict Management and Peace Science*, (2016).

Braw, E. 'NATO's New Frontlines', Issue Brief, *Atlantic Council*, (November 2016), p. 3, available at http://www.atlanticcouncil.org/publications/issue-briefs/nato-s-new-frontlines.

Breedlove, P. 'In a world of instability, NATO is a linchpin for peace', *Washington Post*, (May 2, 2016) available at https://www.washingtonpost.com/opinions/in-a-world-of-instability-nato-is-a-linchpin-for-peace/2016/05/02/dfd113de-0e52-11e6-8ab8-9ad050f76d7d_story.html?utm_term=.bce4d6274b11 (Last accessed December 18, 2016).

Brooks, R. *How Everything Became a War and the Military Became Everything: Tales from the Pentagon*, (New York: Simon & Schuster, 2016), pp. 1–448.

Brown, A. 'Questioning the mythology of the strong leader', *Leadership, Vol. 11, no. 3*, (2015).

Bruneau, T. 'Challenges in building partner capacity: Civil–military relations in the United States and new democracies', *Small Wars & Insurgencies, Vol. 26, no. 3*, pp. 429–445.

Brynjar, L. 'Jihadism in the Arab World after 2011: Explaining its Expansion', Middle East Policy, Vol. 203 (Winter), no. 4, (2016).

Bull, H. *The anarchical society: a study of order in world politics*, (New York: Columbia University Press, 1977).

Bureau of Diplomatic Security, 'Introduction The Foundations Of Diplomatic Security', The History of the Bureau of Diplomatic Security of the United States Department of State, Department of State (1st ed.), (Washington D.C.: Global Publishing Solutions, 2011).

Burns, E., Michael Corcoran, Michael Gibbons, Christian Heckmann, Laurence Kinsella, Adiele Pommier, 'The Security Governance Initiative: An Effective Approach to Security Sector Assistance', SIPA Capstone Project in Coordination with the RAND Corporation, (Columbia University, RAND Corporation, May, 2016).

Butterfield, H. *The Statecraft of Machiavelli*, (London: G. Bell & Sons, 1955).

Bush, G. W. 'Presidential Address to the Nation', Statement by President Bush in the White House Treaty Room, (Oct. 7, 2001), available at https://georgewbush-whitehouse.archives.gov/news/releases/2001/10/20011007-8.html (Last accessed December 1, 2015).

Buzan, B., Waever, O. & de Wilde J. *Security: A New Framework for Analysis*, (Boulder, CA: Lynne Rienner, 1998), pp. 1–237.

Byman, D. & Waxman, M. The Dynamics of Coercion: American Foreign Policy and the Limits of Military Might, (New York: Cambridge University Press, 2002).

Byman, D. 'Downbound Training', Brooking.org, (November 29, 2016), para. 2, available at https://www.brookings.edu/blog/order-from-chaos/2016/11/29/downbound-training/.

Capaccio, A. 'Trump's Bigger Army Could Cost $12 Billion by Fanning's Math', *Bloomberg Politics*, (January 19, 2017), available at https://www.bloomberg.com/politics/articles/2017-01-19/trump-s-bigger-army-could-cost-12-billion-by-fanning-s-math (Last accessed January 17, 2017).

Carlson, B. E. 'Who Tells America's Story Abroad?: State's Public Diplomacy or DoD's Strategic Communication', in Gordon Adams & Shoon Murray (eds.), *Mission Creep: The Militarization of U.S. Foreign Policy*, (Washington D.C.: Georgetown University Press, 2014), pp. 145–165.

Carr, A. 'Defence Diplomacy: A tool for security, not strategy', Submission to the *2015 Defence White Paper*, (Canberra, 2015).

Carter, A. & William J. Perry. *Preventive Defense: A New Security Strategy for America*, (Washington, D.C.: Brookings Institution Press, March 1999).

Carter, A. 'U.S.-India Joint Strategic Vision for the Asia-Pacific and Indian Ocean Region', (The White House Office of the Press Secretary, January, 25, 2015), https://obamawhitehouse.archives.gov/the-press-office/2015/01/25/us-india-joint-strategic-vision-asia-pacific-and-indian-ocean-region (Last accessed December 10, 2016).

Carter, A. 'Remarks by Secretary Carter and Defense Minister Parrikar in New Delhi, India', U.S. Department of Defence, (December 8, 2016), available at https://www.defense.gov/News/Transcripts/Transcript-View/Article/1025104/remarks-by-secretary-carter-and-defense-minister-parrikar-in-new-delhi-india.

Catignani, S. 'Getting COIN' at the Tactical Level in Afghanistan: Reassessing Counter-Insurgency Adaptation in the British Army', *Journal of Strategic Studies, Vol. 3, no. 4*, (2011).

Cavanaugh, M. L. 'The Enemy-informed after Action Review', The Modern War Institute, (January 27, 2016), available at http://mwi.usma.edu/1391-2/ (Last accessed December 20, 2016).

Center for Strategic and International Studies, 'American Military Culture in the Twenty-First Century', *A Report of the CSIS International Security Program*, (Washington D.C.: The CSIS Press, 2000), pp. 1–148.

Chadwick, L. 'Military trainees at defense universities later committed serious human rights abuses', *National Security*, January 17, 2017), available at https://www.publicintegrity.org/2017/01/17/20591/military-trainees-defense-universities-later-committed-serious-human-rights-abuses (Last accessed January 26, 2017).

Cheney, D. *Defense Strategy for the 1990's: The Regional Defence Strategy*, U.S. Department of Defence, (1993), available at http://nsarchive.gwu.edu/nukevault/ebb245/doc15.pdf (Last accessed December 10, 2016).

Chaudhuri, R. & Farrell, T. 'Campaign disconnect: operational progress and strategic obstacles in Afghanistan, 2009–2011', *International Affairs, Vol. 87, no. 2*, (2011), pp. 271–296.

Chairman of the Joint Chiefs of Staff, *National Military Strategy of the United States of America: Shape, Respond, Prepare Now: A Military Strategy for a New Era*, (Washington, D.C., 1997).

Challans, T. 'Emerging Doctrine and the Ethics of Warfare', *School of Advanced Military Studies (SAMS)*, Joint Services Conference on Professional Ethics (JSCOPE): Emerging Doctrine and the Ethics of Warfare, (Fort Leavenworth, Kansas, 2006).

Chaturvedy, R. R. 'China's Strategic Access to Gwadar Port: Pivotal Position in Belt and Road', *RSIS Commentary, No. 5* (January 5, 2017).

Cheney, D. *Defense Strategy for the 1990's: The Regional Defence Strategy*, U.S. Department of Defence, (1993), available at http://nsarchive.gwu.edu/nukevault/ebb245/doc15.pdf (Last accessed December 10, 2016).

Cheyre, J. E. 'Defence Diplomacy', In Andrew Cooper, Jorge Heine, and Ramesh Thakur (eds.), *The Oxford Handbook of Modern Diplomacy*, (Oxford: Oxford University Press, 2013).

Chye, T. S. 'Strengths and Weaknesses of the ADMM and ADMM-Plus', *The Future of the ADMM/ADMM-Plus and Defence Diplomacy in the Asia Pacific*, Rajaratnam School of International Studies, (February 2016).

Clancy, J. & Crossett, C. 'Measuring Effectiveness in Irregular Warfare', *Parameters*, (Summer 2007), pp. 88–100.

Clapper, J. R. *Statement for the Record Worldwide Threat Assessment of the US Intelligence Community Senate Armed Services Committee*, (Office of the Director of National Intelligence, February 9, 2016), pp. 1–30.

Clark, W. 'An Army of One?' *Washington Monthly*, (September, 2002), available at http://www.unz.org/Pub/WashingtonMonthly-2002sep-00019?View=PDF (Last access December 10, 2016).

Clinton, H. Secretary of State, Testimony before the Senate Appropriations Committee, (Washington, D.C., April 30, 2009), available at http://www.state.gov/secretary/rm/2009a/04/122463.htm (Last accessed December 10, 2016).

Clinton, Hillary. 'Remarks at the Launch of the Asia Society's Series of Richard C. Holbrooke Memorial Addresses', The Asia Society, New York, (U.S. Dept. State, February 18, 2011) available at https://20092017.state.gov/secretary/20092013clinton/rm/2011/02/156815.htm (Last accessed December 2, 2017).

Clinton, D. 'The Distinction between Diplomacy and Foreign Policy in American International Though and Practice', in Paul Sharp & Geoff Wiseman, *American Diplomacy*, (Leiden: Brill, 2011).

Clohesy, A. M. Politics of Empathy, (London: Taylor and Francis, 2013), pp. 1–160.

Codevilla, A. 'Tools of Statecraft: Diplomacy and War', *Foreign Policy Research Institute, Vol. 13, no. 1*, (2008).

Cohen. W. S. Annual Report to the President and the Congress, Secretary of Defense, Department of Defence, Chapter 4, (Washington D.C: U.S. Government Printing Office,1997), available at http://archive.defense.gov/Transcripts/Transcript.aspx?TranscriptID=674.

Codevilla, A. 'Tools of Statecraft: Diplomacy and War', *Foreign Policy Research Institute, Vol. 13, No. 1*, (2008).

Cohen, R. *Theatre of power: the art of diplomatic signalling*, (New York: Longman, 1987).

Cohen, R. 'Putting Diplomatic Studies on the Map', *Diplomatic Studies Programme Newsletter*, (May 4, 1998).

Collier, P. *The Bottom Billion: Why the poorest countries are failing and what can be done about it*, (New York: Oxford University Press).

Collingburn, A. 'Aussie diggers: building partner capacity', *The Strategist*, Australian Strategic Policy Institute, (September 12, 2016), available at https://www.aspistrategist.org.au/aussie-diggers-building-partner-capacity/ (Last accessed December 12, 2016).

Combs II, R. (Lt. Col). *Assessing Strategic Effectiveness in the War on Terrorism*, (Carlisle Barracks, PA: U.S. Army War College, 2006).

Commonwealth of Australia, *Australia in the Asian Century*, (Canberra: Department of Prime Minister& Cabinet, 2012).

Commonwealth of Australia, *Defence White Paper*, (Canberra: Department of Defence, 2013).

Congressional Budget Office, *Options for Reducing the Deficit: 2014 to 2023*, (November, 2013).

Conley-Tyler, M., Abbasov, A., Gibson, N., Teo, F. 'Domestic Public Diplomacy: Discussion Paper-International Experience', *Australian Institute of International Affairs*, (2012).

Conliffe, F. 'Military Development and Diplomacy in Afghanistan', *Canadian Military Journal, Vol. 9, no. 4*, (2009).

Constantinou, C. & James Der Derian, *Sustainable diplomacies*, (Basingstoke: Palgrave Macmillan, 2010).

Constantinou, C. M. & S. O. Opondo. "Engaging the 'ungoverned': The merging of diplomacy, defence and development', *Cooperation and Conflict*, (2015).

Cooley, A. 'U.S. Bases and Democratization in Central Asia', *Orbis, Vol. 52, no. 1*, (2008).

Cooper, H. 'Trumps Team's Queries about Africa Point to Skepticism about Aid', *The New Yok Times*, (January 13, 2017) available at https://www.nytimes.com/2017/01/13/world/africa/africa-donald-trump.html?_r=0 (Last accessed January 20, 2017).

Cottey, A. & A. Forster, 'Strategic Engagement: Defence Diplomacy as a Means of Conflict Prevention', *The Adelphi Papers, Vol. 44*, pp. 15–30.

Cordesman, A. 'The Missing Metrics of "Progress" in Afghanistan (and Pakistan)', *Center for Strategic & International Studies*, Paper Presented at the Conference on "Peacebuilding in Afghanistan: Taking Stock and Looking Ahead" Ottawa, Canada, (December 10–11, 2007).

Cordesman, A., Ashley Hess, & Nicholas Yarosh, *Chinese Military Modernization and Force Development–A Western Perspective*, (Washington D.C.: Center for International and Strategic Studies, 2012).

Country Reports on Terrorism 2014, Bureau of Counterterrorism, (Washington D.C: The United States Department of State, June 2015).

Cowan, G. & A. Arsenault, 'Moving from Monologue to Dialogue to Collaboration: The Three Layers of Public Diplomacy', *The ANNALS of the American Academy of Political and Social Science, Vol. 616*, no. 1, pp. 10–30.

Shepard Cowper-Coles, *Cables form Kabul*, (London: Harper Press, 2011), pp. 1–323.

Cragin, K. & Scott Gerwehr, *Dissuading Terror: Strategic Culture and the Struggle Against Terrorism*, (Santa Monica, CA: RAND Corporation, 2005), pp. 1–136.

Crenshaw, M. 'Coercive Diplomacy and the Response to Terrorism', in Robert Art & Patrick Cronin (eds.), *The United States and Coercive Diplomacy*, (Washington, D.C.: United States Institute of Peace Press, 2003), pp. 305–357.

Criekemans, D. 'Exploring the Relationship between Geopolitics, Foreign Policy, and Diplomacy. In The Present and Future of Diplomacy and Diplomatic Studies', *International Studies Review, Vol. 13*, (2011), pp. 713–716.

Crocker, R. 'Diplomacy in a Non-Polar World', *The Yale Journal of International Affairs, Vol. 8, Iss. 2*, (Summer 2013), pp. 100–111.

'CSDP Capabilities', European Union External Action, (August 2016), available at https://eeas.europa.eu/headquarters/headquarters-homepage/5393/csdp-capabilities_en.

Dean, P. 'Australia, Maritime Strategy and Regional Military Diplomacy Australia, Maritime Strategy and Regional Military Diplomacy', In Justin Jones (ed.), *A Maritime School of Strategic Thought for Australia: Perspectives*, Sea Power Series No, 1, (Canberra, 2013).

Defence Security Cooperation Agency, 'International Military Education & Training', available at https://web.archive.org/web/20130530024557/http://www.dsca.osd.mil/home/international_military_education_training.htm.

Defence Security Cooperation Agency, *Vision 2020*, (U.S. Department of Defence, October 2014), pp. 1–26.

Department of the Army, *Field Manual 3–07, Stability Operations*, (October 2008).

Department of the Army, *Army Special Operations Forces Unconventional Warfare, FM 3-05.130*, (Washington D.C., Army Doctrine Publication, September 2008).

Department of the Army, 'Foreward', *ADP 3-05 Special Operations*, (Washington D.C.: Army Doctrine Publication, 2012).

Der Derian, J. *On Diplomacy: Mediating Estrangement*, (Oxford: Blackwell Publishing, 1987).

Der Derian, J. *Antidiplomacy: Spies, Speed, Terror, and War*, (Oxford: Basil Blackwell Press: 1992).

Djalal, D. P. 'An Independent, Active And Creative Foreign Policy For Indonesia', *Strategic Review: The Indonesian Journal of Leadership, Policy and World Affairs' Vol. 2, no. 1*, (January-March, 2012), pp. 40–46.

Dobbins, J., Seth G. Jones, Keith Crane, Andrew Rathmell, Brett Steele, Richard Teltschik, & Anga Timilsina, *The UN's Role in Nation-Building: From the Congo to Iraq*, (Santa Monica, CA, RAND Corporation, 2005).

Donnelly, T. 'Rebuilding America's Defences: Strategy, Forces and Resources for a New Century', *A Report of The Project for the New American Century*, (Washington D.C.: PNAC, 2000).

Dorman, A. M. 'The United Kingdom: Innocence Lost? in Gale A. Mattox & Stephen M. Grenier, (eds.), *Coalition Challenges in Afghanistan: The politic of Alliance*, (Stanford, CA: Stanford University Press, 2015), pp. 108–122.

Dorman, A. & Matthew Uttley, 'Defence and Intelligence Diplomacy', in Alison Holmes & Simon Rofe (eds.), *Global Diplomacy: Theories, Types, and Models*, (Boulder CO: Western Press, 2016).

Dos Santos Lersch, D. & Josiane Simao Satri, 'The Establishment of Foreign Military Bases and the International Distribution of Power', *Disarmament and International Security Committee. Vol. 2*, (2014).

Douglas, F. 'Waging the inchoate war: Defining, fighting, and second-guessing the 'Long War', *Journal of Strategic Studies, Vol. 30, no. 3*, (2007), pp. 391–420.

Drew, D. M. & Donald M. Snow, Making Twenty-First-Century Strategy, (Maxwell AFB: Airforce University Press, 2006), pp. 1–288.

du Plessis, A. 'Defence diplomacy: conceptual and practical dimensions with specific reference to South Africa', *Strategic Review for Southern Africa*, vol. 30, no. 2, (2008), pp. 87–119.

Dunford, J, (Gen.). 'Meeting Today's Global Security Challenges', *Center for Strategic & International Studies*, (29th March, 2016).

Edwards, L. C. 'Foreword', in *Armed Diplomacy: Two Centuries of American Campaigning*, U.S. Fort Leavenworth, Kansas: Army Training & Doctrine Command, 2003).

Emmers, R. 'The Five Power Defence Arrangements and Defense Diplomacy in Southeast Asia', *Asian Security, Vol. 8, no. 3*, (2012), pp. 271–286.

EPSC Strategic Center, 'In Defence of Europe Defence Integration as a Response to Europe's Strategic Moment', *EPSC Strategic Notes, Issue. 4*, (June 15, 2015).

Epstein, S. B. & Lynn M. Williams, 'Overseas Contingency Operations Funding: Background & Status', *CRS Report for Congress R44519*, (Washington D.C.: Congressional Research Service, June 13, 2016).

Erickson, P., Mushin Hassan, Leigh Ann Killian, Gordon LaForge, Sarah Levit-Shore, Lauren Rhode, & Kenneth Sholes, *Lessons from the Civilian Surge in Afghanistan, 2006–2014*, (New York: Woodrow Wilson School of Public and International Affairs, 2016), pp. 1–120.

Eronen, O. 'PRT Models in Afghanistan: Approaches to Civil-Military Integration', *Civilian Crisis Management Studies, Vol. 1, no. 5*, (CMC Finland; 2008).

EU Police Mission in Afghanistan comes to a successful close after nine years of progress', European Union External Action, December 14, 2016), available at https://eeas.europa.eu/headquarters/headquarters-homepage/17259/eu-police-mission-afghanistan-comes-successful-close-after-nine-years-progress_en.

Europe Needs a Military Schengen', European Defence Agency, Issue 12, (January 2017), available at https://www.eda.europa.eu/webzine/issue12 (Last accessed February 2, 2017).

Evans, G., Australia's Regional Security, Ministerial Statement by Senator the Hon. Gareth Evans, QC, Minister for Foreign Affairs and Trade, Canberra, (December 1989).

Fair, C. C. *The Counterterror Coalitions: Cooperation with Pakistan and India*, (Santa Monica, CA: RAND Corporation, 2004).

Farrell, T. 'The dynamics of British military transformation', *International Affairs, Vol. 8, no. 4*, (2008), pp. 777–807.

Farrell, T. & Gordon, S. 'COIN MACHINE', *The RUSI Journal, Vol. 15, no. 3*, (2009).

Farrell, T. 'Improving in War: Military Adaptation and the British in Helmand Province, Afghanistan, 2006–2009', *Journal of Strategic Studies, Vol. 3, no. 4*, (2010), pp. 567–594.

Farrell, T. & Rynning, S. 'NATO's Transformation Gaps: Transatlantic Differences and the War in Afghanistan', *Journal of Strategic Studies, Vol. 33, no. 5*, (2010).

Feickert, 'U.S. Military Operations in the Global War on Terrorism: Afghanistan, Africa, the Philippines, and Columbia', (Congressional Research Service, August 26, 2005).

Feith, D. 'DoD News: Special Briefing on the Russian Visit', U.S. Department of Defence, (January 16, 2002) available at http://fas.org/news/usa/2002/160102a.htm.

Felbab-Brown, V. 'Afghanistan's terrorism resurgence: Al-Qaida, ISIS, and beyond', Testimony Transcript Subcommittee on Terrorism, Non-proliferation, & Trade of the House Foreign Affairs Committee, *Brookings*, (April 27, 2017), available at https://www.brookings.edu/testimonies/afghanistans-terrorism-resurgence-al-qaida-isis-and-beyond/ (Last accessed April 28, 2017).

Fetic, S. 'Fields of Classic Diplomacy with which Defence Diplomacy Interacts Horizontally: Preventative Diplomacy and Coercive Diplomacy', *Military Art and Science*, Vol. 1, no. 73, (2014).

Finney, N. 'A Culture of Inclusion: Defence Diplomacy and Development as a Modern American Policy', *Small Wars Journal*, (September 26, 2010).

Fishstein, P. & Wilder, A. *Winning Hearts and Minds? Examining the Relationship Between Aid and Security in Afghanistan*, (Medford, MA: Feinstein International Centre, Tufts University, 2012).

Fitzsimmons, M. 'Hard Hearts and Open Minds? Governance, Identity and the Intellectual Foundations of Counterinsurgency Strategy', *Journal of Strategic Studies, Vol. 3, no. 3*, (2008).

Fleming, B. 'Farwell to the GWOT: What we learned from the Global War on Terror', *Canadian Defence & Foreign Affairs Institute*, (September 2011).

Floyd, N. 'Dropping the Autopilot: Improving Australia's Defence Diplomacy', *Policy Brief, Lowy Institute for International Policy, Vol. 20*, (2010).

Foley, F. 'Why inter-agency operations break down: US counterterrorism in comparative perspective', *European Journal of International Security, Vol. 1, no. 2*, (2016).

Foley, R. T., Griffin, S. & McCartney, H. 'Transformation in Contact: Learning the Lessons of Modern War', *International Affairs, Vol. 8, no. 2*, (2011), pp. 253–270.

Ford, M. 'Influence without power? Reframing British concepts of military intervention after 10 years of counterinsurgency', *Small Wars & Insurgencies*, Vol. 25, no. 3, (2014).

Ford, L. 'Cross-Strait Series: The Rise of Intra-Asian Defense Cooperation', Panel Discussion at The Atlantic Council, (March 7 2017), available at https://youtu.be/lOHuO2_n3QE.

'Foreward', *Defence Diplomacy Plan*, Defence Ministerio De Defensa Espana, (2012).

Franke, V. C. & Dorff, R. H. *Conflict Management and "Whole of Government": Useful Tools for U.S. National Security Strategy?* (Carlisle PA, U.S. Army War College, 2012).

Freeman, C. *The Diplomats Dictionary*, (Washington D.C.: National Defence University Press, 1994), pp. 1–603.

Freeman, C. 'The Incapacitation of US Statecraft and Diplomacy', in Paul Sharp & Geoff Wiseman, (eds.), *American Diplomacy*, (The Hague: Brill, 2012).

Freeman, C. 'Too Quick to Draw: Militarism and the Malpractice of Diplomacy in America', Remarks to the Academy of Philosophy and Letters, (2015).

Frühling, S. 'The 2013 Defence White Paper: Strategic Guidance Without Strategy', *Security Challenges, Vol. 9, no. 2,* (2013).

Frum, D. 'Trump will Inherit the Biggest NATO Build-up in Europe Since the Cold War', *Defence One*, (January 10 2017) available at http://www.defenseone.com/ideas/2017/01/trump-will-inherit-biggest-nato-buildup-europe-cold-war/134465/?oref=defenseone_today_nl (Last accessed January 15, 2017).

Galster, S. 'Afghanistan: The Making of U.S. Policy, 1973–1990', *National Security Archive*, (October 9 2001).

Garamone, J. 'Votel Pledges Support for Special Operations Forces', *DOD News*, (July 10, 2014), available at https://fas.org/sgp/crs/row/RL30588.pdf (Last accessed December 12, 2016).

Gaston, E. 'The Leahy Law and Human Rights Accountability in Afghanistan: Too little, too late or a model for the future?', *Afghanistan Analysts Network*, (March 5, 2017) available at https://www.afghanistan-analysts.org/the-leahy-law-and-human-rights-accountability-in-afghanistan-too-little-too-late-or-a-model-for-the-future/.

Gates, R. 'How Others Defense Themselves', *Foreign Affairs, Vol. 89, no. 3,* (May/June 2010), pp. 2–6, available at https://www.foreignaffairs.com/articles/2010-05-01/helping-others-defend-themselves (Last accessed December 10, 2016).

George, A. & Simons, W. E. *The Limits of Coercive Diplomacy*, (Boulder CA: Westview Press, 1994).

Gindarsah, L. 'Strategic hedging in Indonesia's defense diplomacy', *Defense & Security Analysis, Vol. 32, no. 4,* (2016), pp. 336–353, DOI: 10.1080/14751798.2016.1233695.

Giustozzi, A. 'Auxiliary Force or National Army? Afghanistan's 'ANA' and the Counter-Insurgency Effort, 2002–2006', Small Wars & Insurgencies, Vol. 1, no. 1, (2007), pp. 45–67.

GPRA Modernization Act of 2010, (Update to the Government Performance and Results Act of 1993, P.L. 103–62, 107 Stat. 285), (January 5, 2010), available at https://www.gpo.gov/fdsys/pkg/BILLS-111hr2142enr/pdf/BILLS-111hr2142enr.pdf (Last accessed December, 2015).

Goldberg, J. 'The Obama Doctrine', *The Atlantic*, (April, 2016), available at http://www.theatlantic.com/magazine/archive/2016/04/the-obama-doctrine/471525/ (Last accessed December 2, 2016).

Goodman, M. 'The Militarization of U.S. Foreign Policy', *Policy Brief, Vol. 9, no. 1*, (Silver City, NM & Washington, DC: Foreign Policy in Focus, February 2004).

Gompert, D., Richard Kugler & Michael Libicki, *Mind the Gap: Promoting a Transatlantic Revolution in Military Affairs*, (Washington D.C.: National Defence University Press, 1999), pp. 1–99.

Gompert, D. C., Hans Binnendijk & Bonny Lin, *Blinders, Blunders, and Wars: What America and China Can Learn?* (Santa Monica, CA: RAND Corporation, 2014).

Goepner, E.W. 'Measuring the Effectiveness of America's War on Terror', *Parameters, Vol. 46*, no. 1, (Spring, 2016), pp. 107–120.

Green, D. R. The Road to Mosul: Reports from the field. *The Washington Institute*, 22 September 2016. https://www.youtube.com/watch?v=XBd-69FgrzI (Last accessed December 2, 2016).

Grenier, S. M. 'United States: Examining Americas Longest War', in Gale A. Mattox & Stephen M. Grenier (eds.), Coalition Challenges in Afghanistan: The Politics of Alliance, (Stanford, CA: Stanford University Press, 2015).

Grimmett, R. 'Instances of Use of United States Armed Forces Abroad, 1798–2006', CRS Report for Congress, (Washington D.C.: Congressional Research Service, January 8, 2007), pp. 1–42.

Grossman, M. 'Seven Cities and Two Years: The Diplomatic Campaign in Afghanistan and Pakistan', *Yale Journal of International Affairs, Vol. 8, Iss. 2*, (Summer 2013), pp. 65–75.

Grossman, M. 'A Diplomacy for the 21st century: back to the future?', *The Foreign Service Journal*, (September 2014), available at http://www.afsa.org/diplomacy-21st-century-back-future.

Haacke, J. 'The concept of flexible engagement and the practice of enhanced interaction: intramural challenges to the 'ASEAN way', *The Pacific Review, Vol. 12, no. 4*, (1999), pp. 581–611.

Hallams, E. 'The Transatlantic Alliance renewed: the United States and NATO since 9/11', *Journal of Transatlantic Studies, Vol. 7, no. 1*, (2009).

Hallams, E. & Benjamin Schreer, 'Towards a 'post-American' alliance? NATO burden-sharing after Libya', *International Affairs, Vol. 88, no. 2*, (2012).

Hamilton & Richard Langhorne, *The Practice of Diplomacy: Its Evolution, Theory and Administration*, (Hoboken: Taylor & Francis, 2010).

Hammer, M. 'Domestic Diplomacy: Making US Foreign Policy Less Foreign', *The Ambassadors Review, Spring*, (2013).

Handel, M. *Masters Of War: Classical Strategic Thought*, (London Frank Cass Publishers, 2005).

Hanlon, Q. & Richard Shultz Jr. *Prioritizing Security Sector Reform, a New U.S. Approach*, (United States Institute of Peace, 2016), pp. 1–350.

Harkavy, R. *Thinking About Basing*, (U.S., Naval War College: Bilbliogov, 2012).

Harlow G. D. & George C. Maerz (eds.), Measures Short of War: the George F. Keenan Lectures at the National War College 1946–47, (Washington D.C.: National Defence University Press, 1991).

Hanauer, L. & Stephanie Pezard, *Security Cooperation amidst Political Uncertainty: An Agenda for Future Research*, (Santa Monica CA: RAND Corporation, 2014), pp. 1–32.

'Heart of Asia', Ministerial Conference, 14 June 2012', available at http://www.unodc.org/afghanistan/en/Events/heart-of-asia-ministerial-conference.html (Last accessed August 10, 2016).

Heinl, C. 'Cybersecurity: Fostering transparency, trust & predictability among militaries in Asia', *focus: Peace & Security Dialogue, Issue no. 2*, (Malaysia: The Institute of Strategic & International Studies, 2016), pp. 22–23.

Henrikson, A. 'What can public diplomacy achieve', *Discussion Papers In Diplomacy*, Netherlands Institute of International Relations 'Clingendael' (2013).

Henrikson, A. 'United States Contemporary Diplomacy: Implementing a Foreign Policy of Engagement', in Pauline Kerr & Geoff Wiseman (eds.), *Diplomacy in a globalizing world: Theories and practices*, (New York: Oxford University Press, 2013).

Herbert, S. 'State legitimacy in Afghanistan and the role of the international community', *Helpdesk Research Report 1068*, GSDRC Applied Knowledge Services, (Birmingham: UK, University of Birmingham, 2014).

Hills, A. 'Defence diplomacy and security sector reform', *Contemporary Security Policy, Vol. 21, no. 1*, (2000).

Hocking, B. 'The Ministry of Foreign Affairs and the National Diplomatic System', in Pauline Kerr & Geoff Wiseman (eds.), *Diplomacy in a globalizing world: Theories and practices*, (New York: Oxford University Press, 2013).

Hoffman, F. G. 'Neo-Classical Counterinsurgency', *Parameters, Summer Issue*, (2007), pp. 1–17.

Holbrooke, H. *To end a war*, (New York: Modern Library, 1999).

Holmes, J. R. "A Striking Thing': Leadership, Strategic Communications, and Roosevelt's Great White Fleet', *Naval War College Review, Vol. 61, No. 1*, (Winter 2008), pp. 51–67.

Hoobler, G. 'Management of issues and relationships during international conflict management: or how (not?) to end a war', *The International Journal of Conflict Management, Vol. 14, no. ¾*, (2003).

Hooker, R. & Joseph Collins, *Lessons Encountered: Lessons from the Long War*, (Washington D.C., National Defense University Press, 2015).

Horne, C., Stephen Shellman & Brandon Stewart, *Nickel and DIMEing the Adversary: Does it work or PMESII them off?* ISA's 49th Annual Convention, Bridging Multiple Divides, Hilton San Francisco, (San Francisco, CA: International Studies Institute, 2008), pp. 1–55.

Homayun Qayoumi, M. 'Afghanistan During the Transformation Decade: Implications for the New U.S. Administration', Center for Strategic & International Studies, (March 3, 2017), approx. 6:00, available at https://www.youtube.com/watch?v=Hld3tsqEo-I.

Howlett, D. *The Future of Strategic Culture*, (Defense Threat Reduction Agency, October 31, 2006).

Huijgh, E. (2011). Changing Tunes for Public Diplomacy: Exploring the Domestic Dimension. Domestic Dimensions. Clingendael.

Hunt, J. P. 'The 800-Pound Gorilla and Stability Operations', *Small Wars Journal*, (June 30, 2010), available at http://www.dtic.mil/dtic/tr/fulltext/u2/a523630.pdf (Last accessed December 2, 2016).

Huntington, S. *The Soldier and the State: The Theory and Politics in Civil Military Relations*, (Cambridge, MA: Belnap Press of Harvard University Press, 1957), pp. 1–278.

Inboden, W. 'The Role of a Strong National Defence', *2016 Index of U.S. Military Strength*, (The Heritage Foundation, 2016).

Independent Panel on Canada's Future Role in Afghanistan, (January 2008), pp. 1–94.

Indonesian Defense White Article, (Jakarta: Ministry of Defence, 2002).

Indonesian Defense White Article, (Jakarta: Ministry of Defense, 2008).

International Institute for Strategic Studies (IISS), 'New Challenges to Defence Diplomacy', *Strategic Survey*, Vol. 100, (1999).

International Institute for Strategic Studies, *The Military Balance 2015*, (London: Routledge, 2015).

International Monetary Fund, *IMF Country Report No. 11/330*, (Washington D.C.: International Monetary Fund Publication Services, November 2011), pp. 1–144.

ISAF Commander's Counterinsurgency Guidance, Headquarters International Security Assistance Force, (2009), pp. 1–7.

Jackson, R. 'Untangling the Web: A Blueprint for Reforming American Security Sector Assistance', Open Society Foundations, (January 2017).

Jaishankar, D. 'India's Military Diplomacy', *Defence Primer: India at 75*, Observer Research Foundation, (2016).

James, A. (1993). 'Diplomacy.' *Review of International Studies, Vol. 19*, no. 1, pp. 91–100.

Jentleson, B. Coercive Diplomacy: Scope and Limits in the Contemporary World, *Policy Analysis Brief*, (The Stanley Foundation, December 2006).

Jervis, R. 'U.S. grand strategy: Mission impossible', *Naval War College Review, Vol. 51, no. 3*, (1998).

Joint Declaration of the ASEAN Defence Ministers on Promoting Defence Cooperation for a Dynamic ASEAN Community, (Vientiane, Laos, May 25, 2016).

Joint Publication 1, *Doctrine for the Armed Forces of the United States*, (March 25, 2013).

Joint Chiefs of Staff, *Military Operations Other Than War, J-7 Operational Plans & Interoperability Directorate*, Joint Doctrine Joint Force Employment Briefing Modules, (U.S. DoD, June 1995).

Joint Chiefs of Staff, *JP5–0 Joint Operation Planning*, (August 11, 2011).

Joint Chiefs of Staff, *FM 3-24 Counterinsurgency*, (2014).

Johnston, D. *Joint Press Conference, Senator the Hon David Johnston, Minister for Defence & the Hon Julie Bishop MP*, Minister for Foreign Affairs, (National Press Club, Tokyo, June 12 2014), available at http://foreignminister.gov.au/transcripts/Pages/2014/jb_tr_140612c.aspx?w=tb1CaGpkPX%2FlSoK%2Bg9ZKEg%3D%3D.

Jönsson, C. & K. Aggestam, 'Trends in Diplomatic Signalling', in J. Melissen, (ed.), *Innovation in Diplomatic Practice*, (New York: Palgrave, 1999).

Jönsson, C. & Hall, M. 'Communication: An Essential Aspect of Diplomacy', *International Studies Perspective, Vol. 4*, (2003).

Jönsson, C. & Hall, M. *The Essence of Diplomacy*, (New York: Palgrave Macmillan, 2005).

Joshi, S. 'Introduction', *Whitehall Papers Vol. 85, no. 1*, (Royal United Services Institute, 2015), pp. 1–15.

Kagan, D., Gary Schmitt & Thomas Donnelly, 'Rebuilding America's Defences: Strategy, Forces and Resources for a New Century', *A Report of The Project for the New American Century*, (Washington D.C., Project For The New American Century, 2000).

Kapstein, E. & Kathuria, K. 'Economic Assistance in Conflict Zones: Lessons from Afghanistan', *CGD Policy Paper 013*, (Washington D.C: Center for Global Development, 2012).

Kattelman, K. 'Party Structure, Information, and Coalition Durability: The Relevance of NATO in the Global War on Terror', *Studies in Conflict & Terrorism*, (2016).

Katzman, K. 'Afghanistan: Post-Taliban Governance, Security and U.S. Policy', *CRS Report for Congress RL30588*, (Washington D.C.: Congressional Research Service, November 8, 2016).

Kay, S. & Khan, S. 'NATO and Counter-insurgency: Strategic Liability or Tactical Asset?' *Contemporary Security Policy, Vol. 2, no. 1*, (2007), pp. 163–181.

Keenan, G. 'Part 5: Practical Deductions from Standpoint of US Policy', *The Long Telegram*, (February 22, 1946), available at http://nsarchive.gwu.edu/coldwar/documents/episode-1/kennan.htm.

Kelly, T. 'U.S. Foreign Policy and Diplomacy', Remarks at the Asia Pacific Center for Security Studies, (Fort DeRussy, Waikiki, April 17 2014), available at https://www.state.gov/t/pm/rls/rm/2014/225003.htm (Last accessed December 10, 2016).

Kelton, M. & Jackson, A. P. 'Australia: Terrorism, Regional Security, and the U.S. Alliance', in Gale a. Mattox & Stephen M. Grenier (eds.), Coalition Challenges in Afghanistan: The Politics of Alliance, (Stanford, CA: Stanford University Press, 2015), pp. 225–241.

Kerr, P. & Geoffrey Wiseman (eds.), *Diplomacy in a globalizing world: Theories and practices*, (New York: Oxford University Press, 2013), pp. 1–406.

Kerry, J. 'Statement of Senator John F. Kerry, Nominee for Secretary of State', Conformation Before the Senate Committee on Foreign Relations, (Washington, DC January 24, 2013) available at https://www.state.gov/secretary/remarks/2013/01/203455.htm (Last accessed December 12, 2016).

Kilcullen, D. 'Australian Statecraft: The Challenge of Aligning Policy with Strategic Culture', *Security Challenges, Vol. 3, no. 4*, (2007), pp. 45–65.

Killcullen, D. *Blood Year. Islamic State & the Failures of the War on Terror*, (London: Hurst & Co, 2016).

Kleiner, J. *Diplomatic practice between tradition and innovation*, (Hackensack, NJ: World Scientific, 2010).

King, A. 'The Internationalization of the Armed Forces', in J. Soeters, P. van Fenema and R. Beeres (eds.), *Managing Military Organizations: Theory and Practice*, (New York: Routledge, 2011).

King, A. *The Transformation of Europe's Armed Forces, From the Rhine to Afghanistan*, (New York: Cambridge University Press, 2011).

Knabbs-Kellar, G. & Wirajuda, 'Indonesia: Diplomacy as nation building', The Lowy Interpreter, (May 5, 2016) available at https://www.lowyinstitute.org/the-interpreter/indonesia-diplomacy-nation-building.

Koch, M. T. & Sullivan, P. 'Should I Stay or Should I Go Now? Partisanship, Approval, and the Duration of Major Power Democratic Military Interventions', *The Journal of Politics, Vol. 72, no. 3*, (2010).

Kohn, R. H. 'The Erosion of Civilian Control of the Military in the United States Today', *Naval War College Review LV: No. 3*, (2002), pp. 9–59.

Koshy, N. Under the Empire: India's New Foreign Policy, (New Delhi: LeftWord Books, 2006).

Kousary, H. 'The Afghan Peace Talks, QCG and China-Pakistan Role', The Diplomat, (July 8, 2016), available at http://thediplomat.com/2016/07/the-afghan-peace-talks-qcg-and-china-pakistan-role/ (Last accessed January 2, 2017).

Krepon, M. & Jenny S. Drezin, 'Declaratory Diplomacy and Confidence Building', *Report 27*, (Washington D.C.: The Henry L. Stimson Center, 1999).

Kronstadt, K. A. 'Pakistan-U.S. Relations: Issues for the 114th Congress', *CRS Report for Congress R44034*, (Washington D.C.: Congressional Research Service, May 14, 2015), pp. 1–21.

Kreps, S. 'Elite Consensus as a Determinant of Alliance Cohesion: Why Public Opinion Hardly Matters for NATO-led Operations in Afghanistan', *Foreign Policy Analysis, Vol. 6, no. 3*, (2010), pp. 191–215.

Kucera, J. 'Afghanistan Looks to Army Expansion', Jane's Defense Weekly, (October 13, 2004).

Kuwayama, D. 'United States Provincial Reconstruction Teams', *Provincial Reconstruction Teams: Lessons and Recommendations*, (Woodrow Wilson School of Public & International Affairs, January 2008).

L'Estrange, M. 'International Defence Engagement: Potential and Limitations', *Review of Security Challenges, Vol. 9, no. 2*, (2013).

Lachowski, Z. 'Foreign Military Bases in Eurasia', *SIPRI Policy Paper No. 18*, Stockholm International Peace Research Institute, (June 2007).

Langhorne, R. 'Contemporary Diplomacy', *Global Society, Vol. 23, no. 1*, (2009), pp. 97–104.

Larsdotter, K. Regional Support for Afghan Insurgents: Challenges for Counterinsurgency Theory and Doctrine', *The Journal of Strategic Studies, Vol. 37, no. 1*, (2014), pp. 135–162.

Lawson, M. L. 'Does Foreign Aid Work? Efforts to Evaluate U.S. Foreign Assistance', *CRS Report for Congress R42827*, (Congressional Research Service, June 23, 2016).

Leahy, P. 'Military diplomacy, Defence Diplomacy: Is the game worth the candle? *The Centre of Gravity Series (paper 17)*, (Canberra: Australian National University, 2014).

Lesser I. O. 'Coalition Dynamics in the War Against Terrorism', *The International Spectator, Vol. 37, no. 2*, (2002).

Levy, J. S. 'Deterrence and Coercive Diplomacy: The Contributions of Alexander George', *Political Psychology, Vol. 29, no. 4*, (2008).

Libby, I. L. *Defense Planning Guide, FY1994–1999*, U.S. Department of Defence, (February 29, 1992), available at http://nsarchive.gwu.edu/nukevault/ebb245/doc04.pdf (Last accessed December 10, 2016).

Liddell Hart, B. H. *Strategy*, (2nd ed.), (New York: Frederick A. Praeger, 1967).

Lindley-French, J. 'What America is Stuck With NATO', *Europe's World*, (October 2006), available at http://europesworld.org/2006/10/01/why-america-is-stuck-with-nato/#.WHwPiVN95hE (Last accessed December 18, 2016).

Lindley-French, J. 'Making Canada's Role in NATO More Effective', *Canadian Global Affairs Institute*, (July 2016).

Livingston, I. S. & O'Hanlon, M. Afghanistan Index, Brookings, (October 31, 2016), pp. 1–31.

Lovegrove, S. 'Permanent Secretary of the UK MOD, The UK's Defense Approach: Key Themes for the Year Ahead', *Speech at the Atlantic Council*, (March, 6, 2017) available at http://www.atlanticcouncil.org/events/webcasts?start=10.

Loy, J. L. State, Foreign Operations, and Related Programs Appropriations for 2014, Testimony before the House Appropriations Subcommittee on State-Foreign Operations, (Washington D.C.: U.S. Government Printing Office, March, 2013).

Lubold, G. 'U.S., Pakistan Build Military Ties, One Office at a Time', *Christian Science Monitor*, (May 11, 2009), http://www.csmonitor.com/USA/Military/2009/0511/p21s01-usmi.html/ (Last accessed December 12, 2016).

Lushenko, P. & Hardy, J. 'Panjwai: a tale of two COINs in Afghanistan, Small Wars & Insurgencies, Vol. 27, no. 1, (2016), pp. 106–131.

Mahapatra, C. 'Washington's War & Diplomacy in Afghanistan', *Perspectives-Journal of Defence Studies, Vol. 5, no. 1*, (January 2011).

Maley, W. 'Afghanistan on a knife-edge', *Global Affairs, Vol. 2, no. 1*, (2015).

Mandelbaum, 'Foreign Policy as Social Work', *Foreign Affairs Vol. 75, no. 1*, (January/February 1996), available at https://www.foreignaffairs.com/articles/haiti/1996-01-01/foreign-policy-social-work (Last accesses September 12, 2016).

Manor, I. 'Is NATO Sending Russia Mixed Signals on Social Media', *Exploring Digital Diplomacy, 2016*), available at https://digdipblog.com/ (Last accessed May 11, 2016).

Manwaring, M. 'Defence, Development and Diplomacy (3D): Canadian and U.S. Military Perspectives', *Colloquium Brief*, (U.S. Army War College, Queens University, and the Canadian Land Forces Doctrine and Training System: Strategic Studies Institute, 2006).

Mandelbaum, M. 'Foreign Policy as Social Work', *Foreign Affairs* Vol. 75, no. 1, (January/February 1996), p. 18 available at https://www.foreignaffairs.com/articles/haiti/1996-01-01/foreign-policy-social-work (Last accessed December 10, 2016).

Manson, C. *Status of Force Agreement (SOFA): What is it and how has it been utilized?*, (Washington D.C.: Congressional Research Service, 2012).

Marks, E. 'The State Department: No Longer the Gatekeeper', in Gordon Adams & Shoon Murray (eds.), *The Militarization of US Foreign Policy*, (Washington D.C.: Georgetown University Press, 2014).

Mattingly, G. *Renaissance Diplomacy*, (New York: Dover, 1955).

Mattis, J. *Foreign Policy Research Institute', Defense Showstoppers Conference*, Reserve Officers Association, Washington D.C., (2009).

Mattis, J. Reflections with General James Mattis-Conversations with History, University of California Public Television, (March 20, 2014), available at https://www.youtube.com/watch?v=HOc38ZwEO8s (Last accessed January 4, 2017).

Mattis, J. N. 'Testimony: Hearing to review the budget and readiness of the Department of Defense', U.S. Senate Committee on Appropriations, (Washington D.C., March 22, 2017).

Mattox, G. A. Going Forward: Lessons Learned', in Gale A. Mattox & Stephen M. Grenier (eds.), *Coalition Challenges in Afghanistan: The Politics of Alliance*, (Stanford, CA: Stanford University Press, 2015).

Mattox, G. A. & Grenier, S. M. (eds.), *Coalition Challenges in Afghanistan: The politic of Alliance*, (Stanford, CA: Stanford University Press, 2015), pp. 288–303.

Mazzetti, M. & Eric Schmitt, 'In Secret, Obama Extends U.S. Role in Afghan Combat', *New York Times*, (November 22, 2014), available at https://www.nytimes.com/2014/11/22/us/politics/in-secret-obama-extends-us-role-in-afghan-combat.html (Last accessed December 10, 2016).

McCain, J. 'Opening Statement on the Situation in Afghanistan', Testimony, Senate Armed Services Committee, (February 9, 2017), para. 3, available at http://www.armedservices.senate.gov/imo/media/doc/2917%20Situation%20in%20Afghanistan%20(McCain)2.pdf.

McCain, J. Select Committee On Russia Now A 'Requirement', *For The Record, MSNBC*, (March 23, 2017) available at https://www.youtube.com/watch?v=8ZsIyopdIiE (Last accessed March 23, 2017).

McCormack, T. 'Human security and the separation of security and development', *Conflict, Security & Development, Vol. 11, no. 2*, (2011).

McCready, D. 'Coercive Diplomacy in U.S. Foreign Policy', *Military Review*, (September/October, 2005), p. 84.

McChrystal, S. Commander of NATO International Security Assistance Force and U.S. Forces in Afghanistan, *Commanders Initial Assessment*, (August 30, 2009), available at http://www.washingtonpost.com/wpdyn/content/article/2009/09/21/AR2009092100110_pf.htl (Last accessed December 2, 2016).

McMaster, H. R. 'The Future of War', Center for Strategic & International Studies, (May 4, 2016), approx. 35:30, available at https://www.youtube.com/watch?v=YVzGd2CElRo&t=1s (Last accessed January 3, 2017).

McNerney, M., A. O'Mahony, T. S. Szayna, D. Eaton, C. Baxter, C. P. Clarke, E. Cutrufello, M. McGee, H. Peterson, L. Adrienne Payne & C. Trenkov-Wermuth, *Assessing Security Cooperation as a Preventive Tool*, (Santa Monica, CA: RAND Corporation, 2014).

Mearsheimer, J. *Anarchy and the Struggle for Power' in The Tragedy of Great Power Politics*, (New York: W.W. Norton Company, 2001).

Mekay, E. 'War on Terror Leaves Foreign Aid Largely Intact', *Inter Press Service News Agency*, (2005).

Melissen, J. *Innovation in diplomatic practice*, (New York: St. Martin's Press, 1999).

Michel, C. 'Dispelling Myths About Special Operations Forces', *War on the Rocks*, (March 17 2016), available at http://warontherocks.com/2016/03/dispelling-myths-about-special-operations-forces/ (Last accessed December 10, 2016).

Miller, P. *Armed State Building: Confronting State Failure, 1898–2012*, (London: Cornell University Press, 2013).

Miller, P. 'How Does Jihadism End? Choosing Between Forever War and Nation Building', *War on the Rocks*, (September 11, 2016), available at https://warontherocks.

com/2016/09/how-does-jihadism-end-choosing-between-forever-war-and-nation-building/ (Last accessed December 18, 2016).

Mitzen, J. 'Reading Habermas in Anarchy: Multilateral Diplomacy and Global Public Spheres', American Political Science Review, Vol. 99, no. 3, (August 2005), pp. 401–417.

Moens, A. 'American Diplomacy and German Unification', *Survival, Vol. 33, no. 6*, (November/December 1991), p.p. 531–545.

Moens, A. 'Canada's Defence Policy Renewal: Broad Capabilities in an Allies and Partners Framework, *The Conference of Defence Associations Institute*, (March 2016).

Molan, Jim, 'How much is enough in Afghanistan?', *Australian Army Journal, Vol. 6, no. 2*, (Winter 2009), pp. 15–31.

Jim Molan, 'Afghanistan worth doing, even badly', the interpreter, The Lowy Institute, (August 10, 2009) available at https://www.lowyinstitute.org/the-interpreter/afghanistan-worth-doing-even-badly (Last accesses August 10, 2016).

Molan, Jim, quoted in Nigel Floyd, 'Dropping the Autopilot: Improving Australia's Defence Diplomacy', *Policy Brief*, Lowy Institute for International Policy, Vol. 20, (2010).

Moroney, J., Thaler, D. & Holger, J. Review of Security Cooperation Mechanisms Combatant Commands Utilize to Build Partner Capacity, (RAND Corporation, National Defence Research Institute, 2013).

Moss, T., D. Roodman & D. Standley, 'The Global War on Terror and U.S. Development Assistance: USAID allocation by country, 1998–2005', *Centre for Global Development, Working paper no. 62*, (August 2005).

Munoz, A. *U.S. military information operations in Afghanistan: effectiveness of psychological operations 2001–2010*, National Defense Research Institute, (Santa Monica, CA: RAND Corporation, 2012).

Murray, S. *Reordering diplomatic theory for the twenty-first century—A tripartite approach*, Department of International Relations and Diplomacy, Faculty of Humanities & Social Science, (Gold Coast, Australia: Bond University, 2006).

Murray, S. 'Ambassadors and the Geographic Combatant Commands', EMC Chair Conference Paper, (2011), pp. 1–4.

Muthanna, K. A. 'Military Diplomacy', Perspectives, *Journal of Defence Studies, Vol. 5, no. 1*, (January 2011), pp. 1–15.

Nagl, J. *Learning to Eat Soup with a Knife: Counterinsurgency lessons from Malaya and Vietnam*, (Chicago: University of Chicago Press, 2002).

National Archives of Australia, NAA: M4251, 44, *Personal papers of McMahon, General correspondence Prime Minister Gorton*, (Jan –March, 1971), pp. 1–184.

National Defense University, *JFSC Pub 1, Joint Staff Officers Guide*, (Washington, D.C.: U.S. Government Printing Office, 2000).

National Security Presidential Directive 44, (Washington D.C.: The White House, December 2005), available at https://fas.org/irp/offdocs/nspd/nspd-44.html.

NATO, *Multiple Futures Project: Navigating Towards 2030*, (2009), pp. 1–74.

NATO, Allied *Joint Doctrine for Counterinsurgency (COIN): AJP-3.4.4*, (2011).

Nau, H. R. Conservative Internationalism: Armed Diplomacy Under Jefferson, Polk, Truman, and Reagan, (Princeton, NJ: Princeton University Press, 2013), pp. 1–321.

Newnham, R. 'Coalition of the Bribed and Bullied? U.S. Economic Linkage and the Iraq War Coalition', *International Studies Perspectives, Vol. 9, no. 2*, (2008).

Nichiporuk, B. 'U.S. Military Opportunities: Information-Warfare Concepts of Operation', Khalilzad, Z., Shapiro, J., (eds.), *Strategic appraisal United States air and space power in the 21st century*, (Santa Monica, CA: RAND, Project Air Force, 2002).

Nicolson, H. *The evolution of diplomatic method: being the Chichele lectures delivered at the University of Oxford in November 1953*, (London: Constable, 1955).

Nicholson, J. W. *Statement For The Record By General John W. Nicholson Commander U.S. Forces—Afghanistan Before The Senate Armed Services Committee On The Situation In Afghanistan* , (Washington D.C., February 9, 2017), available at http://www.armed-services.senate.gov/imo/media/doc/Nicholson_02-09-17.pdf.

Nolan, J. *Diplomacy and Security in the Twenty-first Century*, Institute for the Study of Diplomacy, (Washington D.C., Edmund A. Walsh School of Foreign Service, Georgetown University, 2009).

Nye, J. 'Soft Power', *Foreign Policy, No. 80, Twentieth Anniversary*, (1990).

Nye, J. *The Paradox of American Power*, (London: Oxford University Press, 2002).

Obama, B. 'Statement by the President on the End of the Combat Mission in Afghanistan', The White House Office of the Press Secretary, (December 28, 2014).

Orme, C. *Professional Military Education and Simulation*, (Australian Defence Force College, February 2013), pp. 1–13.

O'Toole, M. 'Trump's Memorial Day Message: "We Don't Win With Military"', *Foreign Policy*, (May 30, 2016), available at https://foreignpolicy.com/2016/05/30/trumps-memorial-day-message-we-dont-win-with-military/ (Last accessed December 10, 2016).

Palazzo, A. 'The future of war debate in Australia: Why has there not been one? Has the need for one now arrived? , *Australian Defence Force Journal, No. 189*, (2012), pp. 5–20.

Pant, H. V. 'Ash Carter Comes Calling: Where do US India Defense Ties Go From Here?', *The Diplomat*, (April 25, 2016).

Pandit, R. 'U.S. offers big-ticket military tie-ups', The Times of India, (December 31, 2016), available at http://timesofindia.indiatimes.com/india/us-offers-big-ticket-military-tie-ups-with india/articleshow/56264990.cms (Last accessed January 10, 2017).

Pape, R. A. *Bombing to Win: Air Power and Coercion in War*, (Ithaca, NY: Cornell University Press, 1996).

Paterson, P. 'Training Surrogate Forces in International Humanitarian Law: Lessons from Peru, Colombia, El Salvador, and Iraq', *JSOU Report 16-9*, (MacDill Air Force Base, Florida, 2016), pp. 1–69.

Paris, R. & Sisk, T. D. 'Managing Contradictions: The Inherent Dilemmas of Postwar Statebuilding', *Research Partnership on Postwar Statebuilding*, International Peace Academy, (2007).

Payne, K. 'Fighting on: emotion and conflict termination', *Cambridge Review of International Affairs, Vol. 28, no. 3*, (2014), pp. 480–497.

Peoples Republic of China, *White Paper on China's National Defense*. The Information Office of the State Council of the People's Republic of China, (1998).

Peoples Republic of China, The Central Conference on Work Relating to Foreign Affairs, Ministry of Foreign Affairs of the People's Republic of China, (November 14, 2014), available at http://www.fmprc.gov.cn/mfa_eng/zxxx_662805/t1215680.shtml (Last accessed January 10, 2017).

Peoples Republic of China, China's Policies on Asia-Pacific Security Cooperation, Ministry of Foreign Affairs of the Peoples Republic of China, (2017), available at http://www.fmprc.gov.cn/mfa_eng/zxxx_662805 (Last accessed April 2017).

Perl, R. 'Combatting Terrorism: The Challenge of Measuring Effectiveness', *CRS Report for Congress*, (Washington D.C.: Congressional Research Service, March 12, 2007).

Perry, W. Annual Report to the President and the Congress, (Washington DC :Office Of The Secretary Of Defense, March, 1996), p. viii available at http://www.dtic.mil/docs/citations/ADA307329 (Last accessed December 18, 2016).

Peoples Republic of China, *White Paper on China's National Defense*. The Information Office of the State Council of the People's Republic of China, (1998).

Perry, W. *Annual Report to the President and the Congress*, (Washington DC :Office Of The Secretary Of Defense, March, 1996).

Perry, W. 'Message of the Secretary Of Defense', *Annual Report to the President and the Congress* (March 1996).

Peterson, J. E. 'Foreign Military Presence and Its Role in Reinforcing Regional Security: A Double-Edged Sword', *Arab Gulf States Security: Internal and External Challenges*, The Emirates Center for Strategic Studies and Research, (Abu Dhabi: I. B. Tauris, 2008).

Petraeus, D. 'Testimony to Congress, *The Long War Journal*, (March 5, 2011), available at http://www.longwarjournal.org/archives/2011/03/full_text_of_general_petraeus.php (Last accessed January 20, 2017).

Pettyjohn, S. U.S. Global Defense Posture, 1783–2011, (Santa Monica, CA: RAND Corporation, 2012).

Phillips, C. D. *Towards a Theory of Strategic Communication: A Relationship Management Approach*, (Carlisle Barracks: United States War College, 2012).

Pigman, G. A. *Contemporary diplomacy: representation and communication in a globalized world*, (Cambridge, UK, Polity, 2010).

Ping, J. *Middle Power Statecraft: Indonesia and Malaysia*, (University of Adelaide: Department of Politics, 2003).

Pomper, S. 'Don't Follow the Bear: Soviet Attempt to Build the Afghan Military', *Military Review, Vol. 85, no. 5*, (2005), pp. 26–29.

Preble, C., Emma Ashford & Travis Evans (eds.), 'Our Foreign Policy Choices: Rethinking America's Global Role', *CATO Institute*, (Washington D.C.: CATO Institute Press, 2016), pp. 1–113.

Priest, D. *The Mission: Waging War and Keeping Peace with America's Military*, (W. W. Norton and Company, 2003).

Putnam, R. D. 'Diplomacy and Domestic Politics: The Logic of Two-Level Games', *International Organization, Vol. 42, no. 3*, (1988).

Qurban-Ali, D. 'From "Defence, Diplomacy, and Development" to "Danger, Distrust and Disaffection": A review of lessons learned from Canada's war in Afghanistan and its effect on Canadian defence policy, 2001–2014', (January 14, 2015).

Rahbek-Clemmensen, J. Beyond 'The Soldier and the State': The Theoretical Framework of Elite Civil-Military Relations, (London School of Economics and Political Science, 2013).

Rand, D. H. & Tankel, S. 'Security Cooperation & Assistance" Rethinking the Return on Investment,' The Center for a New American Security, (August, 2015), available at https://s3.amazonaws.com/files.cnas.org/documents/CNAS-Report_Security-Cooperation_FINAL.pdf (Last accessed January 20, 2017).

Rasmussen, M. V. 'What's the Use of It?': Danish Strategic Culture and the Utility of Armed Force', *Cooperation & Conflict: Journal of the Nordic International Studies Association, Vol. 40, no. 1*, (2005).

Reynolds, K. *Defence Transformation: To What, For What?*, (Carlisle, PA: Strategic Studies Institute Army War College, November 2006), pp. 1–84.

Reveron, D. 'From Confrontation to Cooperation', in Gordon Adams & Shoon Murray (eds.), *The Militarization of US Foreign Policy*, (Washington D.C.: Georgetown University Press, 2014).

Reveron, D. *Exporting Security: International Engagement, Security Cooperation, and the Changing Face of the U.S. Military* (*2nd ed.*), (Washington D.C.: Georgetown University Press, 2016).

Reinert , P. J. & John F. Hussey 'The Military's Role in Rule of Law Development', *Joint Force Quarterly, Vol. 77, 2nd Quarter*, (2015).

Richards, D. 'CGS General Sir David Richards in his own words', *RUSI Commentary*, (August 26, 2009), available at https://rusi.org/commentary/cgs-general-sir-david-richards-his-own-words (Last accessed December 12, 2016).

Ricks, T. 'Rumsfeld Gets Earful From Troops', *Washington Post*, (December 9, 2004), available at http://www.washingtonpost.com/wp-dyn/articles/A46508-2004Dec8.html (Last accessed December 10, 2017).

Rietjens, S. & Bollen, M. 'Linking Provincial Reconstruction Teams to Security Enhancement in Afghanistan', Journal of Peacebuilding & Development, Vol. 3, no. 2, (2007).

Rietjens, S., Joseph Soeters & Paul C. van Fenema, 'Learning from Afghanistan: Towards a compass for civil-military coordination', Small Wars & Insurgencies, Vol. 24, no. 2, (2013).

Roberts, I. *Satow's Diplomatic Practice* (6 ed.), (New York: Oxford University Press, 2006)

Rolfe, J. 'Regional Defence Diplomacy: What is it and what are its limits?', *CSS Strategic Background Paper*, (Wellington, New Zealand: Centre for Strategic Studies, 2015).

Roosevelt, T. Letter to Henry L. Sprague, January 26, 1900, American Treasures of the Library of Congress, http://www.loc.gov/exhibits/treasures/trm139.html (Last accessed January 12, 2017).

Rojansky, M. 'George Keenan is Still the Russia Expert America Needs', *Foreign Policy*, (December 22, 2016), available at http://foreignpolicy.com/2016/12/22/ (Last accessed January 10, 2017).

Rosenfeld, E. 'Applications of U.S. Status of Force Agreement to Article 98 of the Rome Statute', *Washington University Global Studies Law Review, Vol 2, no. 1*, (January 2003).

Ross Jr. T. W. 'Pentagon unveils major policy to evaluate security cooperation programs', *Modernizing Foreign Assistance Network*,(January 17, 2017), available at http://modernizeaid.net/2017/01/pentagon-unveils-major-policy-evaluate-security-cooperationprograms/?utm_campaign=shareaholic&utm_medium=twitter&utm_source=socialnetwork.

Rotmann, P., Tohn, D. & Wharton, J. 'Learning Under Fire: Progress and Dissent in the US Military', *Survival, Vol. 5, no. 4*, (2009), pp. 31–48.

Rovner, J. 'Warring Tribes Studying War and Peace', *War on the Rocks*, (12th April, 2016), available at https://warontherocks.com/2016/04/warring-tribes-studying-war-and-peace/ (Last accessed December 10, 2016).

Rumsfeld, D. 'A new kind of war', *New York Times*, (September 27, 2001) available at http://www.nytimes.com/2001/09/27/opinion/a-new-kind-of-war.html (Last accessed October 10, 2016).

Russell, G. 'Machiavelli's Science of Statecraft: The Diplomacy and Politics of Disorder', *Diplomacy & Statecraft, Vol. 16, no. 2*, (2005), pp. 227–250.

Saideman, S. M. & Auerswald, D. P. 'Comparing Caveats: Understanding the Sources of National Restrictions upon NATO's Mission in Afghanistan', *International Studies Quarterly Vol. 56, No. 1* (2012).

Satow, E. *A guide to diplomatic practice* (2nd ed), (London: Longmans Green & Co., 1922), 1–462.

Schadlow, N. 'War and the Art of Governance', *Parameters*, (Autumn, 2003).

Scharre, S. 'Losing the Peace is Still Losing', War on the Rocks, (October 17, 2016), available at http://warontherocks.com/2016/10/losing-the-peace-is-still-losing/ (Last accessed January 10, 2017).

Schelling, T. C. *Arms and Influence*, (New Haven, CT: Yale University Press, 1996).

Schirch, L. & Aaron Kishbaugh, 'Leveraging '3D' Security: From Rhetoric to Reality', *Foreign Policy in Focus Policy Brief*, Vol. 11, no. 2, (November 15, 2006).

Schmidt, J. R. 'Last Alliance Standing? NATO after 9/11, *The Washington Quarterly, Vol. 30, no. 1*, (2007).

Schneider, C. 'Culture Communicates: U.S. Diplomacy that Works', *Discussions Papers in Diplomacy*, (Netherlands Institute of International Relations 'Clingendael', 2004).

Scobell, A., Ely Ratner & Michael Beckley, *China's Strategy Toward South & Central Asia: An Empty Fortress*, (Santa Monica, CA: RAND Corporation, 2014).

Sending, O., Vincent Pouliot, & Iver Neumann, 'The Future of Diplomacy', *International Journal, Vol. 66, no. 3*, (2011).

Seng Chye, T. 'Strengths and Weaknesses of the ADMM and ADMM-Plus', *The Future of the ADMM/ADMM-Plus and Defence Diplomacy in the Asia Pacific*, Rajaratnam School of International Studies, (February 2016).

Seymour, Claudia. 'Social Psychological Dimensions of Conflict', Guy Burgess and Heidi Burgess (eds.), *Beyond Intractability*, (Conflict Information Consortium, University of Colorado, Boulder, 2003).

Special Inspector General for Afghanistan Reconstruction (SIGAR), *Quarterly Report to the United States Congress*, (January 30, 2017).

Singh, B. & S. S. Tan, 'From 'Boots' to 'Brogues': The Rise of Defence Diplomacy in Southeast Asia', *RSIS Monograph*, (Singapore: S. Rajaratnam School of International Studies, 2011), pp. 1–128.

Shanghai Cooperation Organization and Counter-Terrorism Fact Sheet, (June 3, 2011), available at http://tbinternet.ohchr.org/Treaties/CCPR/Shared%20Documents/KAZ/INT_CCPR_NGO_KAZ_102_9347_E.pdf; 'Shanghai Convention on Combating Terrorism, Separatism and Extremism', Council on Foreign Relations, (June 15, 2001), available at http://www.cfr.org/counterterrorism/shanghai-convention-combating-terrorism-separatism-extremism/p25184.

Sharp, P. 'Who needs diplomats?' in Jovan Kurbalija (ed.) Modern Diplomacy, (Malta: Diplo Foundation: 1998), pp. 110–115.

Sharp, P. 'Obama, Clinton and the Diplomacy of Change', in Paul Sharp & Geoff Wiseman (eds.), *American Diplomacy*, (Leiden: Brill, 2011).

Sharp, P. 'Diplomacy in International Relations Theory and Other Disciplinary Perspectives', in Pauline Kerr & Geoff Wiseman (eds.), *Diplomacy in Globalizing World: Theories and Practices*. (New York, Oxford University Press, 2013).

Shea, J. 'How did NATO survive the Cold War? NATO's transformation after the Cold War from 1989 to the present', Video lecture by Jamie Shea, Deputy Assistant Secretary General for External Relations and acting NATO Spokesman, *NATO*, (November 6, 2003), available at http://www.nato.int/cps/en/natohq/opinions_20526.htm?selectedLocale=en.

Shifrinson, Joshua R. Itzkowitz, 'Deal or No Deal? The End of the Cold War and the U.S. Offer to Limit NATO Expansion', *International Security, Vol. 40, no. 4*, (Spring 2016), pp. 7–44.

Shriver, R. 'Cross-Strait Series: The Rise of Intra-Asian Defense Cooperation', *Panel Discussion at The Atlantic Council*, (March 7, 2017).

Smith, A. *An Inquiry into the Nature and Causes of the Wealth of Nations*, Edwin Cannan, (ed), (Library of Economics and Liberty, 1904).

Smith, L. W. *AFCEA International and the U.S. Naval Institute Conference*, San Diego CA. (February, 2000).

Smith, E. 'Effects Based Operation: Applying Network Centric Warfare in Peace, Crisis and War', *DoD Command and Control Research Program*, (Library of Congress, 2002).

Smith, S. & Owens, P. 'Alternative Approaches to International Theory', in Baylis, J., Smith, S. & Owens, P. *The Globalisation of World Politics*, (London: Oxford University Press, 2008).

Smith, S., Hadfield, A. & Dunne, T. *Foreign policy: Theories, actors, cases* (2nd ed.), (Oxford: Oxford University Press, 2012).

Sofer, S. 'Old and new diplomacy: a debate revisited', *Review of International Studies, Vol. 14, no. 3*, (1988), pp. 195–211.

Sorokin, G. L. 'Arms, Alliances, and Security Trade-offs in Enduring Rivalries', *International Studies Quarterly, Vol. 38, no. 3*, (1994).

Special Inspector General for Afghanistan Reconstruction, *Quarterly Report to the United States Congress*, (Arlington, Virginia, January 30, 2017), pp. 1–269.

Stapleton, B. & Michael Keating, 'Military and Civilian Assistance to Afghanistan 2001–14: An Incoherent Approach', Afghanistan*: Opportunity in Crisis Series, No. 10*, (Chatham House, 2015).

Staten, C. 'U.S. Foreign Policy Since World War II; An essay on reality's corrective qualities', *American Diplomacy*, (August 2005), available at http://www.unc.edu/depts/diplomat/item/2005/0709/stat/staten_reality.html (Last accessed December 10, 2016).

Stewart, P. 'U.S. commander seeks to ease human-rights rules that limit training', *Reuters*, (March 6, 2013), available at http://www.reuters.com/article/us-usa-military-rights-idUSBRE9251NB20130306.

Stoltenberg, J. 'Trident Juncture shows NATO capabilities 'are real and ready', NATO Press Release, (November 4, 2015).

Story, W. C. 'Joint Combined Exchange Training (JCET) and Human Rights: Background and Issues for Congress', *CRS Report for Congress, RL30034*, (Washington D.C.: Congressional Research Service, January 26, 1999), available at http://congressionalresearch.com/RL30034/document.php.

Storey, I. 'China's Bilateral Defense Diplomacy in Southeast Asia', *Asian Security, Vol. 8, no. 3*, (2012), pp. 287–310.

Suh, H, Harry Krejsa & Mira Rapp-Hooper, The Rebalance is Dead,! Long Live the Rebalance!, War on the Rocks, (March 16, 2017), available at https://warontherocks.com/2017/03/the-rebalance-is-dead-long-live-the-rebalance/.

Sullivan, P., Brock F. Tessman & Li Xiaojun, 'US Military Aid and Recipient State Cooperation', *Foreign Policy Analysis, Vol. 7, no. 3*, (2011).

Suri, J. 'War and Diplomacy in the Age of Extremes', *Foreign Policy Breakthroughs:* Imperial & Global Forum, (2015).

Szayna, T. S., Grissom, A., Marquis, J. P., Young, T-D., Rosen, B. & Huh, Y. *U.S. Army Security Cooperation: Toward Improved Planning and Management*, (Santa Monica, CA, RAND Corporation, 2004).

Tago, A. 'When Are Democratic Friends Unreliable? The Unilateral Withdrawal of Troops from the `Coalition of the Willing', *Journal of Peace Research, Vol. 46, no. 2*, (2009), pp. 219–234.

Tan, S. S. & Bhubhindar Singh, 'Introduction', *Asian Security*, Vol. 8, no. 3, (2012), pp. 221–231.

Tan, S. S. 'The ADMM and ADMM-Plus: Progressing Slowly But Steadily?', *The Future of the ADMM/ADMM-Plus and Defence Diplomacy in the Asia Pacific*, Rajaratnam School of International Studies, (February 2016).

Tanenhaus, S. 'The World: From Vietnam to Iraq; The Rise and Fall and Rise of the Domino Theory', *The New York Times*, (March 23, 2003) available at http://www.nytimes.com/2003/03/23/weekinreview/the-world-from-vietnam-to-iraq-the-rise-and-fall-and-rise-of-the-domino-theory.html (Last accessed December 16, 2016).

Tanner, M. & James Bellacqua, 'China's Response to Terrorism', *CNA Report for the U.S.-China Economic and Security Review Commission*, (June 2016).

Tarnoff, C. & Marian L. Lawson, 'Foreign Aid: An Introduction to U.S. Programs and Policy', *CRS Report for Congress R40213*, (Washington D.C.: Congressional Research Service, June 17, 2016).

Tarrosy, I. 'Unconventional Diplomacy' in a New Era of Summit Diplomacy', *Tradecraft Review: Periodical of the Military National Security Service*, (2014/2 Special Issue).

Taylor, B. John Blaxland, Hugh White, Nick Bisley, Peter Leahy, See Seng Tan, 'Defence Diplomacy: Is the Game Worth the Candle?', Centre *of Gravity Discussion papers.* (Canberra: ANU College of Asia & the Pacific, 2014).

Thannhauser, S. & Christopher Luehrs, 'The Human and Financial Costs of Operation in Afghanistan & Iraq', in Richard D Hooker & Joseph J. Collins (eds.), *Lessons Encountered: Learning Lessons from the Long War*, (Washington D.C.: National Defence University Press, 2015), pp. 421–440.

Theros, M. & Mary Kaldor, *A Century Foundation Report*, The Century Foundation, (2011).

Thornhill, P. 'A Funny Thing Happened When These Military Officers and Academics Got Together', *Defense One*, (April 3, 2016), available at http://www.defenseone.com/ideas/2015/04/funny-thing-happened-when-these-military-officers-and-academics-got-together/109303/ (Last accessed September 18, 2016).

Thorton, S. *Press Briefing*, (March 14, 2017) available at https://fpc.state.gov/268444.htm (Last accessed March 24, 2017).

Three Levels of War, *Air and Space Mentoring Guide, Vol. 1*, USAF College of Aerospace Doctrine, Research and Education. (Maxwell AFB: Air University Press, 1997).

Torbati, Y & Robin Emmott, 'Despite fatigue, NATO commits to fund Afghan forces to 2020', (Reuters, July 9 2016), available at http://www.reuters.com/article/us-nato-summit-afghanistan-idUSKCNoZPoAC (Last accessed December 16, 2016).

UK House of Lords, House of Commons, Joint Committee on the National Security Strategy, *National Security Strategy and Strategic Defence and Security Review 2015*, (House of Lords and the House of Commons, July 10, 2016), pp. 1–51.

UK Ministry of Defence, *Strategic Defence Review Modern Forces For The Modern World*, (Whitehall, London: MOD, July 1998).

UK Ministry of Defence, *Policy Paper No. 1: Defence Diplomacy*, (Whitehall: Director General Corporate Communication, 2000).

UK Ministry of Defence, 'Part 10: Countering Insurgency', *British Army Field Manual, Vol. 1*, (London: Ministry of Defence, 2009).

UK Ministry of Defence, *UK Defence Doctrine Joint Doctrine Publication 0-01* (5th Edition), Ministry of Defence Development, Concepts and Doctrine Centre, (Whitehall, November 2014).

UK Ministry of Defence, *International Defence Engagement Strategy: defence engagement 2014/2015*.

Ucko, D. *The New Counterinsurgency Era: Transforming the U.S. Military for Modern Wars*, (Washington D.C.: Georgetown University Press, 2006).

U.S. Advisory Commission on Public Diplomacy, 'Public Diplomacy: Model for the Assessment of Performance', *Assessing U.S. Public Diplomacy-A Notional Model*, (Austin, Texas: The LBJ School of Public Affairs, 2010), pp. 1–151.

USAID, 'Provincial Reconstruction Teams', *USAID Afghanistan,* (Summer 2007), available at http://www.usaid.gov/locations/asia_near_east/documents/countries/afghanistan/afgh_prt_jul2007.pdf (Last accessed January 2, 2017).

U.S. Air Force, Three Levels of War, USAF College of Aerospace Doctrine, Research and Education, *Air & Space Power Mentoring Guide, Vol. 1,* (Maxwell AFB, AL: Air University Press, 1997), pp. 1–3.

U.S Army Field Manual 3–0 Operations, (Washington D.C.: Department of the Army, February 2001).

U.S. Army *Field Manual 3-24/Marine Corps Warfighting Publication 3-33.5, Counterinsurgency*, (Washington D.C.: Department of the Army, December 2006).

U.S. Army, Security Force Assistance. Field Manual 3-07.1, (Washington, DC: U.S. Department of the Army, May 1, 2009).

U.S. Army, The Army Capstone Concept-TRADOC Pam 525-3-0,Operational Adaptability: Operating under Conditions of Uncertainty and Complexity in an Era of Persistent Conflict 2016–2028, (United States Department of the Army, December 21, 2009), pp. 1–58.

US Army *FM 6-0, Commander and Staff Organisation and Operations*, (May 2014).

U.S. Army, *The United States Army Exchange Program with People's Liberation Army of China*, (May 16, 2011), available at http://www.army.mil/standto/archive/2011/05/16/ (Last accessed December 8, 2016).

U.S. Army Doctrine Publication, *6-0 Mission Command*, (2012).

U.S. Army Special Operations Command, *ARSOF Next: A Return To First Principles*, (2015), pp. 1–48, accessed at http://www.soc.mil/swcs/SWmag/archive/ARSOF_Next/ARSOF%20Next.pdf.

U.S. Congress, *Building Partnership Capacity and Development of the Interagency Process*, 11th Cong., 2nd sess., (House Committee on Armed Services , April 15, 2008).

U.S. Defense Science Board, Task Force on Strategic Communication, *Report of the Defense Science Board Task Force on Strategic Communication*, (Washington D.C: Office of the Under Secretary of Defense for Acquisition, Technology, and Logistics, 2004).

Department of Defence, Public Affairs Qualification Course, National Security and Public Affairs, (Fort George G. Meade, MA: The Defence Information School, ND).

U.S. Department of the Defense, *Military Operations Other Than War, J-7 Operational Plans & Interoperability Directorate*, Joint Doctrine Joint Force Employment Briefing Modules, (Washington D.C., June 1995).

U.S. Department of Defence, 'Introduction', *Transformation Planning Guidance*, (April, 2003).

U.S. Department of Defence, *Quadrennial Defence Review Report*, (Washington D.C., February 6, 2006).

U.S. Department of Defense, Quadrennial Defense Review: *Execution Roadmap: Building Partnership Capacity*, (Washington, DC: U.S. Department of Defense, May 22, 2006), pp. 1–24.

U.S. Department of Defence, National Military Strategic Plan for the War on Terrorism, JCOS, (2006).

U.S. Department of Defense, *Principles of Strategic Communication*, (Washington, DC: U.S. Department of Defense, Aug. 15, 2009).

U.S. Department of Defence, *Report on the Assessment of U.S. and Coalition Plans to Train, Equip, and Field the Afghan National Security Forces' Report No. SPO-2009-007*, (Washington D.C.: Office of the Assistant Inspector General, September 30, 2009), pp. 1–224.

U.S. Department of Defense, *Report on Strategic Communication*, (December 2009).

U.S. Department of Defense, Quadrennial Defense Review Report, (Washington, DC: U.S. Department of Defense, February 2010).

U.S. Department of Defence (a), *Vision 2020*, (Defence Security Cooperation Agency, October 2015).

U.S. Department of Defence (b), 'Report on Enhancing Security and Stability in Afghanistan', *DoD Report to Congress*, (Washington D.C.: U.S. Department of Defence, June 2015).

U.S. Department of Defence (c), 'Regional Defense Combating Terrorism Fellowship Program', *Report to Congress FY2015*, (Washington D.C.: U.S. Department of Defence, 2015), pp. 1–86.

U.S. Department of Defence, *Secretary of Defence: Annual Report to Congress*, (Washington D.C.: Department of Defence, 2016).

U.S. Department of Defence, U.S. Joint Publication 1–02, *Department of Defense Dictionary of Military and Associated Terms*, (February 15, 2016), pp. 1–394.

U.S. Department of Defense, General Dunford, *Defense Media Activity*, (26th April, 2016), available at http://www.defense.gov/News-Article-View/Article/743160/dunford-explores-ways-to-better-integrate-counter-extremism-efforts.

U.S. Department of the Defense, 'Joint Press Conference with Secretary Carter and President Ghani in Kabul, Afghanistan', Department of Defence, (July 12, 2016), available https://www.defense.gov/News/Transcripts/Transcript-View/Article/835506/joint-press-conference-with-secretary-carter-and-president-ghani-in-kabul-afgha (Last accessed December 18, 2016).

U.S. Department of the Defense, *DoD Instruction 5132.14 Assessment, Monitoring, And Evaluation Policy For The Security Cooperation Enterprise*, (Washington D.C.: Department of Defence, January 13, 2017).

U.S. Department of the Defense, *Instruction-Stability Operations*, (September 16, 2009), pp. 1–15, available at http://www.dtic.mil/whs/directives/corres/pdf/300005p.pdf (Last accessed January 12, 2017).

U.S. Department of State, 'Transformational Diplomacy', *Strategic Plan: Fiscal Years 2007–2012*, (Washington D.C.: U.S. Government Printing Office, 2007).

U.S. Department of State, 'Introduction The Foundations Of Diplomatic Security', *The History of the Bureau of Diplomatic Security of the United States Department of State*, (*1st ed.*), Bureau of Diplomatic Security, (Washington D.C.: Global Publishing Solutions, 2011).

U.S. Department of State, *Congressional Budget Justification FY2013*, (2013), available at http://www.state.gov/documents/organization/181061.pdf.

U.S. Department of State, 'Leading Through Civilian Power', *Quadrennial Diplomacy Development Review*, (Washington D.C.: U.S. Department of State, 2010), pp. 1–242.

U.S. Department of State, 'Enduring Leadership in a Dynamic World', *Quadrennial Diplomacy and Defence Review*, (Washington D.C.: U.S. Department of State, 2015), pp. 1–90.

U.S. Department of State, *Country Reports on Terrorism 2014*, Bureau of Counterterrorism, (Washington D.C: The United States Department of State, June 2015), pp. 57–60.

U.S. Department of State, *Annual Report on Assistance Related to International Terrorism Fiscal Year 2016*, (Washington D.C., February 22, 2017).

U.S. Government, 3D Planning Guide: Diplomacy, Development and Defense, (Washington D.C.: Government Printing Office, 2012).

U.S. Government Accountability Office, *Report to Congressional Requesters, Overseas Contingency Operations*, (Washington D.C.: U.S. GOA, January 2017).

U.S. Government Accountability Office, *Foreign Assistance, GAO-17–316*, (Washington D.C.: U.S. GOA, March 2017), pp. 1–88.

U.S. Government Accountability Office, *Building Partner Capacity: Inventory of Department of Defense Security Cooperation and Department of State Security Assistance Efforts*, GAO-17–255R, (Washington D.C.: U.S. GOA, March 2017), pp. 1–63.

Foreign Assistance Act of 1961, (Public Law 87–195), available at https://legcounsel.house.gov/Comps/Foreign%20Assistance%20Act%20Of%201961.pdf (Last accessed December 12, 2016).

U.S. Government, *The National Security Strategy for Engagement and Enlargement*, (Washington D.C.: U.S. Government Printing Office, 1995).

U.S. Government, National Security Presidential Directive (NSPD) 44: *Management of Interagency Efforts Concerning Reconstruction and Stabilization*, (Washington D.C.: The White House, December 7, 2005) availableat https://fas.org/irp/offdocs/nspd/nspd-44.html.

U.S. Government, 'Redefining America's Military Leadership', *The National Military Strategy of the United States of America*, (Washington D.C.: U.S. Government Printing Office, 2011).

U.S. Government, *3D Planning Guide: Diplomacy, Development and Defense*, (Washington D.C.: Government Printing Office, 2012).

U.S. Government, 'Introductory Message', *U.S. Civil-military Strategic Framework for Afghanistan*, (Washington D.C: Dept. of State/Dept. of Defence, 2013).

U.S Government, *The National Security Strategy of the United States*, (Washington D.C.: U.S. Government Printing Office, 2015).

U.S. Government, *Report on the Legal and Policy Frameworks Guiding the United States' Use of Military Force and Related National Security Operations*, The White House, (Washington D.C., December 2016).

U.S. Joint Chiefs of Staff, *Joint Publication 1*, (2013).

U.S. Joint Warfighting Center, Commanders Handbook for an EBA Approach to Joint Operations, (24 February 2006).

U.S. Joint Forces Command, *Commander's Handbook For An Effects-Based Approach to Joint Operations*, Draft (Suffolk, VA: U.S. Joint Forces Command, 2006).

U.S. Joint Operation Command, *Joint Publication 3–16 Multinational Operations*, (March 2007).

U.S. Joint Publication 1-02, *Department of Defense Dictionary of Military and Associated Terms*, (February 15, 2016).

U.S. Joint Warfighting Center, *Commanders Handbook for an EBA Approach to Joint Operations, U.S.* Joint Warfighting Center, (24 February 2006).

U.S. National Security Strategy, (*Washington D.C.: The White House Printing Office, 2015*).

U.S. Secretary of Defence, *Annual Report to Congress*, (Washington D.C.: Department of Defence, 2016).

U.S. Senate, 'Embassies as Command Posts in the Anti-Terror Campaign', *A Report to Members of the Committee on Foreign Relations*, (Washington D.C.: U.S Government Printing Office, December 15, 2006), pp. 1–25.

U.S. Senate, 'Afghanistan: U.S. Policy and International Commitments', United States Senate Committee on Foreign Relations, (September 15, 2016), available at http://www.foreign.senate.gov/hearings/afghanistan-us-policy-and-international-commitments-091516 (Last accessed December 18, 2016).

Van Um, E. & Pisoiu, D. 'Dealing with uncertainty: the illusion of knowledge in the study of counterterrorism effectiveness', Critical Studies on Terrorism, Vol. 8, no. 2, (2014).

Von Clausewitz, C. 'War as an Instrument of Policy', *On War*, (Hertfordshire: Wordsworth Editions Limited, 1997).

Von Hlatky, S. & Trisko Darden, J. 'Cash or Combat? America's Asian Alliances during the War in Afghanistan', *Asian Security, Vol. 10, no. 4*, (2015).

Von Hlatky, S. 'Allies by Association? The Significance of America's Asian Alliances for NATO', in Alexander Moens & Brooke A. Smith-Windsor (eds.), *NATO and Asia-Pacific* (Rome: NATO Defence College Research Division, 2016).

Von Hlatky, S. 'NATO's Public Diplomacy in the Grey Zone of Conflict', *CDP Blog*, USC Center on Public Diplomacy, (2016).

Wallin, M. 'Military Public Diplomacy: How the Military Influences Foreign Audiences', *American Security Project* White Paper, (2014), available at https://www.americansecurityproject.org/wp-content/uploads/2015/02/Ref-0185-Military-Public-Diplomacy.pdf.

Walt, Stephen M. 'Testing Theories of Alliance Formation: The Case of Southwest Asia', *International Organization, Vol. 42, no. 2*, (1988), pp. 275–316.

Walt, S. M. 'Beyond bin Laden: Reshaping U.S. Foreign Policy', *International Security, Vol. 26, no. 3*, (2001).

Walt, S. M. 'Alliances in a Unipolar World', *World Politics Vol. 61, No. 1* (2009).

Watson, A. *Diplomacy: the dialogue between states*, (London: Routledge, 1984).

Watson, B. 'State of the Army', *Defence One*, (January 2017), available at http://www.defenseone.com/ideas/2017/01/state-defense-2017/134708/ (Last accessed January 19, 2017).

Watts, S. 'A Competing Risks Approach to Security Sector Assistance for Fragile States', *LAWFARE Foreign Policy Essay*, (May 1, 2016) available at https://www.lawfareblog.com/competing-risks-approach-security-sector-assistance-fragile-states (Last accessed December 10, 2016).

Watts, J. 'Cross-Strait Series: The Rise of Intra-Asian Defense Cooperation', Panel Discussion at The Atlantic Council, (March 7 2017), available at https://youtu.be/lOHuO2_n3QE.

Webber, M., Ellen Hallams & Martin A. Smith. 'Repairing NATO's Motors', *International Affairs, Vol. 90, no. 4*, (2014).

White Paper of the Interagency Policy Group's Report on U.S. Policy toward Afghanistan and Pakistan, (Washington D.C.: The White House, February 2009).

Weinberger, C. The Uses of Military Power', Remarks Prepared for Delivery by the Hon. Casper W. Weinberger, Secretary of Defence, to the National Press Club, Washington D.C., (November 28, 1984), available at http://www.pbs.org/wgbh/pages/frontline/shows/military/force/weinberger.html (Last accessed August 18, 2016).

Wilkins, A. 'To Say It Like It Is: Norway's evaluation of its part in the international intervention', *Afghanistan Analysts Network*, (August 23, 2016), available at https://www.afghanistan-analysts.org/to-say-it-like-it-is-norways-evaluation-of-its-part-in-the-international-intervention/ (Last accessed December 10, 2016).

Willard, J. 'Military Diplomacy: An Essential Tool of Foreign Policy at the Theater Strategic Level', School of Advanced Military Studies, (Fort Leavenworth, Kansas: United States Army Command and General Staff College, 2006), pp. 1–71.

Williams, E. 'Out of Area and Very Much in Business? NATO, the U.S., and the Post-9/11 International Security Environment', *Comparative Strategy, Vol. 27*, (2008).

Wilson, D. & Conway, G. E. 'The Tactical Conflict Assessment Framework: A Short-lived Panacea', *The RUSI Journal, Vol. 154, no. 1*, (2009).

Winger, G. 'The Velvet Gauntlet: A Theory of Defence Diplomacy', in A. Lisiak & N. Smolenski (eds.), *What do I do?, Vol. 33*, (Vienna: IWM Junior Visiting Fellows Conference, 2014).

Wiseman, G. 'What is Non-Provocative Defence?', *Concepts of Non-Provocative Defence*, (London: Palgrave Macmillan, 2002).

Wiseman, G. 'Pax Americana: Bumping into Diplomatic Culture', International Studies Perspectives, Vol. 6, no. 4, (2005), pp. 409–430.

Wiseman, G. 'Distinctive Characteristics of American Diplomacy', in Paul Sharp & Geoff Wiseman (eds.), *American Diplomacy*, (Leiden: Brill, 2011).

White, H. 'Grand Expectations, Little Promise', *Defence Diplomacy: Is the game worth the candle?, The Centre of Gravity Series (paper 17)*, (Canberra: Australian National University, 2014), pp. 10–11.

Wright, M. *Systems of states*, (London: Leicester University Press, 1977).

Wright, A. & Jeremy Herb, 'Democrats' role for Mattis: The anti-Trump', *Politico*, (January 12, 2017), available at http://www.politico.com/story/2017/01/james-mattis-confirmation-hearing-takeaways-233550.

Yarchi, M. 'Terror Organizations' Uses of Public Diplomacy: Limited versus Total Conflicts', *Studies in Conflict & Terrorism, Vol. 39, no. 12*, (2016), pp. 1071–1083.

Zaidi, S. A. 'Who Benefits from U.S. Aid to Pakistan', *Policy Outlook*, (Carnegie Endowment for International Peace, 2011).

Zdzislaw Lachowski, 'Foreign Military Bases in Eurasia', *SIPRI Policy Paper No. 18*, Stockholm International Peace Research Institute, (June 2007), available at http://books.sipri.org/files/PP/SIPRIPP18.pdf (Last accessed December 2, 2016).

Zicheng Y. & Zhang Qingmin, 'China's Contemporary Diplomacy', In Pauline Kerr & Geoff Wiseman, *Diplomacy in a globalizing world: Theories and practices*, (New York: Oxford University Press, 2013), pp. 282–299.

Zimmerman, S. R. 'The Afghan Government at War', in in Gale A. Mattox & Stephen M. Grenier (eds.), Coalition Challenges in Afghanistan: The Politics of Alliance, (Stanford, CA: Stanford University Press, 2015).

Zinni, A. *Testimony before the United States Senate Foreign Relations Committee, Hearing on "Strengthening National Security Through Smart Power—A Military Perspective,"* (March 5, 2008), http://foreign.senate.gov/hearings/2008/hrg080305a.html (Last accessed December 10, 2016).

Zyck, S. A. & R. Muggah, 'Preventive Diplomacy and Conflict Prevention: Obstacles and Opportunities, Stability', *International Journal of Security and Development, Vol. 1, no. 1*, (2012).

www.ingramcontent.com/pod-product-compliance
Lightning Source LLC
Chambersburg PA
CBHW031326230926
51848CB00001B/110